1990

University of St. Francis
G   362 11068 S458

W9-AOH-025

3 0301 00068742 2

CASH
AND
INVESTMENT
MANAGEMENT

for the Health Care Industry

Alan G. Seidner

President
The Alan G. Seidner Company
Pasadena, California

William O. Cleverley

Professor of Health Care Finance
and Accounting
Graduate Program in Hospital
and Health Services Management
The Ohio State University
Columbus, Ohio

LIBRARY
College of St. Francis
JOLIET, ILLINOIS

AN ASPEN PUBLICATION®
Aspen Publishers, Inc.
Rockville, Maryland
1990

Library of Congress Cataloging-in-Publication Data

Seidner, Alan G.
Cash and investment management for the health care industry/
Alan G. Seidner, William O. Cleverley.
p. cm.
"An Aspen publication."
ISBN: 0-8342-0101-1
1. Health facilities--Business management. 2. Health facilities--Finance.
3. Cash management. I. Cleverley, William O. II. Title.
RA971.3.S45   1989   362.1′1′0681--dc20   89-17593
CIP

Copyright © 1990 by Aspen Publishers, Inc.
All rights reserved.

Aspen Publishers, Inc., grants permission for photocopying for limited personal or
internal use. This consent does not extend to other kinds of copying, such as copying for
general distribution, for advertising or promotional purposes, for creating new collective
works, or for resale. For information, address Aspen Publishers, Inc., Permissions
Department, 1600 Research Boulevard, Rockville, Maryland 20850.

Editorial Services: Marsha Davies

Library of Congress Catalog Card Number: 89-17593
ISBN: 0-8342-0101-1

Printed in the United States of America

1 2 3 4 5

G
362.11068
S458

To Gary Koger, CPA, Fellow, Healthcare Financial Management Association, for his kindness and support over the years.
Alan G. Seidner

134,894

Table of Contents

v

Acknowledgments

The authors wish to express their sincere appreciation to those who contributed to the quality of the material in this text. Specifically, we wish to express sincere appreciation to Richard Bort, a consultant in cash and treasury management, for his substantial contribution to the area dealing with cash management and the overall application of his editorial skills. Also, Dennis Rognerud of Ziegler Securities deserves our appreciation for his information and continued support of the authors' work on this publication.

Chapter 1

Introduction to Cash and Investment Management

INTRODUCTION

Few topics in finance are more important than cash and investment management. Cash is the lifeblood of a business operation. A firm that controls its access to cash and generation of cash will usually survive and thrive. A firm that ignores or poorly manages its cash position may fail. Experience has shown that more firms fail for a lack of ready cash than for any other reason, even firms with sound profitability. It is extremely important, therefore, to recognize and appreciate that profit and cash management are not the same thing.

It would seem logical to expect that great volumes of literature would be devoted to such an important topic as cash and investment management. Unfortunately, this is not the case. Although a major portion of a financial manager's time is devoted to working capital problems, relatively little space is devoted to them in most financial management textbooks. A typical text often contains only several chapters that deal with working capital management and perhaps a single chapter that discusses cash management.

Cash management is probably more important in the health care industry than in many other industries, but often it is less understood. Health care financial executives frequently advance through the accounting route. While finance texts provide little coverage to cash management, accounting texts provide almost no coverage. Health care financial executives traditionally think of cash management in terms of receivables control. They often believe that better cash management will result if accounts receivable can be reduced or the collection cycle shortened. While accounts receivable management in health care organizations is clearly important, limiting attention to this one area is myopic. Good cash management should focus not only on the acceleration of receivables, but also on the complete cash conversion cycle. Reduction of the cash conversion cycle, along with the related investment of surplus funds, should be the critical objective of financial managers.

Many hospitals and health care firms are often willing to let their banks handle most of their cash management decisions. While this strategy is acceptable in some situations, it may produce less than optimal performance. Risks are sometimes unnecessarily increased or yields on investments sacrificed. Real or perceived conflicts of interest also exist when the bank is represented on the hospital's governing board.

Why is cash and investment management of importance to health care executives? Hospitals have very large sums of investable funds compared with firms of similar size in other industries. For example, in 1987 the average hospital maintained a $13.3 million investment, or 19 percent of its total assets, in either short-term cash, marketable securities, or other investments (see Table 1-1). Hospitals and other health care firms are also more likely to have greater investment management needs than other industries for several reasons:

Table 1-1 Percentage Balance Sheet All U.S. Hospitals, 1983–1987

	1983	1984	1985	1986	1987
Assets					
Cash and Marketable Securities	5.21%	5.75%	6.46%	6.55%	6.15%
Net Accounts Receivable	15.84	16.17	16.14	15.73	16.17
Inventory	1.44	1.34	1.27	1.18	1.17
Other Current Assets	2.45	2.53	2.50	2.22	2.35
Total Current Assets	24.93%	25.79%	26.36%	25.68%	25.83%
Other Investments	11.81	12.41	13.23	13.96	13.20
Net Fixed Assets	54.22	52.56	50.70	48.94	48.85
Other Assets	9.04	9.24	9.71	11.42	12.11
Total Assets	100.00%	100.00%	100.00%	100.00%	100.00%
Liabilities and Fund Balance					
Current Liabilities	13.91%	13.59%	13.43%	12.77%	12.66%
Long-Term Liabilities	37.02	36.50	35.56	36.61	35.75
Other	1.52	1.88	2.16	2.05	2.15
Fund Balance	47.55	48.03	48.85	48.57	49.44
Total Liabilities and Fund Balance	100.00%	100.00%	100.00%	100.00%	100.00%

Source: Adapted from *Hospital Industry Financial Report 1983–1987* by W.O. Cleverley, p. 135, with permission of Healthcare Financial Management Association, © 1987.

- Most hospitals are voluntary, not-for-profit firms and must set aside funds for replacement of plants and equipment. Investor-owned firms can rely on the issuance of new stockholders' equity to finance some of their replacement needs.

- Hospitals are increasingly beginning to self-insure all or a portion of their professional liability risk. This requires that rather sizable investment pools be available to meet estimated actuarial needs.

- Many hospitals receive gifts and endowments. While these sums may not be large for individual hospitals, they can provide additional sources of investment.

- Many hospitals also have rather sizable funding requirements for defined benefit pension plans and debt service requirements associated with the issuance of bonds. These funds are usually held by a trustee.

With greater investments in the hospital industry, one should expect to find greater levels of investment income. For the average hospital in 1987, approximately 29 percent of its total net income was derived from nonoperating revenue sources. Much of this nonoperating revenue is clearly related to investment income. A comparable figure for the manufacturing sector is 14 percent.

CASH AND INVESTMENT MANAGEMENT STRUCTURE

Effective cash management is often related to the cash conversion cycle, as depicted in Figure 1-1. In its simplest form, the cash conversion cycle represents the time that it takes a firm to go from an outlay of cash to purchase the needed factors of production, such as labor and supplies, to the actual collection of cash for the produced product or service, such as a completed treatment for a given patient. Usually the objectives in cash management are to minimize the collection period and to maximize the payment period. Trade-offs often exist; for example, accelerating receivables collection may result in lost sales, and delaying payments to vendors could result in increased prices.

The primary tool used in cash planning is the cash budget. Cash balances are affected by changes in working capital over time. Working capital may be defined as the difference between current assets and current liabilities. The following items are usually included in these two categories:

Current Assets
Cash and investments
Accounts receivable
Inventories
Other current assets

Current Liabilities
   Accounts payable
   Accrued salaries and wages
   Accrued expenses
   Notes payable
   Current position of long-term debt

The cash budget focuses on four major activities that affect working capital:

1. purchasing of resources
2. production/sale of service
3. billing
4. collection

These activities represent time intervals in the cash conversion cycle. The purchasing of resources relates to the acquisition of supplies and labor, such as the level of inventory necessary to maintain realistic production schedules and the staff required to ensure adequate provision of services. Production and sale are virtually the same in the health care industry; there is no inventory of products or services. However, there is a delay between the production of service and final delivery. A patient may be in the hospital for 10 or 15 days before discharge, which could be regarded as the final point of sale. Billing represents the interval between the re-

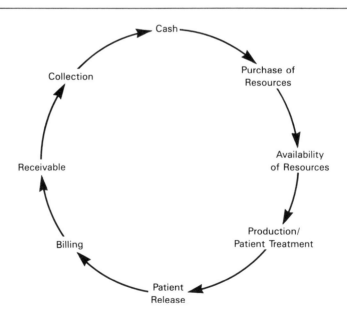

Figure 1-1 Cash Conversion Cycle

lease or discharge of a patient and the generation of a bill. Collection represents the time interval between the generation of a bill to the actual collection of the cash from the patient or the patient's third-party payor.

Estimating these four time intervals is critical to cash budgeting and, therefore, cash planning. For example, the average collection period will dramatically influence the need for cash assets. In periods when sales are expected to increase, a long collection period will require the hospital to finance a larger amount of working capital in the form of increased receivables. The hospital must pay for its factors of production (i.e., supplies and labor) at the beginning of the cycle and wait to receive payment from its customers at the end of the cycle.

The above example also illustrates why a focus on a static measure of liquidity, such as a current ratio, sometimes can be deceiving. A rapid buildup in sales results in a large increase in accounts receivable which increases the current ratio. Liquidity position, however, might not be improved in this case. The speed with which these receivables can be turned into cash is also an extremely important measure of liquidity.

The major purpose of the cash budget, an example of which is shown in Table 1-2, is to prepare an accurate estimate of future cash flows. With this estimate, the firm can arrange for short-term financing from a bank through a line of credit if it projects a period of cash deficiency, or it can invest surplus funds. Since yields are usually higher on longer-term investments, an investment for a 6-month term is likely to result in greater income than an investment broken down into two 3-month cycles. The cash budget, then, is the key document in terms of providing information regarding short-term investment and short-term financing decisions. A key factor in these projections is the desired level of cash balances that the firm would like to maintain. Firms that set low cash requirement levels are assuming more risks.

The entire cash management process can be broken down into five sequential steps:

1. Understand and manage the cash conversion cycle. In most situations, the objective is to minimize the required investment in working capital, where working capital is defined as current assets less current liabilities.
2. Develop a sound cash budget that accurately projects cash inflows and cash outflows during the planning horizon.
3. Establish the firm's minimum required cash balance. This level should be set in a manner consistent with the firm's overall risk assumption posture.
4. Arrange for working capital loans during those periods when the cash budget indicates short-term financing will be needed.
5. Invest cash surpluses in a way that will maximize the expected yield to the firm, subject to a prudent assumption of risk.

Table 1-2 A Sample Cash Budget

	1st Quarter			2nd Quarter	3rd Quarter	4th Quarter
	January	February	March			
Receipts from operations	$300,000	$310,000	$ 320,000	$1,000,000	$1,100,000	$1,100,000
Disbursements from operations	280,000	280,000	300,000	940,000	1,000,000	1,000,000
Cash available from operations	$ 20,000	$ 30,000	$ 20,000	$ 60,000	$ 100,000	$ 100,000
Other receipts						
Increase in mortgage payable						
Sale of fixed assets		20,000		500,000		
Unrestricted income—endowment	-0-		40,000	40,000	40,000	40,000
Total other receipts	$ -0-	$ 20,000	$ 40,000	$ 540,000	$ 40,000	$ 40,000
Other disbursements						
Mortgage payments						
Fixed asset purchase			150,000	$ 480,000	150,000	
Funded depreciation			30,000	130,000	30,000	30,000
Total other disbursements	$ -0-	$ -0-	180,000	610,000	180,000	30,000
Net cash gain (loss)	$ 20,000	$ 50,000	$(120,000)	$ (10,000)	$ (40,000)	$ 110,000
Beginning cash balance	100,000	120,000	170,000	50,000	40,000	-0-
Cumulative cash	$120,000	$170,000	$ 50,000	$ 40,000	$ -0-	$ 110,000
Desired level of cash	100,000	100,000	100,000	100,000	100,000	100,000
Cash above minimum needs (financing needs)	$ 20,000	$ 70,000	$ (50,000)	$ (60,000)	$ (100,000)	$ 10,000

MANAGEMENT OF WORKING CAPITAL

The management of working capital items is related to short-term bank financing and investment of cash surpluses, which are discussed in subsequent sections of this chapter. The balance sheet for ABC Medical Center in Table 1-3 presents a useful way to examine the relevant items of working capital management. As examples, the following two categories are discussed: (1) receivables and (2) accounts payable and accrued salaries and wages.

Receivables

Industry experience suggests that receivables constitute the most critical, but not exclusive, area of importance in cash management. In general, accounts receivable usually represent about 60 to 70 percent of a hospital's total investment in current assets. ABC Medical Center has $8,778,677 of receivables, or 51.6 percent of its total current assets, in 1987. This value is below the range cited above largely because ABC Medical Center has a relatively low value for days in accounts receivable, 50.3 days. This situation, of course, is favorable and is an objective of most financial managers. In general, the following objectives are usually associated with accounts receivable management.

- Minimize lost charges.
- Minimize write-offs for uncollectible accounts.
- Minimize the accounts receivable collection cycle.

All three objectives are important, but our attention will be directed at the third, minimizing the collection cycle. Figure 1-2 provides a schematic predicting intervals involved in the entire accounts receivable cycle. The following intervals usually exist in the hospital inpatient accounts receivable collection cycle:

- admission to discharge
- discharge to bill completion
- bill completion to receipt by payor
- receipt by payor to mailing of payment
- mailing of payment to receipt by hospital
- receipt by hospital to deposit in bank

The schematic in Figure 1-2 also provides estimated time that could be involved in each interval, but these numbers vary widely among hospitals and payor cate-

Table 1-3 ABC Medical Center—Consolidated Balance Sheets, June 30, 1987 and 1986

	Assets	
	1987	1986
Current assets		
Cash	$ 1,216,980	$ 362,442
Investments	4,042,407	4,597,806
Patient accounts receivable (1987, $7,356,120; 1986, $6,253,629), less allowance for uncollectibles	5,892,339	5,143,471
Other receivables		
Medicare	2,672,612	2,113,655
Miscellaneous	213,726	164,631
Inventories	1,302,598	1,174,295
Prepaid expenses	1,021,972	249,455
Current portion of deferred receivable from Medicare	454,404	502,904
Assets held by trustee	180,000	247,181
Total current assets	16,997,038	$14,555,840
Other assets		
Investments	$ 10,642,621	$10,983,125
Accounts receivable—affiliated companies	4,510,105	2,036,436
Note receivable—affiliated company	700,000	700,000
Assets held by trustee		
Temporary cash account	—	59,643
Construction fund	2,717,846	4,018,948
Sinking fund	6,751,942	6,112,530
Interest receivable	118,142	94,231
Self-insurance funds	10,942,749	7,875,602
Unamortized debt issuance expenses	934,535	954,078
Investment in ABC Insurance, Ltd.	209,655	—
Deferred receivables from Medicare	2,620,162	3,074,567
Prepaid pension cost	840,499	—
Unamortized past service cost	1,784,160	—
Total other assets	$ 42,772,416	$35,909,160
Property, plant, and equipment		
Land	$ 1,654,394	$ 1,649,912
Buildings	36,505,277	34,504,398
Improvements to land and leaseholds	1,272,205	1,263,959
Fixed equipment	8,812,615	8,713,615
Movable equipment	20,290,037	15,461,276
Capitalized leases	2,998,295	3,293,693
Total property, plant, and equipment	$ 71,532,823	$64,886,853
Less allowance for depreciation	27,763,195	22,037,503

Table 1-3 continued

	$ 43,769,628	$42,849,350
Construction and other work in progress	4,396,463	3,869,866
	$ 48,166,091	$46,719,216
Total assets	$107,935,545	$97,184,216

	Liabilities and Fund Balances	
	1987	*1986*
Current Liabilities		
Accounts Payable Trade	$ 2,297,672	$ 2,531,257
Accrued salaries and wages	1,366,777	1,035,496
Accrued liability for compensated absences	1,232,586	1,119,800
Accrued Medicare liability	317,302	1,881,895
Accrued indigent care assessment	1,170,001	1,061,742
Other accrued liabilities	611,230	444,916
Current portion of long-term debt	1,528,910	1,442,420
Total current liabilities	$ 8,524,478	$ 9,517,526
Other liabilities		
Accounts payable—affiliated companies	$ 1,993,815	—
Self-insurance liabilities	8,904,000	$ 7,048,000
	$ 10,897,815	$ 7,048,000
Long-Term Debt, Less Current Maturities		
Series B bonds, less unamortized discount		
(1987, $1,144,348; 1986, $1,186,425)	$ 45,745,652	$46,063,575
Notes payable	3,902,113	1,888,504
Capital leases payable	127,535	595,407
	$ 49,775,300	$48,547,486
Fund Balance		
Unrestricted		
Operations	$ 29,909,968	$24,781,866
Board designated	8,259,181	6,792,182
	38,169,149	31,574,048
Restricted	568,803	497,156
	$ 38,737,952	$32,071,204
	$107,935,545	$97,184,216

Figure 1-2 Accounts Receivable Collection Cycle in Days

gories within hospitals. They are intended only to show the relative importance of each interval in the overall accounts receivable collection cycle. The total number of days represented in Figure 1-2 is 66, which is reasonably close to the national average of 71 days during 1987.

Admission to Discharge (Seven Days)

Shortening this interval is not the critical objective from an accounts receivable perspective. This does not imply, however, that a reduction in length of stay is not an objective, because it clearly is. With fixed prices per case, reduced length of stay is particularly desirable from a cost-management viewpoint.

In terms of managing the accounts receivable cycle, the real solution appears to be what takes place during this interval to expedite later collection. The following specific suggestions are provided:

- Determine whether interim billings are possible for long-length-of-stay patients. Some third-party payors permit interim billings if the length of stay exceeds a specified time interval. Often this is 21 days. While there may be relatively few patients in this category, it is important to recognize that the absolute value of accounts receivable represented by these patients can be quite large.
- Use advance deposits for nonemergent admissions. If insurance coverage can be verified, estimates of the total deductible and copayment amounts can be made. They can be requested from the patient prior to or at admission. In situations where this is not possible, a financing plan should be developed jointly between the hospital and the patient. Many patients appreciate being told before the fact what their insurance will pay and what their individual liability is likely to be.
- Obtain required insurance and eligibility information prior to admission for nonemergent patients. For emergency admissions, obtain the same data during the hospital stay. This will permit the preparation of a bill at, or shortly after, discharge.

Discharge to Bill Completion (15 Days)

Ideally this interval should be reduced as much as possible. While this may be an objective, there are clearly some cost/benefit trade-offs to be evaluated. For example, speeding up the processing of bills is desirable only if the cost involved does not exceed the benefits of quicker bill preparation. Basic suggestions include the following:

- Implement more timely billing and remove bottlenecks. Usually bills are not prepared at discharge so that late charges can be posted. If there is a constant delay in certain ancillary departments, corrective steps should be taken to improve posting. A holding period in excess of two to three days is probably not reasonable.
- Develop educational programs to show the effects of delays in completion of medical charts by physicians. Quite often, the major reason for delay in billing is an incomplete medical chart. Physicians must be informed of the effect these delays have on the hospital. Some hospitals have suspended admitting privileges of physicians who are constantly delinquent. While this strategy may not be useful in many hospitals, it is worth considering in some situations.

Bill Completion to Receipt by Payor (Four Days)

The estimated four-day length of this time interval is directly related to mail time. Several steps may be useful in shortening this interval.

- Deliver bills to the post office as soon as they are prepared for mailing. Bills may be stacked in nice neat piles and left on a desk for 1 or more days before being mailed.
- Consider electronic invoicing for large payors where this alternative is available. This cuts mail time to zero, and it may reduce the accounts receivable cycle for these payors by as much as four days.
- Try to settle all outpatient accounts at the point of discharge or departure. Each outpatient should be presented with a bill at the point of departure, and payment should be requested at this time.
- Submit a bill for any deductible and copayment amounts for hospital inpatients at the point of discharge. Settlement should take place at this point if the patient has been previously advised of the total amount due.

Receipt by Payor to Mailing of Payment (35 Days)

This interval varies greatly by type of payor. Some self-pay patients may have outstanding accounts for more than a year. Insurance companies may take an inordinate amount of time to settle bills because of disputes over coverage or reasonableness. Steps to be considered include:

- Selling some accounts receivable. Hospitals cannot legally sell bills to financing companies that are payable by Medicare or Medicaid. However, they can sell or borrow against amounts due from self-pay and private-pay patients. This market is growing as firms such as General Electric and Health Care Funding Corporation provide financing for hospital accounts receivable on either a with-recourse or without-recourse basis.
- Using discounts for prompt payment. Many businesses have long provided discounts as financial incentives for early payment. This strategy may be used for self-pay portions of hospital bills and also insurance payors. Sufficiently large discounts can also greatly reduce collection costs and write-offs. How large an inducement should be offered? This decision, of course, is firm-specific, but a five percent reduction for payment at discharge does not seem excessive.
- Setting up a system to respond quickly to third-party requests for additional data. Third-party payors often delay payment until requested information has been received and reviewed. At a minimum, a log should be maintained that shows dates of requests and dates of responses.
- Claiming all bad debts on the Medicare deductible and copayment portion of hospital bills. Medicare is liable for payment of bad debts experienced in these areas. It is important, however, to document reasonable collection efforts on the part of the hospital before Medicare liability for payment can be assured.
- Using frequent telephone follow-up to detect problems or concern with bills. In many situations self-pay hospital bills are not paid because there is a disagreement over the amount of the bill. This type of dispute can be avoided through prompt contact by a nonthreatening hospital employee who inquires about the patient's health and the amount of the bill. Sometimes this may be better handled by an independent party. Where this approach has been used, reductions in bad debt write-offs have been very large.

Payment Mailed to Receipt by Hospital (Four Days)

Mail time is the cause for this four-day interval. These delays cannot be prevented for most small personal accounts. In the case of a government or large insurance payor, a courier service can be used. Checks are picked up as they become available. For large out-of-town payors, a special courier arrangement can be used or direct deposits to an area bank initiated. Relatively large sums of money must be involved for these strategies to be cost-effective.

Receipt by Hospital to Deposit in Bank (One + Day)

Perhaps the only effective way this interval can be shortened is through the use of a lockbox arrangement in which payments go directly to a post office box that is cleaned at least once a day by bank employees. Bank employees deposit all payments, usually photocopy the checks, and send the copies, along with any enclosures, to the hospital for proper crediting. There is usually a cost for this service. The hospital must determine if improvement in the cash flow, plus potential reduction in clerical costs, is worth the fee charged.

Accounts Payable and Accrued Salaries and Wages

Accounts payable and accrued salaries and wages represent spontaneous sources of financing. This means that these amounts are not usually negotiated but vary directly with the level of operations. Table 1-3 shows that ABC Medical Center had $2,297,672 in accounts payable trade and $1,366,777 in accrued salaries and wages in 1987. In addition, $1,993,815 of accounts payable from affiliated companies also existed. These amounts are not small and represent a sizable proportion of ABC's total financing.

Managing accounts payable and accrued salaries is similar to the management of accounts receivable, except in a reverse direction. Instead of acceleration, most financial managers would like to slow payment to these accounts. A number of approaches, as discussed in the literature, attempt to do this. Several relevant approaches for a freestanding hospital are as follows:

- Delay payment of an account payable until the actual due date. A number of hospitals often process invoices upon receipt and initiate payment even when the invoices are not due for several weeks or several months. For example, many invoices for subscriptions to journals are sent out three to five months prior to their due dates. There is no reason to pay these invoices until they are actually due.

- Stretch accounts payable. This technique has been described frequently in the literature and is familiar to most individuals. Stretching accounts payable simply means delaying payment until some point after the due date. While this technique is often used, the ethics of the method is clearly debatable. In addition, delays may cause a hospital's credit rating to deteriorate. Vendors eventually will be unwilling to grant credit, or they may alter payment terms.

- Change the frequency of payroll. Although not a popular decision with employees, lengthening the payroll period can provide a significant amount of additional financing that is virtually free. For example, ABC Medical Center has an estimated weekly payroll of approximately $1,150,000. If ABC changes its payroll period from a weekly to a biweekly basis, it can create an additional source of financing equal to one week's payroll, or $1,150,000.

Investing that money at 8 percent provides $92,000 in annual investment income. Fewer payroll periods may also reduce bookkeeping costs.

- Use banks in distant cities to pay vendors and employees. This method may delay check clearing and create a day or two of float. Float is defined as the difference between the bank balance and the checkbook balance. It also may be a questionable practice, depending upon applicable state laws.
- Schedule deposits to checking accounts to match expected disbursements on a daily basis. A daily cash report can be prepared for each account using information obtained daily through a telephone call to the bank or electronic access to the account. The report can thus reconcile data on beginning cash balances and disbursements expected to be made that day. Separate accounts for payroll are often maintained to recognize the predictability of check clearing. For example, payroll checks issued on a Friday may have a highly predictable pattern of check clearing. Knowledge of this distribution enables the treasurer to minimize the amount of funds needed in the account on any given day to meet actual disbursements and thus maximize the amount of invested funds.

SHORT-TERM BANK FINANCING

Many health care firms may experience a short-term need for funds during their operating cycles. The need for funds may have resulted from a predictable seasonality in the receipt and disbursement of cash or it may represent an unexpected business event, such as a strike. Commercial banks are the predominant sources of short-term loans, but other sources are also available. Several common arrangements used by health care firms to arrange for short-term loans include those discussed below.

Single-Payment Loan

This is the simplest credit arrangement and is usually given for a specific purpose, such as the purchase of inventory. The note can be either on a discount or an add-on basis. In the discount arrangement, the interest is computed and deducted from the face value of the note. The actual proceeds of the loan, then, would be in an amount less than the face of the note. In an add-on note, the interest is added to the final payment of the loan. In this arrangement, the borrower receives the full value of the loan at loan origination.

Line of Credit

A line of credit is an agreement that permits a firm to borrow up to a specified limit during a defined loan period. For example, a commercial bank may grant a $2 million line of credit to a hospital during a specific year. In that year, the hospital could borrow up to $2 million from the bank with presumably little or no additional paperwork required. Lines of credit are either committed or uncommitted. In an uncommitted line, there is no formal or binding agreement on the part of the bank to loan money. If conditions change, the bank could decide not to loan any funds at all. In a committed line of credit, there is a written agreement that conveys the terms and conditions of the line of credit. The bank is legally required to loan money under the line as long as the terms and conditions have been met by the borrower. To cover the costs and risks incurred by the commercial bank in a committed line of credit, the bank charges a commitment fee. The fee is usually based on either the total credit line or the unused portion of the line.

Revolving Credit Agreements

A revolving credit is similar to a line of credit except that it is usually for a period of time greater than 1 year. Revolving credit agreements may be in effect for 2 to 3 years. Most revolving credit agreements are renegotiated prior to maturity. If the renegotiation occurs more than one year prior to maturity, a revolving credit agreement loan may be stated as a long-term debt and never appear as a current liability on a firm's balance sheet. Terms of revolving credit agreements are similar to lines of credit. Interest rates are usually variable and based on the prime rate or other money market rates.

Term Loans

Term loans are made for a specific period of time, usually ranging between two and seven years. The loans usually require periodic installment payments of the principal. This type of loan is frequently used to finance a tangible asset that will produce income in future periods, such as a CT scanner. The asset acquired with the loan proceeds may be pledged as collateral for the loan.

Letters of Credit

Letters of credit are used by some hospitals as a method of bond insurance. A letter of credit is simply a letter from a bank stating that a loan will be made if certain conditions are met. In hospital bond financing, a letter of credit from a bank guarantees payment of the loan if the hospital defaults.

INVESTMENT OF CASH SURPLUSES

The term surplus is confusing, even among financial executives. For the purpose of this discussion, cash surplus is defined as money exceeding a minimum balance that the firm prefers to keep on hand to meet immediate operating expenses and to meet minor contingencies, plus any compensating balance required at its banks.

The balance sheet for ABC Medical Center shown in Table 1-3 lists a cash balance of $1,216,980 plus $4,042,407 in short-term investments as of June 30, 1987. These are the funds that are most often referred to as surplus cash when discussing short-term investment strategy. It is important to note that ABC Medical Center has significant investments in other areas. Most hospitals follow this procedure. For example, ABC Medical Center, as of June 30, 1987, has $10,642,621 in an investments account under the "Other assets" section of the balance sheet. These funds are probably designated for the eventual replacement of the hospital plant. In addition, sizable balances of funds are maintained with a trustee. For example, there is $2,717,846 in the construction fund account, $6,751,942 in the sinking fund account, $118,142 in the interest receivable account, and $10,942,749 in the self-insurance fund account. Most hospitals and health care firms maintain similar fund balances. It is critical for management to make investments that will meet the objectives of each specific fund and maximize the potential yield to the firm.

Often a portion of a firm's investment funds is restricted to money market investments. The term money market refers to the market for short-term securities, including Treasury bills, negotiable certificates of deposit, banker's acceptances, commercial paper, and repurchase agreements. Maturities for money market investments can range from one day to one year. Funds invested in money market securities usually serve two roles. They represent (1) a liquidity reserve that can be used if the firm experiences a need for these funds and (2) a temporary investment of surplus funds that can result in the earning of a return.

If the funds are invested for periods of time longer than one year (for example, the investment of a replacement reserve fund) higher yields often result. These longer-term maturity investments may not be referred to as money market securities.

In evaluating alternative investment strategies, there are usually five basic criteria that should be reviewed. These are

1. price stability
2. safety of principal

3. marketability
4. maturity
5. yield

Price Stability

The importance of price stability, especially for money market investments, cannot be overemphasized. If a firm has a sudden need for cash, most major money market investments can be sold without any serious capital losses. Generally, U.S. Treasury bills are the most creditworthy money market investments, followed closely by other U.S. Treasury obligations and federal agency issues. Investment in securities with long-term maturities are subject to risk if interest rates rise. This explains why money market investments are usually restricted to maturities of less than one year.

Safety of Principal

Financial managers expect that the principal of their investment is generally not at risk. Treasury and federal agency obligations have little risk of principal loss through default. Bank securities, such as negotiable certificates of deposit and banker's acceptances, and corporate obligations, such as commercial paper, are different matters. There may be a loss of principal through default, and care should be exercised in choosing these instruments. Information on banks is available in Polk's *World Bank Directory* and Moody's *Bank and Finance Manual*. There is no reason why a firm should not review the creditworthiness of its banks as carefully as banks review the financial position of loan applicants. It should be noted, however, that erosion of principal can occur through increases in money market interest rates, and these increases will subsequently impact fixed-rate securities.

Marketability

Marketability varies among money market instruments. The term refers to the ability to sell a security quickly and with little price concession prior to maturity. In general, an active secondary trading market must exist to ensure the presence of marketability. Most major money market instruments do have active secondary markets, especially obligations of the U.S. Treasury. Some commercial paper, especially that of industrial firms, may be difficult to redeem prior to maturity.

Maturity

There is a clear relationship between the yield of a security and its maturity that can be summarized in a yield curve. Table 1-4 shows a set of values for Treasury bills on July 6, 1989. Some firms employ a strategy of investment described as "riding the yield curve." This strategy relies on the existence of an upward sloping yield curve. Investments are made in longer-term securities that are sold prior to maturity. Chapter 11 describes this method in some detail.

Yield

Yield is a measure of the investment's return and is an important consideration. Yield is usually affected by maturity, expected default risk of principal, marketability, and price stability. In addition, taxability is often an issue. A tax-exempt health care firm has no incentive to invest in securities that are exempt from federal income taxes.

SUMMARY

Cash and investment management is concerned with decisions that have an impact on operating cash flows of the firm. Ideally, the objective of most cash management systems is to accelerate the collection of cash from customers and to slow down the payment to suppliers and employees. Investment management is very important in many health care firms because of the relative size of their invest-

Table 1-4 Yield to Maturity for Treasury Bills, July 6, 1989

Days to Maturity	Annualized Yield (percent)
7	7.30
14	7.26
21	7.83
28	7.98
35	7.75
42	8.04
49	8.07
56	8.01
63	8.08
70	8.10

ment portfolios. Hospitals, for example, generate about 30 percent of their total net income from nonoperating sources, largely investment income. With so much at stake, health care firms need to improve performance in the cash and investment management area.

Chapter 2

The U.S. Banking System

STRUCTURE OF THE BANKING SYSTEM

The commercial banking system in the United States has a dual nature in two areas. First, some banking institutions are regulated by agencies of the federal government, while others are regulated by agencies of state governments. The second aspect of duality in the U.S. banking system derives from the fact that there are two types of banking institutions in the system: commercial banks and thrift institutions.

The term "thrifts" refers to savings banks, savings and loan institutions, and credit unions. There are approximately 9,000 thrift institutions in the country. They primarily serve consumers who want to save money or to borrow money for consumer purchases. Companies seeking unsecured loans to obtain working capital seldom look to thrifts; they look to commercial banks that also provide the services required by corporations to manage their daily cash flows.

Commercial banks accept deposits on behalf of, and make loans to, all classes of customers—individuals, public organizations, and private organizations. A bank uses the deposits it accepts to make short-term and intermediate-term loans. Banks make intermediate-term loans that meet their customers' capital needs, and short-term loans that enable their customers to manage their short-term and seasonal cash flows.

The dual nature of bank regulation is probably more important to bankers than to financial managers, but a general understanding of banking regulation can be important to good financial management. Most banks are chartered by state agencies, but whether regulatory and supervisory responsibility rests with federal or state agencies, the goal is the same: to monitor the fiscal soundness and operations of banks.

The U.S. Comptroller of the Currency is the primary federal agency that supervises national banks. Banking departments or commissioners in each state supervise state-chartered banks. In addition, any qualified bank that wants its deposits insured must be examined by the Federal Deposit Insurance Corporation (FDIC), which provides that service. All federal and state banks that are members of the Federal Reserve System are required to have their deposits insured by the FDIC. Some thrifts are insured by the FDIC, and others may elect, if qualified, to be insured by the Federal Savings and Loan Insurance Corporation.

To financial managers, one of the most important aspects of banking regulation is interstate banking. The Depository Institutions Deregulation and Monetary Control Act, passed by Congress in 1980, marked the dawn of interstate banking in the United States. The act eliminated federal legal barriers forcing banks to operate in only one state. Similar changes in state laws—many of which allow banks in one state to do business in adjacent states—have followed. Legal restrictions to nationwide interstate banking are expected to be largely eliminated by 1991.

One of the short-term effects of nationwide interstate banking to interest financial managers will be faster funds collection and concentration for those firms operating in more than one state. With nationwide interstate banking, companies receiving mail payments will be able to receive those payments in different regions through lockboxes operated by a single bank. That bank will consolidate the funds internally, eliminating the costly process of initiating funds concentration. The larger and more technologically advanced banks will be able to accept deposits in virtually all business centers and consolidate funds within their own banks when state laws allow them to maintain offices throughout the country.

Bank mergers will be another likely consequence of nationwide interstate banking—a consequence that should work to the benefit of larger companies. Mergers could cut the number of commercial banks by one-third from the current 15,000. Banks serving the same region may merge to create large regional banks. Banks serving different regions may merge to form ''super-regional,'' or even nationwide, banks. Indeed, such mergers are currently in process, as banks serving different states are being bought by bank holding companies. The larger banks should be able to offer large corporations more complete lines of cash management products, better pricing, and more experienced and competent management teams.

These major changes in the banking system have just begun in the late 1980s and probably will not settle into a stable pattern until the late 1990s. Despite such rapid changes, however, business communities around the globe must realize that the U.S. banking system will maintain a certain degree of stability. U.S. banks lubricate the world economy. Because the United States is a huge supplier to world markets and an enormous consumer of their products, financial troubles in this country affect all of its global trading partners. The task of providing worldwide markets with the economic, political, and psychological reassurances they need falls on the federal government in general and the Federal Reserve System in particular.

Regulation and Supervision

Bank regulation means the promulgation of rules that govern the structure and conduct of banking in order to maintain a sound banking system. Regulation must meet this goal by providing a framework of rules and financial profiles within which financial institutions can operate. Supervision, on the other hand, means the examination of individual banking institutions. Banks are continually examined by government regulatory agencies to ensure that they comply with banking laws and are well managed.

Because of the dual nature of the banking system—some banks are chartered by the federal government and others by state governments—banks are supervised by both levels of government. Each state has its own agency to supervise banks. At the federal level, there are three main agencies that supervise banks: the Federal Reserve System, the Office of the Comptroller of the Currency, and the Federal Deposit Insurance Corporation. To avoid overlapping duties, the federal and state agencies have established arrangements to ensure that each agency performs its functions without subjecting financial institutions to potential harm resulting from multiple examinations. The areas covered by the three federal regulators are:

1. Federal Reserve System (Fed). The Federal Reserve System (usually referred to as the "Fed" in financial circles) oversees banks that are members of the Federal Reserve. All national banks are required to be Federal Reserve members, and state-chartered banks may elect to join. Bank holding companies are also subject to regulation and supervision by the Fed.
2. Office of the Comptroller of the Currency (OCC). The OCC grants charters to national banks. Consequently, the OCC regulates, supervises, and examines those banks. Its regulatory duties are much more detailed than those of the Fed. The Fed has only general regulatory and supervisory responsibilities over national banks and reviews financial statements and examination reports prepared by the OCC.
3. Federal Deposit Insurance Corporation (FDIC). The FDIC, in keeping with its role of insuring deposits, directly supervises only insured commercial banks that are not members of the Fed. The FDIC also supervises state-chartered savings banks that elect to buy FDIC protection.

ROLE OF THE FEDERAL RESERVE SYSTEM

Financial managers are concerned with borrowing and investing money. The financial manager of a health care organization, therefore, must be aware of the condition of the economy and the direction and level of interest rates. Almost every financial decision, whether the company is a net borrower or a net investor, is affected by interest rates. High interest rates, for instance, can reduce the availability of credit and slow the collection of accounts receivable. It increases the cost of capital expenditures for plant and equipment. It is crucial for financial managers to gain an understanding of why interest rates change, how those changes affect the economy, and how they affect a manager's own institution. That means understanding the Fed and how it influences the U.S. economy through the manipulation of interest rates.

The weight of the Fed in the economy is probably equal to that of all of the other players combined. Because of the overriding importance of the Fed—not only in terms of its duties to safeguard the banking system but also in terms of its duties to manage the U.S. economy through monetary and credit policies—the next three sections of this chapter are devoted to explaining the Fed. First, its structure is explained. Next, the operations of monetary policy, the tool used by the Fed to regulate the country's economy and thus its banking environment, is detailed. Finally, how the Fed functions in relation to the U.S. Department of the Treasury will be discussed.

Structure of the Federal Reserve System

Congress created the Federal Reserve System as an independent agency of the federal government with the adoption of the Federal Reserve Act on December 23, 1913. Although the Fed is independent, it reports to Congress and works with other federal agencies in developing and executing the country's monetary policy. Congress enacts the banking laws of the land, and the Federal Reserve's Board of Governors adopts additional regulations to implement those laws.

The Fed implements and administers banking laws through regulations ranging from specifications relating to its functions as the nation's central bank, to descriptions of the activities of banks and their holding companies, to rules governing consumer credit transactions. In administering its regulations the Fed has four basic tasks:

1. It manages the monetary policy of the United States.
2. It regulates U.S. banks.

3. It provides banking services as a wholesaler.
4. It acts as fiscal agent for the U.S. Department of the Treasury.

The Fed has three principal components: the Board of Governors, the 12 Federal Reserve Banks and their branches, and the Federal Open Market Committee (see Figure 2-1).

Board of Governors

The Board of Governors' primary responsibilities are to formulate credit and monetary policy and to supervise the 12 district Reserve Banks, bank holding companies, and member banks. The board has seven members, who serve 14-year terms. Each governor is appointed by the President and confirmed by the Senate. The chairman of the Board of Governors probably has more influence on interest rates than any other single person. By virtue of this influence, the chairman's opinions and the actions of the organization he directs must command the attention of health care financial managers, along with financial managers in all industries.

Federal Open Market Committee

The Federal Open Market Committee (FOMC) determines the Fed's policy on the control of money and credit. To determine the degree of control, the FOMC regularly assesses the condition of the U.S. economy and its international trade balance, and it bases its decisions on the most timely and accurate economic data available. To implement monetary policy, the FOMC decides whether to buy or sell U.S. Treasury securities from its portfolio, which is the largest portfolio of U.S. government securities in the world. FOMC decisions alter the amount of money in the banking system, thereby influencing the amount of credit that the financial markets can offer.

The FOMC consists of the seven Fed governors and five of the 12 Reserve Bank presidents. Reserve bank presidents rotate their membership on the FOMC, with the exception of the president of the Federal Reserve Bank of New York, who is a permanent member. The New York bank implements the FOMC's decisions by conducting open market operations; that is, buying and selling U.S. Treasury securities to alter the amount of funds and credit in the banking system.

Federal Reserve District Banks

Each of the 12 Federal Reserve districts serves a geographic region of the United States, and each district has a district Federal Reserve Bank. The 12 district banks, in turn, have 25 branches and 11 regional check processing centers (RCPCs), as shown in Table 2-1.

134,894

College of St. Francis Library
Joliet, Illinois

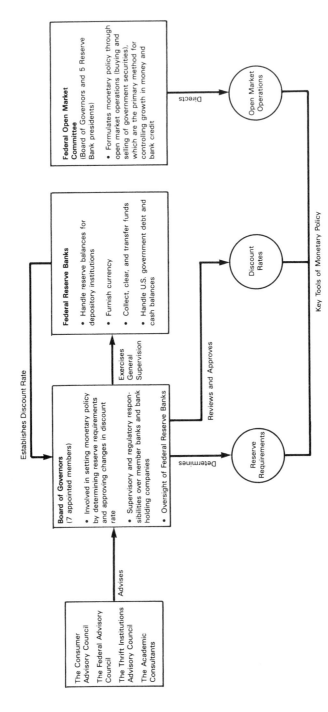

Figure 2-1 The Organization Chart of the Federal Reserve System. *Source:* Board of Governors of the Federal Reserve System.

Table 2-1 Federal Reserve Banks, Branches, and Regional Check Processing Centers

Federal Reserve District	Reserve Bank Headquarters City	Branches	RCPCs
1	Boston	—	Lewiston Windsor Locks
2	New York	Buffalo	Cranford Jericho Utica
3	Philadelphia	—	—
4	Cleveland	Cincinnati Pittsburgh	Columbus
5	Richmond	Baltimore Charlotte	Columbia Charleston
6	Atlanta	Birmingham Jacksonville Miami Nashville New Orleans	—
7	Chicago	Detroit	Des Moines Indianapolis Milwaukee
8	St. Louis	Little Rock Louisville Memphis	—
9	Minneapolis	Helena	—
10	Kansas City	Denver Oklahoma City Omaha	—
11	Dallas	El Paso Houston San Antonio	—
12	San Francisco	Los Angeles Portland Salt Lake City Seattle	—

The Fed can be compared with an electrical power system. The Federal Reserve Banks form the wires through which the electricity generated by the Fed's power plant (the FOMC) flows; the banks are the means by which the Fed's monetary and credit policies and supervisory powers are put into practice. Services performed by the Federal Reserve Banks include

- maintaining reserve and clearing accounts
- accepting deposits and executing payment orders from member and non-member depository institutions
- providing coin and currency
- operating electronic and paper-based payment systems

The Federal Reserve Banks are also fiscal agents, depositories, and custodians for the U.S. Treasury and many foreign central banks, as well as for international organizations such as the International Monetary Fund.

Legally, the district banks are unusual entities. Stock in each district bank is held by that district's member banks—the banks being regulated own the stock of the bank that regulates them. Yet these stockholders do not have the same powers and privileges as the stockholders of private corporations. The selection of Federal Reserve Bank officers, for instance, is not a duty that stockholders may exercise on their own. The board of each Reserve Bank is composed of nine directors. Three directors represent the member banks; three are independent members, which means they are not involved in the lending business; and three are appointed by the Board of Governors. Each bank's chairman and deputy chairman are selected from the Board of Governors' appointees. The board of directors appoints the bank's president, who serves as chief executive officer, and the bank's first vice president. The president and first vice president serve five-year terms and are approved by the Board of Governors.

Member Banks

Only about 5,700 of some 15,000 commercial banks are members of the Federal Reserve System. The law requires that federally chartered banks be members. Banks chartered by the states can become members, but their membership must be approved by the Board of Governors. Although only about 38 percent of U.S. banks are members, member banks hold more than 70 percent of U.S. bank deposits.

The amount of stock that each member holds in its district's Federal Reserve Bank equals 3 percent of the member's capital and surplus. Since 1980, a uniform structure of reserve requirements has governed all depository institutions, whether or not they are members of the Federal Reserve System. All depository institutions may use the credit facilities of the Fed and purchase its services.

Federal Reserve Operations

Monetary policy is the principal tool used by the Fed to achieve its goals with respect to managing the U.S. economy. Essentially, monetary policy consists of the daily activities in which the Fed engages to influence the amount of money and credit in the U.S. economy. Monetary policy is not the same as fiscal policy. Fiscal policy comprises the actions of federal agencies other than the Fed in managing the government's taxation, spending, and debt. Monetary policy, on the other hand, refers to the buying and selling of U.S. securities by the Fed to control the amount of money flowing through the U.S. economy. Monetary policy and fiscal policy, of course, influence each other, but they are established by different agencies of the federal government and influence different elements of the economy.

For its part, the Fed must ensure that there is enough money and credit in the economy for the volume of transactions that people and organizations want to complete. The Fed constantly measures how various forces affect the growth of the economy, price stability, and inflation and deflation. A large part of the economic research and analysis that the Fed uses is undertaken by the 12 Federal Reserve Banks, most of which publish monthly or quarterly journals and other materials. The economics staff of the Federal Reserve Board of Governors and the Federal Open Market Committee (FOMC) use that research to set monetary policy that manages all of the pressures on the economy by influencing the availability of money and credit. Monetary policy is executed by the FOMC in three basic ways:

1. the purchase and sale of U.S. government securities in the open market
2. the adjustment of reserve requirements by the Board of Governors
3. the lending of funds to depository institutions by Federal Reserve Banks

Open Market Operations

The U.S. government securities market is the benchmark for the markets of all other debt securities—long-term and short-term, public and private. The interest rates of all other securities are based on those of government securities of like maturity. As a result, the FOMC, which manages the Fed's investment portfolio, can affect interest rates by influencing the level of supply of debt securities in the marketplace. With a portfolio of government securities valued in mid-1989 at more than $230 billion, the FOMC merely has to buy or sell government securities to exert its influence on the economy.

The trading desk at the New York Fed handles securities trading for the FOMC. Traders at the New York bank conduct almost all of their business with some 43 primary dealers in government securities. These dealers are ready to trade in any issue of government securities and must report their financial conditions to the Fed regularly. By virtue of their constant contact with Fed traders, these securities dealers are the Fed's primary sources of information on interest rates and trading activities in the government securities market.

The interaction of the primary dealers and Fed traders implements decisions made by the FOMC on how much money and credit should be available in the economy. To increase short-term interest rates, the Fed will sell securities in the market, thereby absorbing funds out of the banking system. It obtains quotes from the primary dealers on short-term government securities. After soliciting bids from the dealers for each security, the traders simultaneously sell the securities to the primary dealers at the best prices, but they stay within the dollar limits set by the Fed's trading office. When the Fed sells securities, dealers are forced to finance their purchases either by borrowing from banks or by selling other securities to maintain their liquidity. Conversely, by purchasing securities, the Fed adds funds to the banking system, thereby providing liquidity and tending to force interest rates downward.

Many of the primary dealers also happen to be banks that pay for their securities by using money in the reserve accounts they maintain with the Fed. As a result, the amount of nonearning reserve funds that these dealer-banks have on deposit with the Fed is reduced to less than the reserve level they are required to maintain. To keep their reserves and still pay for the securities transactions, lenders have several options. They may (1) decide not to make as many loans; (2) make it more expensive to borrow (thus reducing the number of customers willing to borrow) by increasing interest rates; (3) sell securities, which increases the supply of securities and thus drives up interest rates; or (4) use some combination of these actions. In any case, the FOMC can cause interest rates to increase by its decision to sell securities.

Reserve Requirements

The Monetary Control Act of 1980 requires that each depository institution maintain reserves against its deposits. This means that a bank cannot lend, or otherwise invest, a certain percentage of the money it takes in as deposits. The act set the level of reserves that banks must maintain at 12 percent of demand deposits, and the Fed's Board of Governors has the power to adjust that percentage in order to achieve monetary policy objectives. There had been no adjustments to this reserve requirement through the second quarter of 1989.

In practice, the Fed would not adjust the level of required reserves very often. The Fed can take other actions to cause a bank's reserves to decline, which then forces the bank to restore reserves at the required level. Banks can increase their reserves either by borrowing from the Fed's discount window or by selling liquid securities. A change in reserves in the banking system ripples through the economy like a stone thrown into a pond.

Fed Funds

Defined as short-term unsecured loans between banks, Fed Funds loans usually are only overnight loans, although they may be extended for a longer period. Fed Funds are important to health care financial managers because an interest rate change on such loans is a key indicator of the supply and demand for money and credit in the economy. It also serves to form the basis for interest rates on short-term loans and yields on short-term money market securities. In fact, there is generally considerable interbank activity in Fed Funds loans because the Fed tends to discourage banks from borrowing at its discount window. It prefers to allow discount window borrowing only when credit is extremely tight and banks do not have enough excess reserves to meet demand, or when a bank's financial condition is so poor that other banks will not extend it credit. The interest rate on Fed Funds, however, is a key indicator of very short-term (one-day) interest rates.

As a result of the Fed's attitude toward discount window borrowing, there is an extremely active market in which banks with excess reserves lend to banks whose reserves fall below the required level. Large regional and money center banks simultaneously lend and borrow in the Fed Funds market. The large banks use the market to offer a service to their smaller correspondent banks; the amount of Fed Funds that a small bank needs or has to offer may not be large enough to attract interest in the market, so the large correspondent meets the small bank's shortage or buys its excess reserves. Because the larger bank quotes a spread to buy and sell small blocks of Fed Funds, it makes a profit while adjusting its own net funds position. The large banks can often make up for their own reserve shortages by buying funds from smaller banks at interest rates below market.

The significance of Fed Funds to the health care financial manager, as mentioned earlier, is the benchmark interest rate for very short-term investments (usually overnight). This rate is the principal determinant of the yield that a hospital can obtain on overnight investments of its pool of liquidity reserves.

Action Advice: Health care financial managers can use the Fed Funds market to the benefit of their companies. By making a Fed Funds loan to a bank instead of investing the money in a certificate of deposit, a financial manager can improve the yield on short-term cash without appreciably increasing risk. A Fed Funds loan is akin to a repurchase agreement but without collateral. A bank must maintain reserves against a certificate of deposit (CD) or checking account balance, but there is no requirement for a bank to maintain reserves against a Fed Funds loan. Consequently, the bank can offer a slightly higher interest rate to an investor on a Fed Funds loan than it can on a CD. Whether a bank will want to make a Fed Funds loan, of course, depends on whether it needs to borrow.

Lending Operations

The Fed conducts its lending operations through its discount window at each Federal Reserve Bank. All depository institutions are required to maintain accounts with the Fed and may borrow from the Fed, whether or not they are members. Even so, the Fed tends to consider the discount window to be the lender of last resort and prefers banks to borrow from other institutions. Loans made through the discount window are designed to accomplish two objectives: (1) to help depository institutions restore their reserves as part of the Fed's open market operations, and (2) to provide the banking and financial system with liquidity when it is under economic stress.

Two types of loans are made through the discount window: advances and discounts. Advances are loans to depository institutions that borrow against collateral, such as pledged securities of the federal, state, and local governments; certain types of mortgage loans; and some forms of business and consumer loans that may include loans made to health care firms and institutions. Most borrowing at the discount window is in the form of advances. Discounts, on the other hand, are loan instruments that the depository institution sells (with recourse) to the Fed at a discount from maturity value. The interest rate that the Federal Reserve Bank charges on advances and discounts is called the discount rate. The discount rate is not a market rate; it is set and periodically adjusted by the Board of Governors. As a result, the discount rate tends to lag behind the market and is not a good indicator of current economic activity.

Activity at the discount window signifies the general condition of credit markets. In periods of tight credit, activity at the discount window increases when institutions that rely heavily on volatile checking account deposits or have heavy short-term loan commitments are forced to adjust their reserves. Indeed, the major reason institutions seek credit at the discount window is to make short-term adjustments in their reserve positions because of a sudden change in deposit levels, a need to fund unexpected loans, or a temporary gap in obtaining funds from other sources.

Federal Reserve Relationships

U.S. Treasury

In addition to their functions in carrying out policy set by the Board of Governors, the Federal Reserve Banks and their branches act as bankers for the federal government. Reserve banks maintain checking accounts for the U.S. Treasury and clear Treasury checks drawn against the accounts. These are the checks that pay the federal government's bills, including social security payments and the salaries and retirement benefits of government employees. Reserve banks are also central collection points for the Department of the Treasury. The department maintains accounts for tax receipts at 15,000 depository institutions, and tax funds deposited in those banks are concentrated at Federal Reserve Banks.

The Federal Reserve Banks also function as the Treasury's fiscal agents in operations that involve issuing, redeeming, and transferring ownership of government securities such as Treasury bills, bonds, and notes. The Fed distributes information on new issues, accepts tenders from the public, collects payment for the securities, and credits the Treasury's account with the proceeds. The Fed also operates the communications network for transferring the ownership of Treasury securities from sellers to buyers. Finally, the Fed issues, services, and redeems U.S. savings bonds and handles the work involved in allowing depository institutions and corporations to issue and redeem savings bonds.

Financial Management Service

Although it is part of the Treasury, not the Fed, the Financial Management Service is another agency that financial managers may want to understand, especially if their organizations do business with nondefense government agencies, such as the Health Care Financing Administration. Financial Management Service (FMS) is the organization that performs cash management functions and pays the bills for the federal government. FMS headquarters are in Washington, D.C. Seven regional financial centers handle the government's collections, payments, accounting, credit administration, and cash management. Cash flow amounting to some $7 billion a day is managed by FMS.

SUMMARY

The banking system in the United States consists of approximately 15,000 commercial banks and 9,000 "thrift" institutions that largely serve consumers and make real estate loans. Bank regulation and supervision by specific agencies depend on the source of the bank's charter, federal or state. The Federal Reserve System regulates banks and the money supply in the nation. It also has a strong influence on interest rates in order to stimulate or moderate the rate of growth and inflation in the economy.

The Fed's principal weapon for economic activity is called "open market operations," in which the Fed buys and sells U.S. Treasury securities to manage the supply of funds available in the banking system, thereby influencing interest rates. Another potential tool to control money supply is the reserve requirement placed on banks. This is not a flexible tool and is not used frequently.

Chapter 3

U.S. Payments System Operation

HISTORY

The history of the modern check began during the 1500s, when Dutch "cashiers" accepted deposits to protect money against bandits. Goldsmiths in late 17th-century England performed essentially the same service. They accepted deposits and then issued receipts that promised to pay either the depositor or someone the depositor designated.

Checks were introduced in the United States in 1681, but were little used for more than a century. The use of checks in drawing against bank account deposits did not increase in popularity in the United States until after the Revolutionary War as cities grew, transportation improved, and a postal system with low rates was developed. By the time of the Civil War, checks had replaced paper currency as the preferred means of settling debts.

The use of checks presented problems, however. The United States did not have a central bank to settle activity between banks, so each bank had to set up accounts with other banks in order to clear transactions made between their customers. As the amount of checks and the number of banks increased, the cost and inconvenience of moving funds in that manner became obvious. It also became apparent that a centralized system for clearing checks was needed to reduce the delays and costs associated with clearing checks. Congress created a centralized system in 1913, with the adoption of the Federal Reserve Act. Under the Act, Federal Reserve Banks and their branches were charged with collecting and clearing checks for their member banks. Because the system cleared checks at par, the process of routing checks through the country became faster and less costly.

HOW CHECKS MOVE

Through its centralized system of clearing checks, the Federal Reserve System (usually referred to as the "Fed") now processes more than 15 billion checks per year. This figure represents about one-third of the total number of checks written annually in this country. The remaining 30 billion checks are cleared by essentially the same methods used before the formation of the Fed. They are processed within a depository institution and then sent to correspondent banks or exchanged in local clearinghouses.

A basic task of a health care financial manager is to design a cash management system that will make the best use of the payment float associated with check clearing and achieve an optimally low cost in terms of bank and other financial charges. Financial managers should understand the multiple check-clearing systems that continue to exist and how each system functions. These systems include the Fed, correspondent banking, and clearinghouses.

Financial managers can then use their knowledge of check-clearing systems to advantage when selecting banks by examining closely the different pricing schedules and service levels of competing banks. They can improve the efficiency of their organizations' cash management systems by selecting banks with optimal check-clearing deadlines and pricing.

For example, a health care institution located in Phoenix may receive sizable checks from fiscal intermediaries that are drawn on banks in Chicago. The health care institution's Phoenix bank has three options for handling checks drawn on Chicago banks. It can (1) deposit these checks with the Fed located 400 miles away in Los Angeles; (2) send the checks to the Chicago Fed, or (3) if the Phoenix bank maintains a depository account with a Chicago correspondent bank, it can send the checks to the Chicago correspondent (see Figure 3-1).

The method the bank uses in its check-clearing operations may result in later deposit deadlines and faster funds availability than in other Phoenix banks. Sending the checks to Los Angeles and obtaining next-day availability, for instance, requires that the Phoenix bank meet an early deposit deadline of perhaps 8:00 p.m. Sending the checks by courier to the Chicago correspondent, however, may extend the deadline to perhaps as late as 5:00 a.m. the next morning and give the Phoenix bank more time to process the checks. The difference in these deadlines can result in availability of hundreds of thousands of dollars one day earlier, which will offer the health care institution greater liquidity and additional interest income or reduced interest expense.

Check Clearing

When a check is deposited into a bank, called the depository bank, that bank credits the customer's account. The check then must be physically moved from the depository bank to the bank on which it is drawn—the drawee bank. The route the check takes from the depository bank to the drawee bank depends on the physical proximity of the two banks, as well as any special arrangements that exist between

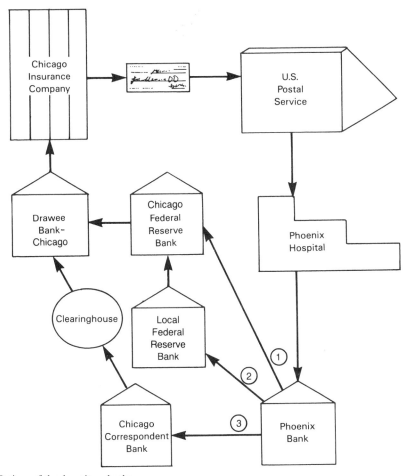

Options of the depository bank:
(1) Deposit to Federal Reserve Bank.
(2) Send directly to drawee bank if it is a correspondent of Phoenix Bank.
(3) Send to correspondent of Phoenix bank located in the same city as the drawee bank, where the check is presented through the Chicago clearinghouse.

Figure 3-1 Route of a Check

them or with another bank. Check-clearing patterns are largely a function of geography. There are three geographical directions in which a check can move:

1. The check can stay in the depository bank, if the check is drawn on that bank.
2. The check can be sent to a local clearinghouse, if the check is drawn on another local bank.

3. The check can be sent to either the Fed or a correspondent bank for deposit, if the check is drawn on a distant bank.

Local Checks

There are two main types of local checks. First, checks drawn on the depository bank itself, called "on-us" checks, are processed within the bank and charged to the issuer's account. Second, checks drawn on other local or regional banks may be exchanged directly between the depository bank and the drawee banks, or they may be deposited with the nearest Federal Reserve System's Regional Check Processing Center. Unlike the 37 Federal Reserve district banks and branches, the 11 Regional Check Processing Centers (RCPCs) provide *only* check-clearing services. However, the district banks and branches also process checks.

Clearinghouse Checks

The term "clearinghouse checks" refers to the bilateral exchange of checks between a depository bank and a drawee bank. This process has been used since bank messengers in 17th-century London discovered that they could meet at one central location to sort their bundles of checks, rather than travel to each bank to deliver checks. The modern clearinghouse works much the same way, with member banks exchanging "on-us" checks that were received by other clearinghouse members. The banks then calculate the net amounts due to and from each other. At the end of the day, perhaps after several clearinghouse meetings, the banks determine their net positions with each other and then settle by transferring funds through either their respective Federal Reserve accounts or their correspondent accounts.

Checks drawn on other local banks generally require zero time or one day to collect. The depository bank receives credit to its account at the end of the day, which is usually one day after the depositor's account has been credited. Exhibit 3-1 shows typical times associated with the processing of clearinghouse checks.

As Exhibit 3-1 shows, clearinghouse checks deposited over the counter during Day No. 1, even early in the day, will not be exchanged with other drawee banks that day, because banks usually do not process the deposits until the evening. There are exceptions, however. For example, checks received by the bank through a lockbox are usually processed by the depository bank early enough to meet the clearinghouse deadlines. Therefore, the funds become collected (and investable) the same day the checks are deposited. Checks drawn on depository institutions that are not members of the local clearinghouse (usually including savings and loans, savings banks, credit unions, and local offices of foreign banks) will clear through other channels, such as correspondent banks, that may lengthen float time. The sooner the depository bank can actually collect the funds represented by

Exhibit 3-1 Clearinghouse Checks and Clearing Float

Day No. 1:

3 P.M.   At the end of the business day, the bank accumulates its deposits and processes them in its proof of deposit and transit departments.

5 P.M.   Processing the checks involves the verification of deposit amounts and sorting of checks by category: "on-us," clearinghouse, and transit (out of town).

11 P.M.   Throughout the night, the bank prepares cash letters—the term bankers use to refer to deposits made with other banks—that will be sent to the Fed and correspondent banks. After cash letters are prepared, clearinghouse checks are sorted and totaled for delivery to the clearinghouse.

Day No. 2:

7 A.M.   The first clearinghouse meeting takes place at about this time. There may be several meetings throughout the day. At these meetings, checks are exchanged among clearinghouse members, and the respective amounts are noted and verified.

2 P.M.   At the final clearinghouse meeting of the day, a bank's net position in relation to each other clearinghouse bank is calculated. Money is transferred through the Fed by each bank that owes funds to each bank that is owed the funds.

---

the check, however, the sooner the depositor can use these funds to make investments or repay debt.

Regional Checks

The Federal Reserve district bank collects and processes checks drawn on banks in the district that do not belong to the clearinghouse. Alternatively, depository banks that are not members of the clearinghouse can use a correspondent bank that is a member of the clearinghouse. When clearing checks through the Fed, the depository bank sends a cash letter (deposit) to the Fed, which credits the bank's Fed account either the same day, next day, or second day, depending on the amount of time it takes for the Fed to present the checks to drawee banks. The Fed has a strict schedule of deadlines for presenting cash letters. When the bank presents its cash letter early enough, it can get same-day availability on its funds if the drawee banks are local. Otherwise, the Fed grants availability in one or two days for checks drawn on banks in most locations in the country.

Transit Checks

Transit checks are checks drawn on banks located outside of the depository bank's Federal Reserve district. They can be cleared in several ways:

- deposited with the Fed or RCPC that serves the depository institution
- sent to the Fed or RCPC that services the drawee bank

- sent directly to the distant drawee bank, if the depository bank has enough checks drawn on that bank to justify the cost of maintaining an account there
- deposited with a correspondent bank in the same city as the drawee bank, in which case the correspondent bank credits the deposit to the sending bank's account and then clears the check through the local clearinghouse

Correspondent Banks

Money center banks provide an alternative to the Fed's check-clearing system. Those banks maintain deposit accounts from other banks, and they attract check-clearing business away from the Fed by offering faster processing and more flexible deposit deadlines and availability schedules. Also, under provisions of the Monetary Control Act of 1980, the Fed is required to charge for its services. Money center banks often price their services lower than the Fed in order to attract deposits from correspondent banks.

Of course, neither alternative is free. Both the Fed and correspondent banks charge for each check deposited with them. Some drawee banks place a handling charge on the bundles of "on-us" checks they receive. Air freight or courier charges are also involved in presenting checks to distant correspondent or drawee banks. Although banks tend to set their charges and funds availability in relation to the Fed's charges and availability, large money center correspondent banks can sometimes offer lower costs, faster availability, or both, because they can sort checks by city and by bank.

Checks that are drawn on banks in small cities and towns are usually deposited with the Fed. As a result, the Fed often has to clear all of the small-town checks, which are the most expensive to clear unless the costs are offset by business from major cities. Even so, the Fed stands ready to clear checks among all depository institutions. Each district bank presents checks directly to banks in its own territory. Checks drawn on banks in other Fed districts are sent to their RCPCs, and at the end of each day the Fed district banks settle with each other through the Fed's Interdistrict Settlement Fund.

Transit checks are associated with clearing float, for which the time period depends, to a large degree, on transportation scheduling. Most of the time, a depository bank can get a check to the drawee bank before the end of the next business day. Clearing float is thus most often limited to one day, assuming that the drawee bank deposits the check on the day it is received.

If the intermediary bank that receives the check from the depository bank, whether a correspondent bank or a Federal Reserve Bank, has to deliver the check to a distant drawee bank, two days of float usually will be involved.

Clearing and settlement of most checks tend to be completed on the business day after deposit. In that case, bankers say the transaction has "next-day settlement" that allows "one-day availability" of funds. The banking environment gives banks an incentive to settle transactions as quickly as possible. This, in turn, causes banks to process and transport checks as quickly as practical from a cost standpoint. Because of cost considerations, it can take two days for checks drawn on banks located far from a Fed check processing center to arrive at the drawee bank. Also, delay on the part of the airline carrying the checks may result in a missed arrival deadline at the correspondent bank. This adds an additional day of float to each check.

Clearing Float

The term "clearing float" refers to the amount of time that passes between the deposit of a check into an account until its payment by the drawee bank. With today's effective transportation system, that delay is usually between zero and three days, as described in the previous section. Clearing float arises when a customer deposits a check in an account and the depository bank simultaneously credits the funds to the customer's account. This reflects the deposit as a liability on the bank's books. To offset the liability, the depository enters a debit in its asset accounts called "Items in Process of Collection." The check that the customer deposited is then entered into the check-clearing system and sent to the bank upon which it is drawn. That bank, in turn, will credit the depository bank's account and charge the account of the issuer of the check.

From the 1970s to the early 1980s, managing payment float was one of the principal concerns of financial professionals who managed corporate cash. The Monetary Control Act of 1980, however, mandated the Fed to take steps to eliminate float; therefore, float management is not as important a function for financial managers as it once was. However, as long as a substantial portion of a company's receipts and disbursements are settled with paper checks, the financial manager must be aware of payment float. Float affects several areas of a health care institution's business:

- configuration of bank accounts
- selection of depository banks
- processing of remittances, either in the business office or by a lockbox processor
- timing of billing, including frequency, and payment terms
- selection of a bank for disbursements

Second Presentment

The Fed has attempted to comply in a number of ways with the mandate of the Monetary Control Act of 1980 to reduce float, including initiating a second presentment (delivery) of checks during the day. The second presentment is supposed to occur by noon, although in practice it typically occurs several hours earlier. Fed check-processing centers process most of their checks early in the morning, and these are presented to the drawee banks in the first presentment. Items that fail to be processed until after the early deadline are presented to the drawee banks a few hours later, rather than being held over to the next day, as was the case prior to about 1983.

Only banks whose check volumes exceed a certain level—approximately $10 million per day—receive second presentments. The volume of checks cleared by smaller banks (most of the commercial banks in the country) does not warrant the extra cost the Fed would incur in making second presentments to them.

Availability Schedules

The schedule of processing deadlines that an individual bank establishes for deposited checks drawn on banks in other locations is called an availability schedule. The bank uses its availability schedule to assign the number of days of float a deposited item will receive.

Most cash management banks publish their availability schedules so that customers will know the exact time of the day that the bank's processing center must receive deposited checks. Customers know beforehand how much float will be associated with a particular check. Availability schedules are generally organized by the geographical location of drawee banks, in terms of their location in relation to RCPCs rather than by city (see Table 3-1).

As a general rule, funds availability on checks processed by the Fed and drawn on a bank in the same Fed district as the Fed processing bank is one day. Two-day availability is generally granted to checks drawn on banks in other Fed districts, especially if the bank is located far from an RCPC. When designing a system for collecting remittances, the financial manager needs to pay particular attention to origination points of remittance checks. Because funds are available sooner when a check remains within a Fed district, district boundaries are as important as mailing times in selecting lockbox banks.

Availability considerations make little difference to health care financial managers who make over-the-counter deposits at a branch office of the bank. Availability deadlines apply to the time when a deposit reaches the bank's central processing office, not the teller's window at the branch. The deadlines become meaningful to the financial manager who delivers deposits directly to the bank's central processing office using a bank's lockbox service. Deposit deadlines may be later at some banks than at others, but the trade-off may be missed airline flights, longer clearing times, and thus later availability.

Table 3-1 Sample of a Portion of a Bank Availability Schedule

FEDERAL RESERVE DISTRICT SEVEN
Effective March 1, 19xx

Location	ABA Number(s)	Deadline	Availability
Chicago:			
City	0710	7:00 P.M.	1
First National Bank	0710-0001	5:00 A.M.	0
Continental Illinois	0710-0003	5:00 A.M.	0
Northern Trust	0710-0015	5:00 A.M.	0
Harris Trust	0710-0028	5:00 A.M.	0
Drovers Bank	0710-0034	8:00 P.M.	1
LaSalle National Bank	0710-0050	8:00 P.M.	1
National Boulevard Bank	0710-0052	8:00 P.M.	1
Central National Bank	0710-0053	8:00 P.M.	1
Exchange National Bank	0710-0054	8:00 P.M.	1
American National Bank	0710-0077	5:00 A.M.	0
RCPC	0711, 0712, 0719	5:00 A.M.	1
Detroit:			
City	0720	7:00 P.M.	1
National Bank of Detroit	0720-0032	8:00 P.M.	1
Michigan National Bank	0720-0080	8:00 P.M.	1
First of America	0720-0091	8:00 P.M.	1
RCPC	0724	5:00 A.M.	1
Michigan National, Lansing	0724-1174	8:00 P.M.	1
Des Moines:			
City	0730	7:00 P.M.	1
United Central Bank	0730-0017	8:00 P.M.	1
Iowa Des Moines National Bank	0730-0022	8:00 P.M.	1
Bankers Trust	0730-0064	8:00 P.M.	1
RCPC	0739	5:00 A.M.	1
Indianapolis:			
City	0740	7:00 P.M.	1
American Fletcher	0740-0001	8:00 P.M.	1
RCPC	0749	5:00 A.M.	1
Milwaukee:			
City	0750	7:00 P.M.	1
Marine Bank	0750-0001	8:00 P.M.	1
First Wisconsin	0750-0002	8:00 P.M.	1
Marshall & Ilsley	0750-0005	8:00 P.M.	1
RCPC	0759	5:00 A.M.	1

It is impossible for banks to track each check through the clearing process. About 45 billion checks clear the banking system each year. Depository institutions can and do track cash letters to make sure that they are dispatched when scheduled. Availability schedules are based on existing routing patterns. Large banks generally establish routing patterns so that checks travel over the most efficient routes. Banks tend to alter routes frequently to reflect changes in airlines' flight schedules and correspondent banks' availability schedules.

Action Advice. The health care financial manager who is interested in monitoring availability should ask the banker several questions:

- How accurately does the published availability schedule correspond to the actual availability obtained by the bank?
- Is the schedule intended to be accurate or does it show only how the bank establishes clearing float? A bank may pad a deadline so it appears earlier than its actual time, thus ensuring that the bank can meet the deadline. In that situation, a bank may charge the customer two days' worth of float, even though most items clear in only one day.
- When was the last time the bank revised its published availability schedule? The schedule may change daily, but it is neither practical nor useful for a bank to publish daily changes. The bank that updates and publishes its availability schedule frequently probably is achieving faster check clearance and lower float than its competitors.

HOW ELECTRONIC FUNDS MOVE

All payment mechanisms serve the purpose of transferring value from the payor to the payee. In abstract terms, value is represented by credit balances on books of the bank. Value is transferred by increasing the payee's balance and reducing the payor's balance. The means by which instructions to make such transfers are given is nothing more than a medium of communication. The medium can be in the form of a paper notice, such as a check or draft, or an electronic message. Because of the physical delivery methods involved, paper checks are slow, and it is difficult to determine the exact time the transaction is completed. Electronic notification is faster and allows both parties to know with certainty when the transaction actually occurs.

There are two main systems of electronic funds transfer: wire transfers and automated clearing house transfers. Two other systems to transfer money electronically are utilized by banks rather than the banks' customers. CHIPS is operated by the New York Clearing House Association; SWIFT is operated by an international consortium of banks.

Wire Transfers

Wire transfer is an electronic notification to transfer funds from one bank account to another by means of the Fedwire. Fedwire is a network of the 12 Federal

Reserve district banks, their 25 branches, and certain eligible U.S. depository institutions. To initiate a wire transfer, the originating financial institution electronically sends a set of instructions to its Federal Reserve district bank or branch. The Fed is instructed to charge the Fed account of the originating institution and to credit the Fed account of the receiving institution. The message may also state the purpose of the transfer and include instructions to credit a specific customer's bank account.

The Fed guarantees to transfer funds on the date the wire was initiated as long as the transfer contains the proper instructions and meets the day's wire transfer deadline. It usually takes only a few minutes for a wire transfer to be completed, unless the transfer is bound for a bank in another Fed district. In that case, the two district banks settle the transaction between themselves through the Interdistrict Settlement Fund, and the wire transfer may take as long as 30 minutes to complete.

Fedwire transfers are used when value must pass immediately or in very large amounts. When an immediate wire transfer is necessary, the financial manager should request the bank to supply the Fedwire number, which indicates the time the wire was sent. The financial manager will then know the wire transfer was handled quickly and efficiently.

Automated Clearing House Transfers

Another means of transferring money electronically is to use the automated clearing house (ACH) system. In many major cities, clearinghouse associations have developed electronic systems for exchanging credits and debits among clearinghouse members and other financial institutions in the region. Table 3-2 lists the names and locations of ACHs.

In ACH parlance, parties making ACH transactions are called the originator and the receiver. The transaction is either a credit, in which funds are sent out, or a debit, in which funds are pulled in. There are also two financial institutions in an ACH transaction, the Originating Depository Financial Institution (ODFI) and the Receiving Depository Financial Institution (RDFI).

As an example of an ACH transaction, Hospital C makes a salary payment to its employee, Davis. The hospital is the originator and its bank is the ODFI. Davis is the receiver and his bank is the RDFI. The transaction is a credit transfer, meaning that Davis's bank account is credited for the amount of the transfer. If Davis were a patient wishing to pay the hospital, an ACH transfer initiated by the hospital still could be used to pay for the transaction, only this time it would be a debit transaction moving funds preauthorized by Davis from his bank account to the bank account of the hospital. The hospital would have to obtain prior permission from Davis to collect payments for his patient account by having the bank transfer

Table 3-2 Names and Locations of Automated Clearing Houses

City	ACH Name	Acronym	FRB District
Atlanta	Georgia ACH Association	GACHA	6 Atlanta
Baltimore	Mid-Atlantic ACH Association	MACHA	3 Philadelphia
Birmingham	Alabama ACH Association	ALACHA	6 Atlanta
Boston	New England ACH Association	NEACH	1 Boston
Charleston, WV	Virginias ACH Association	VACHA	5 Richmond
Charlotte	North Carolina ACH Association	NORCACHA	5 Richmond
Chicago	Midwest ACH Association	MACHA	7 Chicago
Cincinnati	Central Regional Automated Funds Transfer System	CRAFTS	4 Cleveland
Cleveland	Mid-America Automated Payments System	MAPS	4 Cleveland
Columbia, SC	South Carolina ACH Association	SOCACHA	5 Richmond
Columbus, OH	Central Regional Automated Funds Transfer System	CRAFTS	4 Cleveland
Dallas	Southwestern ACH Association	SWACHA	11 Dallas
Denver	Rocky Mountain ACH Association	RMACHA	10 Kansas City
Des Moines	Iowa ACH Association	IACHA	7 Chicago
Detroit	Michigan ACH Association	MACHA	7 Chicago
Indianapolis	Indiana Exchange, Inc.	INDEX	7 Chicago
Jacksonville	Florida Payment Systems, Inc.	FPSI	6 Atlanta
Kansas City	Mid-America Payment Exchange	MAPEX	10 Kansas City
Little Rock	Mid-America Payment Exchange	MAPEX	8 St. Louis
Los Angeles	Calwestern ACH Association	CACHA	12 San Francisco
Louisville	Kentuckiana ACH Association	KACHA	8 St. Louis
Memphis	Southern Financial Exchange	SFE	6 Atlanta
Miami	Florida Payment Systems, Inc.	FPSI	6 Atlanta
Milwaukee	Wisconsin ACH Association	WACHA	7 Chicago
Minneapolis	Upper Midwest ACH Association	UMACHA	9 Minneapolis
Nashville	Tennessee ACH Association	TACHA	6 Atlanta
New Orleans	Southern Financial Exchange	SFE	6 Atlanta
New York	New York ACH Association	NYACH	2 New York
Oklahoma City	Mid-America Payment Exchange	MAPEX	10 Kansas City
Omaha	Mid-America Payment Exchange	MAPEX	10 Kansas City
Philadelphia	Third District Funds Transfer Association	3DFTA	3 Philadelphia
Phoenix	Arizona Clearing House Association	ACHA	12 San Francisco
Pittsburgh	Tri-State ACH Association	TRISACH	4 Cleveland
Portland	Oregon ACH Association	DACHA	12 San Francisco
Richmond	Virginias ACH Association	VACHA	5 Richmond
Salt Lake City	Calwestern ACH Association	CACHA	12 San Francisco
San Francisco	Calwestern ACH Association	CACHA	12 San Francisco
Seattle	Northwest ACH Association	NWACHA	12 San Francisco
St. Louis	Mid-America Payment Exchange	MAPEX	8 St. Louis
Tempe	Arizona Clearing House Association	ACHA	12 San Francisco

money from Davis's account on a certain day of the month. The hospital is still the originator of the transaction and Davis is still the receiver of the transaction. The originating and receiving banks remain the same, although the funds now move in the opposite direction from a credit transfer.

There are three essential differences between wire transfers and ACH transfers:

1. The Fedwire transfer system is geared to handle one transfer at a time, while the ACH system can handle multiple transfers, or batches, at one time.
2. The Fedwire transfer system settles transactions on the same day, while the ACH system is designed to allow transactions to be settled at a specified future date, usually the next day for business-to-business payments and two days later for payments involving consumers.
3. The Fedwire transfer is expensive because of its single-transaction nature and custom message format, while the ACH is inexpensive because of its batch-processed nature and structured message format. In addition, banks realize that a customer will pay more for same-day settlement than for settlement one or two days later.

Private EFT Systems

Two major electronic funds transfer systems are operated in addition to the Fedwire and ACH systems: CHIPS and SWIFT. They are operated by private organizations, rather than by the Federal Reserve System.

CHIPS

CHIPS is the acronym for the Clearing House Interbank Payments System. Operated by the New York Clearing House Association, CHIPS is designed to handle large-dollar payments among its approximately 140 member banks that have offices in New York. It is a computer-based system that allows member banks to clear a high volume of payment transactions daily. The New York Clearing House Association also operates the paper-based New York Clearing House and the New York Automated Clearing House (NYACH). NYACH, one of 29 automated clearing houses (ACHs) in the country, handles the same types of ACH transactions as other regional ACHs.

CHIPS tends to handle transactions related to international business, but all of the transactions involve domestic funds and occur only among the New York offices of financial institutions. For example, if a British bank owes money to a large Chicago bank, the British bank could send a telex to its New York correspondent asking that it charge the British bank's account and pay the Chicago bank. The New York correspondent could either initiate a Fedwire transfer to Chicago or create a CHIPS transfer if the Chicago bank has a New York office that is a member of CHIPS. Unlike Fedwire, CHIPS transfers involve only messages between banks, not the actual transfer of money. CHIPS transactions accumulate through the day and are net settled at the close of business. Each financial institution settles its account with the clearinghouse, rather than with an individual member bank.

SWIFT

The Society for Worldwide Interbank Financial Telecommunications (SWIFT), formed in 1973 by a group of the largest banks in Europe, Canada, and the United States, handles international funds transfers electronically. Based in Brussels, SWIFT had approximately 1,500 member banks in 52 countries by 1988. SWIFT is basically a message system, rather than a true funds transfer system; SWIFT does not move money at the same time it moves the message. SWIFT transactions are settled through correspondent accounts maintained by the sending and receiving banks, through mutual correspondents, or through central banks of the countries involved. Because SWIFT is an international system, messages are in standard formats structured by message type.

RISK IN THE U.S. PAYMENTS SYSTEM

Understanding ''finality of payment'' is the key to comprehension of risk in the payments system. A transaction is complete when payment becomes final. After that, neither party has recourse to the other. Except for Fedwire payments, there is no way to know exactly when a transaction is settled and the payment final until some time after the fact. In an attempt to reduce or eliminate the element of uncertainty that surrounds banking transactions, regulators are trying to make finality of payment more visible and thus allowing it to be recorded.

The Fed has devoted increased attention to risk in the payments system, as evidenced by daylight overdraft caps, reduction of float, and acceleration of return checks back to the bank of first deposit.

Risk in the payments system takes three forms:

1. Systemic risk. This risk results from inefficiencies and processing delays within the system.
2. Credit risk. This risk refers to the potential failure of a corporate payor or a drawee bank or the possibility that daylight overdraft restrictions will freeze a bank's ability to move money.
3. Fraud risk. This risk refers to the possibility that electronic transactions will be tampered with in transit.

The Fed is concerned about risk because a major corporate or bank insolvency could trigger other bank insolvencies. Within the extensive networks of correspondent banks, most banks maintain deposits with at least several, and often many, other banks. The failure of one bank conceivably could result in the collapse of other banks with which it does business. This was a principal consideration, for example, in the Federal Deposit Insurance Corporation's decision in 1984 to support the failed Continental Illinois National Bank of Chicago, which held sizable deposits from perhaps hundreds of correspondent banks.

Costs of a bank failure can be high. When an institution fails, its payments are not honored. The fear in the banking industry is that supervisory agencies cannot cover the payments of a failed bank quickly enough. If a safety net is not erected soon enough to support an insolvent bank, the amount of federal deposit insurance available to cover the failure may be exhausted. This would leave other banking institutions with inadequate insurance protection.

Wire Transfer Risk

There is little risk in the wire transfer system because Fedwire is a true funds transfer system; the execution of both the debit and credit bookkeeping entries are made simultaneously. The moment of finality of payment is very clearly defined. A transaction is aborted if the entry cannot be made. The only risk, therefore, involves daylight overdrafts, the amount of which can be known at any given moment.

Daylight Overdrafts

Banks normally send out wire transfers on a timely basis. A daylight overdraft in an account, however, could cause a bank to delay a wire transfer. A daylight overdraft occurs when a depositor initiates an outgoing wire transfer in anticipation of receiving an incoming wire transfer to cover later that day. As a result, there is a period of time during the day when the depositor's account is overdrawn.

For example, assume that Hospital A's account has a balance of $525,000, and the controller is certain that its outside investment manager will send $750,000 to the account later that day after a sale of securities from its investment portfolio. The hospital has to pay for new equipment costing $750,000 on the same day. At 9:00 A.M., the controller telephones the bank and orders a wire transfer of that amount to pay the equipment supplier. The wire transfer from the investment manager, however, is not received until 11 A.M. If the hospital's bank initiated its wire transfer promptly at 9:00 A.M., the hospital's account would have been overdrawn from 9:00 A.M. until 11 A.M., when the hospital's bank received the wire from the investment bank.

Because banks generally cover companies' accounts in such instances, daylight overdrafts are reflected in the bank's own Fed account. In the mid-1980s, when overdrafts were amounting to $120 billion a day, the Fed decided to limit the amount of daylight overdrafts a depository institution could have with the Fed.

With a rash of bank failures, the Fed became nervous. As a result, in March 1986 "voluntary" limits on daylight overdrafts for each bank were imposed by the Fed. A bank's limit on the amount it may overdraw its Fed account is called the "sender's net debit cap." By adjusting a bank's net debit cap, the Fed can control its exposure to the risk of a sudden bank failure.

Critics of daylight overdraft controls believe they could create gridlock in the financial system. For example, if a major bank is barred from making wire transfers until it receives money from other banks, a problem exists when the other banks are also barred from making wire transfers in order to stay within their net debit caps. What this means to a health care financial manager is that an outgoing wire transfer could be delayed because the originating bank reached the limit of its sender's net debit cap. It may not be the fault of customer companies that the bank reached its cap; the bank could have bought government securities for its own account that were settled out of its Fed account. Financial managers should discuss the daylight overdraft situation with their banks to reduce the possibility that health care firms will face wire transfer delays.

Check Risk

The mere existence of clearing float represents risk in the paper-based payments system. Clearing float essentially represents the double accounting of funds in the banking system; both the payee and payor have the same money on account until a check has cleared. Risk, therefore, exists between the time the depositor's account is credited and the payor's account is charged—a period of up to two days plus the time it takes for the check to be returned to the depository bank. If the check is not honored for some reason (such as insufficient funds, stopped payment, or lack of a signature) it takes even longer for the check to be returned to the depository bank. If the depositor has closed its account and skipped town in the meantime, the depository bank has no recourse when it must accept the dishonored check.

For that reason, banks often place a "hold" on the deposited funds for the length of time it normally takes to return an item. In the late 1980s, because of a perception that banks were holding items too long, Congress passed the Expedited Funds Availability Act, which places limits on the length of time that banks can maintain holds on accounts. To implement the act, the Fed adopted Regulation CC. This essentially requires banks to return dishonored checks to the bank of first deposit within the same time frame that it would take to clear the item to that bank originally.

Automated Clearing House Risk

There are two possible ways for payment risk to arise in the automated clearing house (ACH) system:

1. Failure of the payor. As an example, the originator authorizes an ACH credit transfer and specifies settlement at a future date. If the originator fails before settlement, the payee may receive an invalid payment. ACH payment risk, therefore, can involve credit risk.
2. Failure of the paying bank. An ACH transaction depends on the ability of the paying bank to meet its payment obligation on the settlement date.

SUMMARY

Checks are the basic form of payment in the U.S. economy. They represent an essentially inefficient method of settling payments compared with electronic forms of payment. A check deposited in one bank can be sent to the drawee bank along one of several routes. They include the Fed, correspondent banks of the depository bank, direct transmittal to the drawee bank, and a local clearinghouse. Because a check must be physically moved from the depository bank to the drawee bank, an element of time is involved during which funds in the depository bank are uncollected. To the depositor, this is deposit float. To the issuer of the check, the entire length of time that it takes for the check to reach the drawee bank after the issuer releases it is called disbursing float.

Electronic forms of payment are generally less expensive to operate if they are used for batches of payments. Float is minimized, and the moment of finality of payment is more determinate.

Risk in the payments system affects all users of bank services because of the possibility that the user may be adversely affected by the failure of a bank. The risk of daylight overdrafts, in particular, has caused concern among bank regulators. They can cause delays in the movement of wire transfers between two parties without fault of either party.

Chapter 4

Optimum Cash Management Structures

INTRODUCTION

"Quick" and "accurate" are the key words to remember when structuring a cash management system. A cash management system consists of a series of subsystems to manage receipts, funds concentration, and disbursements, and to provide information and control. The first subsystem that financial managers need to understand is the depository system, the method by which money is transferred from the buyer to the seller. The words "quick" and "accurate" reflect the whole point of depository systems. They are discussed in the first main section of this chapter.

When money is received from customers, funds must be concentrated into a single account so that the organization can use the money for its own payments and investments. The system that performs that function is the concentration system, which is presented in the second main section. The third section covers paper-based (check) disbursements.

DEPOSITORY SYSTEMS

Depository systems are designed to receive funds and deposit them in a bank account so that the funds are available for use as soon as they are collected. The manner in which a depository system is structured depends on the type of business. Health care firms receive most of their payments through the mail in the form of checks. A traditional retailer receives most of its payments at the point of sale by means of cash, credit cards, and checks.

Most nonretail businesses, including many large health care institutions, arrange for customers to remit payments to a lockbox. A lockbox is a post office box from which the mail is collected and processed by a bank or other remittance-processing institution. Use of a lockbox reduces float resulting from mail time, processing time, and clearing time; a lockbox speeds availability of funds to the depositor. Money is available to the depositor more speedily and more accurately, enabling the institution to invest additional funds or to reduce debt, thereby enhancing earnings and cash flow.

The structure of a depository system for a health care provider depends on the size and structure of the organization. Small hospitals often need only one bank account to process patient remittances. Larger operations, however, have a degree of complexity that makes it difficult, if not impossible, to monitor all transactions through one bank account. Divisions or subsidiaries may need to track their own collections and disbursements. In addition, the financial manager may want to track, forecast, and control funds by separating disbursements from receivables. Before designing systems that perform such tasks, however, the financial manager needs to understand the various methods by which funds are received and deposited.

Depository Tools

Funds are received in three basic forms: coin and currency, paper, and electronic messages. Coin and currency tend to be received at the point of sale, as the patient checks out through the hospital's cashier or business office. Paper, in the form of checks and credit card receipts, are received at the point of sale and also through the mail. Electronic funds transfers are usually used for large payments, such as remittance of Medicare payments from a fiscal intermediary. These are sent through the banking system and consist of instructions to the hospital's bank to credit the hospital's account.

The term ''funds'' refers to credit balances on the books of a depository institution. Checks, therefore, are not funds, but are orders to a bank to pay the amount of funds indicated to the entity shown as payee on the check. Similarly, credit card vouchers are not funds either until a bank accepts the charge ticket from the seller and credits its account. In fact, the term funds does not even encompass coin and currency until they are deposited. Because so many laws and regulations govern business transactions, proper accounting dictates that all forms of receipts be deposited before they are used to make payments.

Deposit Methods

The way an institution receives funds generally determines—and sometimes limits—the way it deposits them. Most funds received by health care firms are received through the mail in the form of paper checks. Although most checks come in through lockboxes, many are still received at the firm's business offices and service facilities. These receipts must be transported to the bank. Therefore, it is important to understand the various methods by which banks accept deposits.

Window Deposits

Window deposits are the deposits that everyone is familiar with, the kind taken by a teller at the bank. Window deposits are often called over-the-counter deposits.

Armored Carriers

Armored carriers transport coin, currency, and checks from the depositor's location to a bank. They are used simply because they provide a safe means of transport.

Unarmed Couriers

Armored couriers need not be used to transport checks if there is no coin or currency involved. Checks have no intrinsic value, so unarmed couriers are often used in place of institution personnel to transport checks to the bank for deposit.

Night Depositories

After banking hours, businesses often place sealed bags containing deposits into night depositories. The bank can be granted authority, usually under the control of two people, to open a bag the next day, process the deposit, and credit the customer's account. Otherwise, the bank will hold the bag for the customer to open in the morning.

Credit and Debit Cards

Credit and debit cards are used by consumers in place of cash and checks. The difference between the two forms of cards is that the purchaser's account is charged immediately for funds in a debit card transaction and at some future date in a credit card transaction. In either case, upon accepting payment via plastic card, the seller generates a draft that is sent to the bank that issued the card. Drafts from credit and debit cards are the slips of paper signed by the consumer, which must be delivered to the bank in a manner similar to checks. Some banks, however, allow the seller to transmit the card data to the bank in lieu of delivering the paper. The bank debits the cardholder's line of credit or deposit account and credits the seller's account. Whether paper is delivered or data transmitted, the bank generally credits funds to the seller's account the next day minus a certain percentage of the transaction for the use of the card.

There is a difference between bank-issued credit cards and the "travel and entertainment" and proprietary charge cards such as American Express, Diners Club, Carte Blanche, and Discover Card. The method of collecting on these cards is different from the method used for traditional bank-issued credit cards. Generally, the retailer must mail the card drafts to the card issuer who, in turn, mails a check for the amount of the transaction minus the issuer's percentage fee. Sometimes a card issuer will allow a bank in the region to accept vouchers, in which case the card's deposits and credits are treated in the same manner as bank-issued credit cards.

Lockbox

As noted previously, a lockbox is nothing more than a post office box, except that the box is used only as an address for payments. A bank or other processor collects the mail from the lockbox and processes it for deposit to the boxholder's account. The reason for using a lockbox and the processing services that banks and nonbank processors provide is to convert checks into available funds faster than if the institution collected payments along with its other mail.

Depository Transfer Check

A depository transfer check (DTC) is a check that is drawn routinely against a depository account and deposited into a concentration bank account at another bank. DTCs are used to concentrate funds from many depository banks into one central account. They are also used to fund payroll, interest, and controlled disbursement accounts. Despite the name, DTCs can be either paper checks or electronic funds transfers.

Preauthorized Draft

A preauthorized draft (PAD) is used by institutions when their customers have to make repetitive payments of a fixed amount, such as monthly insurance payments. Like other payments, a PAD is a draft drawn against the bank account of a customer for deposit into the business's account. Before such transfers are made, the payor must authorize the bank to honor the drafts. PADs are in the form of either paper checks or automated clearing house debits.

ACH Transfer

Automated clearing house (ACH) transfers are electronic funds transfers (EFTs) made through the automated clearing house system. Business-to-business transactions are generally settled the next day and consumer transactions in two days. EFT payment instructions move through the payor's and payee's banks.

There are two types of ACH transfers, credit transfers initiated by the payor and debit transfers initiated by the payee.

Wire Transfer

A wire transfer consists of electronic messages between two banks, generally sent through the Federal Reserve System (Fed) as the payment intermediary, to make simultaneous bookkeeping entries at each bank to reflect a payment made by one bank's customer to the other bank's customer. At the same time, the Fed is usually instructed to charge the sending bank's Fed account and credit the receiving bank's Fed account. Wire transfers are settled on the day of initiation. Funds subject to wire transfer, therefore, are said to have "same-day" availability.

Action Advice. When designing a firm's depository operations, financial managers can reduce costs of depositing checks, and thus increase their organizations' cash flows, by performing some of the tasks that banks generally perform for a fee. Banks usually offer lower prices (by a few pennies per item) and faster availability on checks that are pre-encoded with the dollar amount in the MICR line before they are deposited. (MICR stands for "magnetic ink character recognition." The line of characters across the bottom of the check contains the identification numbers of the drawee bank and other information in a special form of ink that enables electronic check processing equipment to "read" the check.)

If an institution deposits a large volume of checks, it may be economical to invest in desktop encoding equipment for pre-encoding checks. Banks also may give discounts of a few pennies per item to organizations that presort checks by drawee bank for local checks and by city for checks drawn on out-of-town banks.

Lockbox Deposits

Health care organizations generally do business more like nonretail firms than retail establishments. One characteristic of a nonretail business, for instance, is that sales are made on credit terms that are generally established prior to the point of sale. Because of the nature of sales, financial managers at nonretail businesses face a different series of challenges—and opportunities—in managing corporate funds.

Health care financial managers must set credit terms and collection policy that encourage patients and third-party payors to remit their payments quickly. Financial managers also must ensure that funds move from payors' bank accounts to their institutions' bank accounts as fast as possible. Finally, they must ensure that payments are accompanied by the necessary data to record the payments properly in patient account records.

Almost all payments are still made by checks, and most checks are remitted by mail. Financial managers must set up systems for the timely handling of these checks. A postal lockbox is the best method to facilitate the handling, depositing, and clearing of checks.

Lockbox Types

A lockbox is a specific address reserved only for customer remittances. It allows an institution to keep checks it receives through the mail separate from other correspondence. The advantages of receiving checks through a lockbox, rather than at the institution's location, include

- earlier deposit and faster funds availability
- lower processing costs
- greater accuracy in deposit processing
- greater flexibility in capturing remittance data
- increased security over the remittances

There are two types of lockboxes, wholesale and retail, with similar general characteristics. The difference between services associated with each type involves the way that remittance data, needed to apply payments to accounts receivable, are captured. An institution that primarily receives a small number of large dollar payments from other organizations should use a wholesale lockbox service in which the remittances are processed manually. An institution that primarily receives a large volume of checks of relatively small dollar amounts should use a retail lockbox service. Comparing how the remittance data are captured under wholesale and retail lockbox services can clarify the differences between the two types.

An institution requires a wholesale lockbox usually when it must receive either a photocopy of the remittance check or have the lockbox processor capture the remittance data electronically. If the receiving firm must apply the payment to specific open invoices rather than to an open account, certain electronic data also must be captured and transmitted by the lockbox processor or furnished by a photocopy of each check. Remittance data include identification of the remitter, invoice numbers and amount of each invoice being paid, as well as any adjustments, such as discounts allowed under credit terms that a payment may contain.

Organizations that use retail lockbox services, such as oil companies, public utilities, department stores, cable television companies, and other consumer-oriented firms, generally do not need as much invoice data as those using a wholesale lockbox. Retail lockbox processors often capture only the total amount paid by a customer without reference to individual invoices because consumer-to-corporate payments are generally made against an open account, not a series of open invoices. Also, payments are generally accompanied by coded paper remittance advices that can be processed by optical scanning or other machines.

The use of optical scanning equipment in retail lockbox processing is warranted by the high volume of items. The precoded advice, or coupon, contains a "scan line," a series of data fields that are scanned by optical character recognition (OCR) equipment. The scan line generally contains the patient's (or customer's) account number and the amount of the statement. The OCR equipment captures the data quickly and accurately. The scan line on the coupon may also include the minimum payment amount, so the lockbox processor can include that information if partial payments are received.

Lockbox Benefits

The collection of incoming checks through a lockbox offers the health care firm five major benefits: faster funds availability, lower cost, increased reliability, easier data capture, and better security.

Funds Availability

A lockbox processor can usually deposit and clear checks faster because it meets earlier deadlines. The U.S. Postal Service generally sorts incoming mail at night. The lockbox processor starts work as mail becomes available late in the evening. Throughout the night, couriers pick up mail at the post office. By 7 A.M. the processor usually has finished processing all incoming mail and can exchange checks with local banks for same-day settlement. There is also enough time to meet deadlines to send cash letters to Fed and correspondent banks. Consequently, float is minimized and same-day availability is maximized.

Lower Cost

Lockbox processors train their staffs specifically for check-processing work. These firms usually achieve high levels of employee accuracy and productivity. Therefore, per-item costs are lower than they would be if an institution performed its own check processing.

Increased Reliability

For the reasons listed above, as well as more direct supervision and backup staffing offered by lockbox processors, these services tend to be highly reliable.

Data Capture

Lockbox processors have the equipment and trained staff needed to capture data from checks or remittance advices and store it on magnetic tape or computer disk for delivery to their clients. The payee institution, therefore, can more easily update its patient accounts.

Better Security

Most lockbox processors have control procedures for receiving checks at the post office and handling checks during processing. These procedures generally result in better security compared with check processing procedures in business offices of many institutions.

Lockbox Processing

There is little mystery, but a lot of labor, in the services required to process remittances sent to a lockbox. Figure 4-1 demonstrates the basic steps in processing a lockbox. These include:

- transporting mail from the post office to the processing center
- sorting mail according to lockbox customers
- opening the envelopes
- removing the contents of the envelopes
- examining each check to ensure that the amount of the check matches the amount of the remittance advice and that the check is signed and dated
- recording manually the amount of each payment on the envelope
- separating each check from the envelope and other contents, which are saved intact
- preparing deposit of all checks
- balancing the amount of the deposit with the amounts written on the envelopes
- making photocopies (optional) of all checks and matching photocopies with their respective envelopes
- delivering packages containing envelopes and their contents to customers
- creating and transmitting or delivering data files of remittance information to customers (optional)

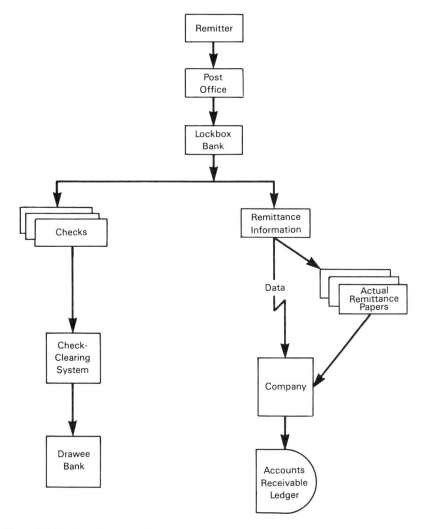

Figure 4-1 Lockbox Processing Steps

ELECTRONIC FUNDS TRANSFER DEPOSITS

Electronic funds transfer (EFT) is another method of depositing and concentrating funds. An institution that receives frequent electronic payments may want its bank to combine EFT remittance data (name of sender, the amount, and reason for payment) with similar data captured from checks that are received in a lockbox department. There is usually no reason why data from EFT payments cannot be consolidated with data from paper payments. It is important that the business office of the recipient receive dollars and remittance data at the same time, and it is advantageous for banks to provide that service. Banks offering consolidated EFT and lockbox data often refer to this as "electronic lockbox" service.

The most useful form of EFT remittances are the various payment formats available through the ACH payment system.

Return Item Funding

The goal of a well-designed cash management system is to move all funds into a concentration account as quickly as possible. A problem of overdrafts in the depository accounts may arise, however, if deposited checks are returned by the drawee bank. The reasons for returning checks are many, including insufficient or uncollected funds, stopped payment, unauthorized signature, and missing endorsement. The depository bank must pay the drawee bank for any returned item immediately and, in turn, must be reimbursed by the depositor. If the depositor's funds are automatically transferred into a concentration account, however, an overdraft arises in the depository account. A challenge is created when the depository account and concentration account are at different banks.

Every business, including those in health care, that accepts checks as payment must expect some checks to be returned. Consequently, procedures must be established to handle returned checks. Methods of avoiding an overdrawn depository account include:

- cash funds
- depository imprest fund
- local check

Cash Funds

A hospital may use cash funds to cover returned checks of relatively small amounts. The cashier's office in effect "buys" the return item from the depository bank by withdrawing currency from the till. Such disbursements are generally accounted for at the end of the day as "paid out." Return items tend to deplete limited amounts of coin and currency on hand. As a result, use of cash funds is often impractical, particularly if returns are frequent in number or large in amount.

Depository Imprest Funds

When the incidence of return items is expected to exceed the amount of cash on hand, two variations of deposit concentration systems may be used. They are the positive balance imprest fund and the variable deposit report.

Positive Balance Imprest Fund. The depository account is operated with a positive balance level rather than the usual imprest balance of zero. Funds are maintained in the account to cover return items, even as daily deposits are swept out of the account. There are three principal drawbacks to this method. First, return items are not accounted for until the imprest balance is refunded, a delay that may be longer than the normal accounting cycle. Second, positive balance imprest funds must be consciously refunded; if they are not refunded often enough overdrafts will still occur. Finally, companies with many depository accounts may tie up excessive amounts of funds. This method also may take more administrative time than return item management is worth.

Variable Deposit Report. Depository accounts retain their zero balance imprest levels under this method. Instead of maintaining a positive balance to cover return items, the amount of the deposit that is reported each day to the concentration system is reduced by the amount of return items received that day. If, for example, the amount of the day's deposit is $1,000 and there is a return item for $150, only $850 will be reported into the concentration system so that there will be money left in the account to cover the return item. The disadvantage of variable deposit reports is that business units may become lax in reporting each day's deposits, especially if the amount of the actual deposit is allowed to differ from the amount that is reported and concentrated.

Local Check

Satellite business units or subsidiaries are often operated separately from the main business unit. They may include home health care, magnetic resonance imaging, medical office buildings, equipment rental operations, and medical supplies. Checking accounts may be set up with the bank of the main office to pay for miscellaneous petty cash disbursements, travel expense reimbursements, and other expenditures of the satellite units. Such accounts also may be used to buy return items from the depository bank. The disadvantage of using local checks for this purpose is the lack of limitation on the dollar amount of checks that can be drawn on the account. As a result, the satellite unit can use the checking account for unauthorized purposes.

FUNDS CONCENTRATION SYSTEMS

Objectives of Funds Concentration

Funds concentration systems are used by decentralized organizations to meet two principal goals of cash management—control and earnings enhancement. These goals are met by moving funds from the point of deposit, or the point at which the institution first gains control over funds, to a central concentration account where the institution can gain maximum value from the funds. Indeed, a well-designed funds concentration system functions like a trap. It encourages funds to come in, but it requires a deliberate act to release them.

The components of a funds concentration system that expedite movement of funds to a central account are paper depository transfer checks and their electronic counterparts, ACH debit transfers, wire transfers, and deposit consolidation techniques. The tool that links these components in a well-functioning system is the concentration bank's balance reporting service.

Control

An institution gains control over funds, in a cash management sense, upon their arrival at a point in the system where they can be used by the financial manager to make disbursements, to pay debts, or to invest. Until the funds reach that point, they are either uncontrolled or are subject to control by organizations or individuals other than the institution or its financial manager. Such other organizations or individuals may not have the financial manager's objectives in mind. Managers of satellite business units, for instance, may place a higher priority on delivering health care services than on moving funds to a point at which the head office gains control of them. Unit managers may want to retain high balances in their accounts to compensate for bank services rendered locally that may not have been authorized by the head office.

There are several ways that a concentration system allows head office financial managers to gain control over funds.

- Funds move into the hands of the head office personnel. Fewer people handle a greater amount of funds; the head office environment is more structured and is also audited.

- Deposits are channelled toward a concentration account. As a result, the integrity of incoming funds is preserved without being disturbed by offsetting disbursements, and the flow of funds can be monitored for use in cash forecasts. Tracking and forecasting the individual components of incoming funds allows the financial manager to notice and investigate unanticipated changes in the flow. Use of a concentration account also increases control by allowing organizations with multiple divisions or subsidiaries to track each unit's funds independently of the others.

- Short-term forecasting is more accurate when the flow of incoming funds is not disrupted by the flow of outgoing disbursements. More reliable short-term forecasts enable the financial manager to reduce borrowings or to increase investments.

- The organization's exposure to risk of depository bank failure is lessened by maintaining lower balances in depository banks that serve decentralized units. This may be important to institutions that use many depository banks, especially when some are smaller and lesser-known local banks. Such banks can be used with greater confidence if funds are continually moving to a more secure concentration bank.

Earnings Enhancement

Concentration systems make earnings enhancement possible by pooling funds from the individual business units into larger available sums to invest or pay debts. With larger investment sums, yields can be improved by utilizing more economic sizes of available instruments in the money markets. Leaving relatively small sums spread out in many depository accounts will significantly reduce investment funds. Concentrated into a single account, however, these small amounts can make investments in the short-term money markets worthwhile.

Similarly, an institution that borrows at the parent level to support the operations of its subsidiary units may find that sound funds concentration devices and techniques will help to reduce the balances of short-term or revolving loans. Borrowers generally save money by using concentrated funds to reduce debt, because interest rates on loans are usually higher than money market yields on instruments with similar maturities and credit qualities. Greater efficiency also is obtained from funds concentration when an institution has some operating units with negative cash flows and others with positive flows. By pooling funds through a concentration system, the overall funding position is more evenly balanced and borrowings generally reduced.

Funds concentration systems can also enhance earnings because they take advantage of inefficiencies in the banking system. Two primary banking inefficiencies are float and slippage. The banking system, rather than the depositor's concentration system, suffers the consequences of these inefficiencies. In fact, a concentration system uses these inefficiencies to the depositor's advantage by allowing dual balances to exist simultaneously in the depository bank and in the concentration bank.

A typical concentration system uses DTCs to concentrate funds from the field depository banks. The float associated with the checks gives the depositor dual balances; funds from the transfer check are credited to the concentration account, but the balances also exist in the depository account until the transfer check clears.

The funds in the depository bank also may be used to compensate that bank for services rendered. When the depository account is credited with deposits of coin and currency or local checks, it contains a significant amount of collected balances, which produce credits to offset the depository bank's account service charges.

When a DTC takes longer to clear than the depository bank's availability schedule suggests, it is said that "slippage" has occurred. For example, the concentration bank may grant next-day availability on depository transfer checks, but it may take two days before the DTC actually clears the depository bank. As a result, the depositor has collected funds in both the depository and concentration accounts for one day.

The slippage that caused the check to take an extra day to clear could be the result of external considerations. Inclement weather may cause delays in air traffic, for instance, which would thus delay the delivery of checks. Most checks, as they make their way through the clearing system, are physically transported aboard commercial aircraft. Because Federal Reserve deadlines must be met for checks to clear on time, a delay of even a few hours at an airport can increase float by a full day. Banks, however, set their availability schedules on the basis of normal check-clearing times. When slippage upsets the schedules, it is the bank, not the concentration customer, that pays.

System Architecture

A typical funds concentration system consists of a master concentration bank account and depository bank accounts, along with mechanisms that move funds into the master concentration account. Deposits enter the concentration system by transfers from depository accounts at other banks and depository accounts at the concentration bank belonging to related business units. Figure 4-2 depicts a typical funds concentration system.

Alternatively, funds deposited in the field may be moved to a regional concentration bank, which then moves funds to the master concentration account. An institution uses regional concentration banks to reduce check-clearing times by pooling funds from depository banks located within a single Federal Reserve district. By using a subconcentration system that is confined to a single Federal Reserve district, the institution obtains same-day availability of funds, or at least next-day availability. Upon collection, the regional concentration banks then move funds into the master concentration account by wire transfer that results in same-day credit. Consequently, all funds, no matter where in the country they are deposited, can be concentrated with same-day or next-day availability. When only one account is used to concentrate funds deposited across the country, funds receive a mix of same-day, next-day, and two-day availability.

System Operations

Concentration systems use three methods to transfer funds from depository banks to the concentration bank: (1) DTCs, (2) ACH transfers, and (3) wire

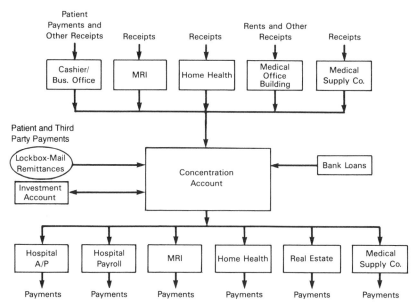

Figure 4-2 A Typical Funds Concentration System

transfers. Each method has its own cost, benefit, and performance characteristics. It is the financial manager's task to select the method or combination of methods that results in the best balance between cost and benefit for the institution.

Depository Transfer Checks

The most common method used to make payments, the paper check, is also the most common method used for concentration of funds. In concentration work, initiation of paper transfer checks has been enhanced by sophisticated telecommunications. Since the early 1970s several systems using nationwide, toll-free telephone networks and computer-linked telecommunications centers have been developed for use in funds concentration. The systems are operated by banks and by independent service bureaus.

Under such a system, an institution requests its concentration bank to maintain a computerized data base listing depository bank information for each of the institution's units that make deposits. The information contains the name and address of the unit's depository bank and the complete MICR line, including the bank's transit routing number and the unit's depository account number. The system operates as follows:

- During the day, each unit making deposits uses the telephone network to report the amount of its daily deposit to the system operator (this may be the concentration bank itself or a service bureau).

- As the system operator receives deposit reports, the depositor's location identification number and deposit amount are entered into the system operator's computer.
- At the day's cutoff time, which is usually about 5 P.M. Eastern time, the system operator ends the unit's file for that day and transmits all deposit data received to the institution's concentration bank. Any deposit reports received by the system operator after the deadline are saved in a computer file for the next day's business.
- After the concentration bank receives the data transmission and enters the data into the bank's computer, it matches the deposit data by location with its data base of depository bank routing information. Then computer-printed DTCs are produced. The DTCs drawn against each respective depository bank are payable to the concentration bank for the amount of each deposit. DTCs are identifiable by their signature areas that usually state:

> "Depository Transfer Check—No Signature Required.
> Not to be Cashed."

- The concentration bank produces all of the DTCs required for the day's activity and prepares a deposit to the institution's concentration account. That deposit is timed to meet check-clearing deadlines and may be made as late as 7 P.M. local time.
- Meanwhile, the system operator sends the customer a report of the deposits that were made by each unit. This provides the accounting needed to distribute credit for the aggregate deposit made to the master concentration account.

While some institutions estimate the balances in their field depository accounts and periodically make transfers to the concentration bank, this is cumbersome and nonautomatic. There are several advantages and benefits of an automated DTC system, compared to making concentration deposits on the basis of estimates of deposit activity. They include

- elimination of uncertainty about the amount of the transfer
- elimination of staff required to estimate and concentrate funds
- reduction of idle balances in the depository banks because transfers are made automatically every day
- elimination of overdrafts in the depository accounts due to inaccurate forecasting
- improved control by financial managers over the depository accounts, because locations that do not report deposits are identified immediately

Intrabank Deposit Consolidation

It is easier to consolidate funds within a single bank than to concentrate funds from multiple banks. Most states allow banks to operate branches in various parts of the state. It is possible to deposit funds directly into a central account from any branch. In such cases, the institution may use a special deposit slip that includes the depositing unit's identification number in the MICR line, thus freeing the financial manager from the cost of employing other methods of funds concentration.

Automated Clearing House Transfers

Many businesses use ACH transfers to concentrate funds from depository bank accounts. ACH transfers are often called electronic DTCs because they closely resemble the functional utility of the paper DTC. Deposit data is reported in generally the same manner as outlined above for reporting DTC data, and the end result is the same. However, there are substantial differences in the way the paper and electronic systems operate. Under the paper DTC system, the concentration bank usually maintains the data base of depository information. Under an ACH system, the data base is usually maintained by either the customer or the tele-communications system operator. The customer, not the bank, matches depository information against the data base and creates a data file that can be processed through the ACH system, rather than the bank producing a paper DTC. The ACH file is then transmitted to the concentration bank that acts as the gateway into the ACH system.

One advantage of using ACH debit transfers for concentration of deposits is their cost. For a large number of transfers, the cost may be less per transfer than paper DTCs. When comparing costs, however, the financial manager must bear in mind that ACH transfers often have a fixed cost per transmission in addition to the per-transfer charge. The fixed cost may add considerable expense if only a few transactions are made. It is also necessary to ensure that the depository banks can handle ACH debit transfers. Banks are accustomed to handling paper DTCs. Their use generally requires that each depository bank have an authorization to honor the DTCs without obtaining an institution signature. As of the late 1980s, however, many banks are in the process of learning how to handle business-type ACH transactions, especially debit transfers.

Wire Transfers

Wire transfers are also used to concentrate funds. Because they are expensive, they should be used only to concentrate a large amount of immediately available funds. Wire transfer fees are usually charged by both the sending bank and the receiving bank. They can range from approximately $10 to as much as $25, depending upon the method used by the financial manager to initiate the transaction and the pricing set by the respective banks. The charges for wire transfers, like charges for other banking services, are usually reflected in the account analysis and paid for with compensating balances rather than by direct charge to the bank account. However, they are costs and must be considered as such.

A simple cost-benefit calculation uses the time value of money to determine whether paying the price of a wire transfer to move funds for immediate use is worthwhile. Assume that the total cost of a wire transfer (including charges at both the sending and receiving banks) is $20. Also assume that receiving available funds in the concentration account one day sooner allows the funds to earn interest for that day at a market rate. Table 4-1 compares various amounts at different interest rates and shows the income that could be earned in one day.

A financial manager should use wire transfers for funds concentration only if the amount of the transfer and the interest rate are high enough to generate more revenue than the cost of making the wire transfer.

As Table 4-1 shows, some amounts will not earn $20 in interest for one day. It would not be economical to use a wire transfer for these amounts. For smaller amounts, the financial manager should use the less expensive DTC or ACH transfer to concentrate the funds.

Action Advice: The financial manager should know the full costs of moving funds by wire transfer, including charges levied by both the sending and receiving banks, and calculate a matrix similar to Table 4-1. With this information, the financial manager can balance the cost of transferring funds with the amount of income that could be generated by the funds produced through a wire transfer.

Balance Reporting

Concentration banks supply a tool, called balance reporting, that is necessary to the successful management of a funds concentration system. Daily balance reports show all of the activity in the concentration account, including incoming and outgoing transactions posted the previous day. These reports are used by a financial manager to monitor deposits, float, concentration transfers, and disbursements. Balance reports are also useful in measuring actual funds flow

Table 4-1 Trade-Off of Benefit versus Cost of Wire Transfers

Amount	Interest Rate		
	11%	9%	7%
$300,000	$91.67	$75.00	$58.33
100,000	30.56	25.00	19.44
50,000	15.28	12.50	9.72

against forecasted funds flow and providing information for accounting purposes. Specific information about the following sources of funds is usually included in balance reporting:

- lockbox numbers and the respective amounts deposited from each lockbox
- DTCs listed by amount and location identification number
- wire transfers, both incoming and outgoing, listed by source and destination
- ACH transfers, both incoming and outgoing, listed by source and destination
- deposit consolidation reports showing the origin of each deposit and the identification number of each respective depositing location
- other activity, such as investment and loan transactions, foreign exchange settlements, and other bank charges and credits

PAPER-BASED DISBURSEMENTS

Paper-based disbursements include funds that move by means of checks and drafts. These are negotiable instruments developed hundreds of years ago as alternatives to coins, currency, precious metals, and shells. A check, a special form of draft, is a written order addressed to the financial institution that holds money on behalf of the party writing the check. The check provides an unconditional instruction to the depository institution (the drawee bank) to pay a certain sum of money to the person to whom the check is made out (the payee) at the time the check is presented. A check has no maturity date; it is payable on demand. A draft, on the other hand, is drawn against the maker rather than a bank, although the payee is usually instructed on the face of the instrument to present it through a certain bank for payment.

The one element that ensures the success of all paper-based financial instruments is negotiability. In fact, information is stated on checks in a way to ensure negotiability. For instance, if a check stated, ''Pay to Jack Johnson,'' the drawee bank would be able to honor the check only if Jack Johnson walked into the bank and presented the check. Because most checks are not cashed in person at the drawee bank, checks state, ''Pay to the Order of Jack Johnson.'' In that way, the check can move through the banking system and still be negotiable, as long as Jack Johnson's signature or endorsement appears on the check.

An entire body of law governing negotiable instruments and banking practices has grown through custom and practice. It is embodied in the Uniform Commercial Code (UCC) and in laws adopted by each state. Financial managers should be familar with these laws. (Most law libraries have copies of the UCC. Article 3 of the UCC, entitled ''Commercial Paper,'' details all the common forms of negotiable instruments including checks, drafts, notes, and certificates of deposit. Article

4, "Bank Deposits and Collections," describes the workings of the banking system and the relationship between the payor bank and its depositor.) Under the UCC, an instrument is negotiable only if it

- is signed by the maker
- contains an unconditional promise or order to pay a certain sum of money and includes no other promise, order, obligation, or power
- is payable on demand or at a definite time
- is payable to order or to the bearer

An instrument that meets all of the above requirements is called

- a *draft* (or *bill of exchange*) if it is an order
- a *check* if it is a draft drawn on a bank and payable on demand
- a *certificate of deposit* if it represents an acknowledgment by a bank that it received money with an engagement to repay it
- a *note* if it is a promise other than a certificate of deposit

A check may change ownership many times as it moves through the clearing system. Under law, each owner, called a "holder in due course," must endorse the check. Through its endorsement, the holder guarantees the endorsement of the previous holder. Each endorsement links the holders together, which is important if the check is not honored. In the banking system, the dishonored instrument is called a "return item," but commonly referred to as a "bounced check."

A draft is similar to a check, but it has an important difference. Like checks, drafts are written orders to pay money but it is drawn against the payor rather than a bank. Drafts also move through the bank clearing system. Unlike checks, however, the payor reserves the right to honor or reject the draft when it is presented for payment. Because checks are drawn by the payor and made payable to a payee, the payor generally does not reserve the right to honor or reject checks upon presentment.

Elements of a Check

Because the bulk of business transactions are paid by checks, the financial manager should have detailed knowledge of checks and how they move through the banking system. Checks meet the legal requirements of all negotiable instruments. They are also designed to move physically through the banking system, and many of the physical characteristics of checks are designed to ensure that they move efficiently. In fact, the legal requirements for negotiability generally do not hinder the automated processing of checks. A missing signature, for instance, has not prevented a check from moving through the system and being paid. The physical requirements (see Figure 4-3) a check must meet, in order to be processed through the clearing system, are

- size
- date
- payee
- amount
- signature
- drawee bank
- MICR line

Size

A check must meet certain size requirements prescribed by the Federal Reserve System and the American National Standards Institute. Checks must be at least 7 inches long but cannot be any longer than 8-¾ inches. They must be at least 2-¾ inches wide but no wider than 3-⅔ inches. If a check does not meet these dimensional requirements, it cannot be processed by standard automated check processing equipment.

Date

The date on the face of a check determines when the instrument legally becomes a check; a check is not legally a check until the date of the item is reached. A postdated check, which is not yet legally a check, is similar to a promissory note, because it is payable at a point of time in the future. Postdated checks often are cleared accidentally through the banking system and paid by the drawee bank when the check's date is not scanned properly.

It is also possible for time to run out on a check through the concept of "stale date." A check, in effect, expires after six months. After that time a bank is not obligated to pay the check. However, under the UCC, the bank *may* pay the check and charge the customer's account. Banks may pay stale-dated checks so that the payor's liability is not open to question. If checks automatically became invalid after six months, the payor's obligation to pay would be discharged simply through the passage of time. Payors, then, cannot ask the bank for a refund because the date was not noticed when the bank paid a stale-dated check, unless, of course, the payor had placed a stop payment order with the bank and the bank had accepted that order.

⑨ *Payable If Desired At:*
Main Street Bank
Anytown, U.S.A.

⑧ Citibank
New York, NY

ABC Health Care, Inc.
Anytown, U.S.A.

Check No. 54321

1-8 ③
210 ②

Date July 21, 1987   Pay Exactly $ 1,000,000

To The Order Of:*****Medical Supply Company ******************************

_____ ⑦
Authorized Signature

132054321   021000083   0241739680   0000100000
  ①   ②   ③④   ⑤   ⑥

1   Auxiliary On-Us Field — May be used by maker of the check for any purpose. Usually used to incorporate check number into the MICR line. Example shown incorporates a division/unit/location number — 132 — in addition to check numbers.

2   Federal Reserve Number — "02" indicates the second Federal Reserve District, next digit "1" indicates headquarters office of that district, or the New York Federal Reserve Bank, that services the drawee bank.

3   Drawee Bank's Transit Number — In "1-8" the digit "1" is a vestige of manual processing, but the digit "8" refers specifically to Citibank.

4   Check Digit — The digit "3" results from an algorithm that contains the Federal Reserve Number and the Transit Number to ensure accuracy.

5   On-Us Field — Reserved for the drawee bank's use, this field usually contains the maker's account number at the drawee bank.

6   Amount Field — The amount of the check is encoded here by the bank where the check is first deposited.

7   Signature Line — Check must bear manual or facsimile signature authorized by board of trustees of maker.

8   Drawee Bank — This is the bank on which the check is drawn.

9   Alternate Drawee Bank — This bank has agreed to cash this check even though it is not the drawee.

Figure 4-3 Sample of a Check

Payee

The payee is the party that the payor wants to pay. The payee's name is placed on the face of the check. The payor, or maker, is responsible for naming the payee on the face of the check. If a payee is not named, or the item is made payable to "cash" or to "bearer," any person who comes into possession of the check is entitled to cash it, even if the check was stolen or fraudulently negotiated.

The words "Pay to the order of:" are customarily printed on the face of the check and placed before the space in which the maker is to specify the payee. The phrase has two important components.

1. "Pay to . . ." is the unconditional order given by the maker to the drawee bank. Without that instruction, the drawee bank would not have the authority to pay the item.
2. ". . . the order of . . ." is the phrase that allows the check to become a legally negotiable instrument. Without that phrase, the payee would not be able to transfer ownership of the item to another person. This would prevent the payee from having its bank collect on the item; the payee would have to present the check in person to the drawee bank in order to receive payment.

Amount

The amount of a check or draft must be stated on the face of the item. By custom, the amount is stated twice, once in numerals and once in words. If the amounts conflict, the amount stated in words legally prevails.

Signature

The maker authenticates a check by placing a unique signature or mark on it. That doesn't mean, of course, that all checks must be signed by hand, or even signed at all. Signatures may be made by facsimile. They may be single or joint signatures. They may be omitted. In fact, automated check processing equipment cannot automatically authenticate signatures, at least with the speed and economy that large volumes of checks require. As a result, bank employees authenticate signatures; this is a major weakness in the paper-based payments system.

The signature on an item is of great importance, however. It is the contractual element between the maker and the drawee bank. When the item is a draft drawn by the payee against another party, the signature constitutes the drawer's warranty that it is entitled to the funds. When the item is a draft drawn by the payor against itself, such as a "payable through" draft issued by an insurance company, the signature indicates intent to pay at the time the draft is issued but does not constitute a guaranty or warranty of payment. The signature merely identifies the source of the item.

When the item is a check, the signature signifies that the maker has instructed its bank to charge the maker's account and pay the check upon presentment. The drawee bank can validate the signature only by comparing it to a specimen that it knows is authentic. It does not matter how the check is signed or even if the signature is legible. The only requirements are that (1) the signature is unique and (2) the bank can verify its authenticity.

An organization has a variety of choices in signing checks, but the bank must agree to accept the signature chosen. Problems may exist, for example, if the bank will accept only a single manual signature on a check, and the institution wants two people to countersign a check or wants to use a facsimile.

Facsimile signatures are mechanical reproductions of manual signatures. Their use presents a potential liability because it is possible for the facsimile plate to be used in unauthorized ways. The drawee bank could have no knowledge of unauthorized use. Consequently, the drawee bank generally does not honor a facsimile signature unless the customer signs an agreement that protects the bank against loss in the event the facsimile is misused.

Most organizations that use facsimile signatures place control over the plate with one person authorized to sign checks manually, and that individual personally supervises use of the plate. Unfortunately, a few users do not place such tight security over facsimile signatures. If a facsimile signature is misused, however, any savings that might have resulted from inadequate check-issuing procedures will be immediately offset.

Drawee Bank

The bank to which the maker addresses instructions ordering the payment of a sum of money on the face of the check is the drawee bank. Negotiable items are not always drawn on banks, however. In a warrant, for instance, the maker is the payor, and a bank may be reflected on the document to facilitate its clearance through the banking system. Warrants are frequently used by governmental units to provide the unit's commitment to make payment from its treasury. Also, drafts are not drawn against banks. The name of a bank appears on a draft solely to allow the item to clear through the banking system. On drafts, the name of the bank is preceded with the words ''Payable through (name of bank).'' The drawee of the draft is the maker or institution that is expected to pay the funds, not the bank.

Alternate Drawee Bank. There are occasions when organizations may want to draw checks on a bank in one location and have another bank honor that check as if it were the drawee bank. If an institution has health care facilities in more than one state, for instance, it may be subject to laws requiring payroll checks to be payable (or cashable) at in-state banks. These laws can wreak havoc on a unified payroll system. An institution can solve the problem by arranging to have an in-state bank designated on the face of the check as an alternate drawee. To signify that a bank is an alternate drawee bank, its name is preceded by the words ''Payable if desired at (name of alternate drawee bank).'' Such arrangements are often called ''PID'' arrangements.

Another area in which alternate drawee banks are frequently used is controlled disbursing, especially among banks located in the Western United States. Because of the time difference, East Coast banks can notify West Coast customers of their daily check clearings earlier than West Coast banks can notify these customers. This gives the East Coast banks a competitive advantage. Consequently, some West Coast banks provide controlled disbursing service to their customers through a correspondent bank in an earlier time zone that acts as the draweee bank. The West Coast bank manages the account relationship, including customer service and daily funding, and its name usually appears on the face of the check as an alternate drawee. In Figure 4-3, for example, the drawee bank is Citibank; the alternate drawee bank is Main Street Bank.

In alternate drawee bank arrangements, the routing and transit numbers appearing in the MICR line are those of the drawee bank, even though the alternate drawee bank has agreed to cash the check for the payee. When a check is cashed by the alternate drawee bank, it generally cannot directly charge the payee's account and thus is not reimbursed for the check until it clears. Therefore, the alternate drawee bank suffers clearing float when it cashes these checks. The alternate drawee bank must also notify all of its offices of the PID arrangement. Both steps represent a cost to the alternate drawee bank, so such banks are generally compensated by the issuer for performing PID-related services.

Alternate drawee banks, in addition, often require a written agreement under which the check maker agrees to indemnify the alternate drawee bank from any losses. The alternate drawee bank, for its part, generally agrees to require identification from the payee when cashing such checks. However, the alternate drawee bank generally cannot monitor stop payments or authorized signatures.

MICR Line

Magnetic Ink Character Recognition (MICR) refers to the line of characters printed across the bottom of a check with a special ink containing magnetic particles. The characters can be read by scanning equipment on check-processing machines. The MICR line is a series of numbers and symbols that specify information about how the check is to move through the banking system. The Federal Reserve system requires that all checks contain a MICR line identifying the drawee bank and its Federal Reserve district.

Banks use the information contained in the MICR line to sort and route checks through the clearing system. The MICR line contains information that enables the depository bank to move the check to the drawee bank and to allow the drawee bank to process the item and charge the maker's account. All MICR line information is printed when the check is manufactured, with the exception of the amount of the check, which is encoded into the MICR line by the bank where the check is first deposited.

Endorsements

The endorsement on the back of a check serves two legal purposes: (1) it acknowledges receipt of value and (2) it guarantees all previous endorsements. For instance, Grant issues a check payable to Lee. The check is then endorsed by Lee over to Lincoln who deposits the check in the bank. The depository bank has no way of knowing whether Grant's signature or Lee's endorsement are genuine. The depository bank should know Lincoln's signature and have some confidence in its customer. So by accepting the check and crediting Lincoln's account, the depository bank relies on Lincoln to accept financial responsibility for the check. If it is returned unpaid, Lincoln is responsible for locating Lee and asking to be repaid for the check.

If the check was not endorsed by the payee, the maker can legally demand a refund from the drawee bank and return the item unpaid. A forged endorsement is equivalent to no endorsement. But if a payee is to demand a refund on the grounds that the endorsement was forged, the payee will have to supply to the maker, payor, and drawee bank an affidavit stating that the endorsement was forged.

How Checks Clear

Banks use different methods of routing checks, depending on where the check is deposited and where the drawee bank is located. Financial managers need to understand these methods and the circumstances under which banks employ them so they can plan their receipts and disbursements accordingly. Almost all checks begin their journey through the clearing system in the "proof and transit" operation at the organization's depository institution. From there, checks are routed to a local clearinghouse association, delivered to a Federal Reserve check processing center, or sent to a correspondent bank in another city. Some checks may move through a combination of these steps.

Each step in the clearing process takes a certain amount of time. Financial managers should understand the process for this reason. They should know how much time it takes a bank to clear deposited checks and how it grants availability on checks. For instance, the easiest way for a bank to clear checks deposited on banks located in other cities is to send them to the bank's Federal Reserve regional check processing center (RCPC). It is more difficult and expensive to send the checks directly to a distant correspondent or to a Federal Reserve Bank in the other city, but doing so improves funds availability. Consequently, a health care institution wants to deal with a bank whose availability terms match the institution's deposit patterns.

For example, if a hospital's deposits consist mostly of local checks, it should make its deposits at the largest local bank. Many checks will be "on-us" items, and the funds will be immediately available upon deposit. Checks from other local banks will be cleared through the local clearinghouse and receive next-day availability. If the hospital deposits its checks at a small local bank, it will have fewer "on-us" items; also, the bank may not be a member of the local clearinghouse. Funds will not become available as fast at this bank.

It is also advantageous for a health care firm to use a large bank if it has checks drawn on banks throughout the country. Large banks tend to have more "direct send" arrangements with correspondents in other cities and can usually offer faster availability on out-of-town deposits, as well as on local deposits.

An institution must view availability from a different angle when it considers disbursements. Theoretically, it can count on longer check-clearing times by using a smaller bank for disbursements. If the drawee bank is small, located far from a major city, and not a member of a clearinghouse, the length of time it takes for its checks to clear may allow the institution to keep its disbursement funds invested longer.

Disbursement Float

The amount of time that passes from the moment an organization issues a check to the moment the check is charged to the issuer's account by the drawee bank is called disbursement float. The following three components constitute disbursement float:

1. Mail float: the amount of time that the check is in the mail while traveling from issuer to payee.
2. Processing float: the amount of time it takes the payee to open mail and process, endorse, and deposit the check.
3. Clearing float: the amount of time it takes for the check to move from the depository bank to the drawee bank and for the drawee bank to charge the check to the issuer's account. Clearing float is minimal if the depository bank and the drawee bank are the same.

Remote Disbursing

Remote disbursing is the practice that some firms have engaged in when they wanted to increase the length of time it took for their checks to clear. One of the original premises of the practice of cash management was that a firm can increase its working funds by increasing disbursement float.

Remote disbursement schemes involved drawing checks on a bank located away from major cities and airports. Ideally it was in a rural area. Because the bank was not served by a commercial airport or was located far from a Fed Regional Check Processing Center, it took longer for the bank physically to receive checks drawn against it. By establishing disbursing accounts at a remote bank, a firm was able to use disbursement funds for several more days while the checks cleared. When the bank received the firm's checks, it contacted the customer firm by telephone. The firm then sent a wire transfer to the drawee bank to cover the amount of the checks.

The practice of remote disbursing grew rapidly during the 1970s. After passage of the Monetary Control Act of 1980, the Fed persuaded banks to discontinue remote disbursing arrangements where the issuer's only purpose was to delay check presentment.

Controlled Disbursing

Controlled disbursing, a bank product line the Fed has somewhat reluctantly accepted, grew out of financial managers' profitable experiences with remote disbursing. Unlike remote disbursing, however, controlled disbursing is conducted through sizable drawee banks located in major cities. Banks offering controlled disbursing services can inform an organization of the amount of its checks presented for disbursement early enough in the day to allow the organization to fund its account for the exact amount on that day. Health care financial managers like controlled disbursing because early notification of the amount of checks that cleared allows them to complete accurate daily cash forecasts. These, in turn, allow them to determine the organization's cash position early enough to make accurate decisions about borrowing or investing in the money markets that day.

Even though controlled disbursing does not delay disbursements, as remote disbursing did, financial managers are attracted to it on the basis of the early notification it provides. Controlled disbursing is as important to the disbursing operation as lockboxes are to the collection side. Financial managers have willingly dropped efforts to increase float in favor of early notification. Apparently, the Fed accepts the practice because of the fact that most banks providing controlled disbursing are large and have sufficient capital to cover the usual risks.

Many small banks, however, still take longer to clear checks than larger banks. Some of them, through ownership or correspondent affiliations with large banks, offer controlled disbursing services that also increase float. Despite the Fed's banishment of remote disbursing in 1980, controlled disbursing through remote banks is alive and well.

Controlled disbursing does not necessarily result in the best cash management environment. For example, the Fed's high-dollar group sort (HDGS) program, under which the Fed makes a second daily presentment of checks to drawee banks clearing more than $10 million in checks from outside their respective Fed districts, affects controlled disbursing in two ways: (1) On the negative side, financial managers are not notified of the amount of checks that clear until after the second presentment is received and processed. That delay may affect the financial manager's daily cash planning and overnight investment transactions. (2) On the positive side, banks processing a high-dollar volume of check presentments are often highly automated. As a result, they can offer lower per-item pricing for processing an organization's disbursements.

Both of those factors can be used in a controlled disbursing strategy. After the HDGS program went into effect, financial managers started to use drawee banks that processed less than $10 million per day in out-of-district checks and thus were not subject to HDGS. Use of such banks lengthens disbursement float by a small amount. A number of the small, non-HDGS banks often contract their processing to their large correspondent banks. The small banks can then offer lower per-item pricing.

Financial managers who want to select a bank for controlled disbursing must evaluate a number of factors, including clearing float, HDGS, processing efficiency, funding alternatives offered, proximity to the issuer, and pricing.

Remote Mailing

Remote mailing systems, in which checks are mailed from a site located far away from the drawee bank and the payees, can be quite sophisticated. Such systems lengthen disbursement float, because they maximize the amount of time it takes checks to move through the mail to the payees and then to the drawee bank. An institution that processes accounts payable in a central location may also print its own checks with printers located in various offices around the country. After consulting a data base of mail times between check printer locations and payees, the central computer can determine which bank to draw each check on and which location should print it.

Drafts

Drafts are payment orders drawn by the issuer against itself or another nonbank party. If it is to move through the clearing system, a draft must be made payable through a bank that acts as agent for the issuer. Although the agent bank's name and MICR line appear on the face of the draft, they merely permit the item to clear through the banking system and do not make the bank a principal party to the transaction. Accordingly, such drafts are often called payable-through drafts (PTDs).

In many business-to-business situations, PTDs are a viable payment alternative to checks. Some industries routinely use drafts for certain payment purposes. Property and casualty insurance claims are often paid by drafts. Personal-line insurance companies, however, are discontinuing their use because payees complain that they are difficult to cash. Automobile manufacturers use drafts to draw against dealers for car shipments, and livestock, grain, and tobacco purchases are often paid for with drafts.

Drafts move through the clearing system like checks until they reach the agent bank, where they are sorted into a separate category. A PTD differs from a check in that it cannot be charged to the issuer's account without the issuer's prior approval. As a result, a bank generally captures the MICR line of the issuer's drafts received that day, sorts the file by check serial numbers, and lists the amounts of the drafts. The bank then transmits the file to the issuing institution, which completes the processing by verifying the authenticity of the drafts.

The issuer maintains a file of the PTDs it has issued. That file is updated every day; it is checked against the bank's file of drafts presented and any items that have been approved and paid are deleted. As the file is reconciled, new PTDs, whose serial numbers and amounts match in both the institution's and bank's files, are authorized for payment. If serial numbers and amounts do not reconcile, the physical PTD is obtained from the bank and examined before payment is authorized.

It is the issuer's responsibility to ensure that PTDs received from the bank match those that were issued, because the bank is merely an agent for the issuer. After the bank receives the issuer's approval to pay a PTD, it charges the issuer's account for the total of all drafts paid that day, rather than for each item. The bank, however, had to pay for the drafts when it received them through the clearing system. Therefore, a PTD customer must pay interest to the bank if its account is not charged on the same day that the drafts were received. The customer can allow the bank to charge its account for all drafts at the time they are received and later credit the account for any rejected drafts.

Bank charges for processing PTDs are considerably less than for checks, sometimes as much as 75 percent less, because the bank does not verify signatures or update accounts item by item. All the bank does is physically present the drafts and capture, sort, and deliver the data. Costs for such services are charged either at low per-item rates or at a flat rate. There are, of course, costs associated with processing that the issuer performs. These costs, however, are generally offset by elimination of expenses for the bank's account reconcilement and stop-payment services. Companies paying by drafts also maintain reconcilement data and are not required to pay banks for this information. For institutions that issue a large number of payments, drafts can result in significant cost savings compared with checks.

Organizing Disbursement Bank Accounts

A disbursing system must be properly designed and organized to function efficiently. As illustrated in the sections above, efficiency is the key word in managing the flow of funds. Several elements characterize a cost-effective disbursement system that does not suffer from bottlenecks, gaps, and delays. In an efficient system, disbursements are:

- controlled by financial managers
- authorized at either a central hub of financial authority or at regional hubs
- drawn against bank accounts used solely for disbursements
- covered by systematic funds flows
- covered by funds that flow only when checks clear or are requested by decentralized personnel and approved by central financial authority

In addition, a well-planned disbursing system is a well-documented one. Methods for authorizing, generating, and accounting for payments must be well-defined, systematic, and accurate. Further, a well-designed disbursement system works efficiently regardless of the type of payments—paper-based or electronic—that move through the system; the principles are the same. Indeed, many systems use both electronic and paper payments. At this time, the most common form of electronic payment is direct deposit of payroll using the automated clearing house system.

Control of Disbursing Activities

The health care institution's financial management should control disbursing activities, since it is charged with conserving the organization's assets. In order to perform that role, financial managers must have effective systems for accounting, auditing, and control and be capable of adhering to budgets and funding forecasts. At the same time, however, they must respond to the needs of other components of their organizations. The management of disbursements requires that financial managers seek to balance competing forces: funds disbursements must balance with available resources, and requests for disbursement must balance with budget constraints.

At a small- or medium-size health care institution, disbursement activities are usually centered in the headquarters office, and disbursement management is often charged to one person, the controller. The controller's functions expand and divide as the institution grows and becomes more complex. Separate departments may handle accounts payable, accounts receivable, and general ledger accounting. At the same time, an institution may develop data processing (DP), information services (IS), or management information services (MIS) departments. Disbursements will continue to grow in number, dollar amount, and complexity. As a result, the following circumstances may arise:

- an increase in vendor complaints about slow payments
- a clamor from related businesses to institute their own disbursing systems
- a laxity in review and control of disbursements
- an increase in DP overhead

The controller, as the title suggests, is the one who must maintain control and prevent the system from running awry. Trained as an auditor, the controller is responsible for setting up a system where duties are separate and where checks and balances are maintained. As a result, overhead expenditures may have to be increased. This often causes management to face painful decisions of whether or not to spend money it may not have and to make an investment in the growth and future viability of the firm. If management opts to invest, the investment undoubtedly will include computers and software to manage payroll and accounts payable. The institution probably will grant some decentralized disbursement control as well, especially if major related units maintain their own accounting.

Accounts Payable Function

The objective of the accounts payable function is to initiate payment of the organization's legitimate obligations on a timely basis. To accomplish this, the accounts payable system must be able to (1) verify whether, in fact, obligations belong to the firm and not someone else; and (2) determine the proper time to pay each obligation (neither too soon nor too late).

Accounts payable systems produce payments for tangibles, such as goods, materials, merchandise, and equipment; and intangibles, such as services. Tangibles are generally bought on the basis of purchase orders or material release orders when the institution buys large quantities under a blanket purchase order for release over time. When the institution receives tangibles, it creates a document certifying their receipt. After receipt, the seller sends the buyer an invoice. At that point, the accounts payable function takes over; it must match three documents— purchase order, receiving document, and invoice. When these documents match in all respects, the invoice is approved for payment. Making the match, however, is not always easy due to the number of variables involved: merchandise description, quantity, unit price, and any agreements covering such items as freight, insurance, duties, and handling charges. Paying for intangibles requires a different set of procedures because there is no receiving document and usually no purchase order. Therefore, payment authorization is usually based on approval of the invoice by a designated person who is familiar with the transaction.

Bank Account Structures

An organization's bank account system must be designed so that form and function are balanced. A well-designed system first deals with immediate functional concerns. These concerns, however, are tempered by prospects of the institution's growth. Finally, the system manager chooses a bank that can provide information and control services to meet its requirements.

An important objective of a bank account system, from the point of view of disbursing, is to isolate disbursing and depository activities through the use of separate bank accounts. Separating the flow of disbursements from the flow of depository funds makes it easier to monitor and forecast activities, reconcile bank accounts with the general ledger, and control functional duties. Further extension of this concept suggests that the basic components of disbursement, payroll and accounts payable, also should be separated. These functions usually are performed by different people and different departments, so separating them improves accountability and control.

After separating collections and disbursements by functional organization, the financial manager should focus on operation of the bank account system. The most important question now is the funding of disbursing accounts. Several methods are available; the appropriate method should be chosen on the basis of structural design and cost. The funding of disbursing accounts by using imprest accounts, for example, does not require a change in structural design, while using zero-balance accounts does.

Imprest Account

An imprest account is a demand deposit account that maintains a fixed general ledger balance selected by management. As disbursements flow out of the account, the general ledger imprest balance is restored by moving funds from other accounts. Financial managers generally use imprest disbursing accounts when they want to control and review disbursements as they are made.

An imprest account may be used, for instance, when a related business needs to make local disbursements for postage, petty cash, and such things as casual labor. Headquarters normally pays all payroll and operating expenses, but the related unit requires a procedure to make modest disbursements on the spot. In such a situation, the related unit may be given an imprest bank account. Certain designated personnel are authorized to sign checks, and the head office funds the account with an initial deposit. The amount of the initial deposit, which is the account's imprest balance, is based on the expected volume of disbursements and the anticipated frequency of replenishment. For instance, if the unit expects to disburse about $1,000 per month and the head office wants the account to be replenished monthly, the imprest balance should be about $1,000. If the head office wants to have the account replenished weekly, then the imprest balance should be about $250.

The business unit initiates replenishment of its imprest account, so it must keep track of its checkbook (general ledger) balance. Typically, the unit prepares a report listing disbursements made, their amounts and purposes, and the total of disbursements made since the last replenishment. A financial manager at the head office reviews the disbursements and approves the replenishment request, which is accomplished by check or electronic funds transfer. For an imprest account to be successful, disbursements must be reviewed and the unit must make a specific request for replenishment. Perfunctory reviews that never challenge disbursement requests defeat the purpose of an imprest account.

Zero-Balance Account

A zero-balance account (ZBA) is an imprest account for which the bank balance is maintained at a zero level, the "pegged" amount, while the general ledger, or checkbook, balance fluctuates as a lower or negative balance. To maintain the bank balance at zero, the bank must have the authority to draw automatically on a funding source so that it can restore the ZBA to a zero balance after the day's checks have cleared. In most cases, the funding source is the concentration account maintained at the same bank.

A ZBA with a mechanism that automatically funds the account on the same day that checks clear is called a "true ZBA." In a true ZBA, the bank posts all charges to the account and draws a total before making the transfer, which occurs before the books are closed for the day. A ZBA with automatic funding allows the financial manager to monitor disbursements with ease, especially if the institution maintains several ZBAs tied to the concentration account. The financial manager needs only to monitor transfers from the concentration account, rather than to review transfers from several disbursing accounts. Banks generally charge a small premium in return for maintaining each ZBA. The premium covers the cost of daily transfers, a service that regular accounts do not require.

General Accounts

General accounts are demand deposit accounts that combine the collection function and the disbursing function into a single bank account. General accounts require neither special bank services nor special operating procedures. There are no particular advantages associated with general accounts, but there may be some disadvantages. It is difficult to reconcile the mixed transactions in a general account with the general ledger. Accordingly, it is advisable to use general accounts only when the organization tends to make a lot of deposits and only a few disbursements, or vice versa.

SUMMARY

There are many ways to channel remittances from customers, fiscal intermediaries, and patients into the organization's cash flow system, depending on whether the payor mails the payment, delivers it in person, or pays electronically. Therefore, the financial manager must design a system to accommodate various forms of remittance. Lockboxes are particulary effective where checks are mailed, and a network of lockbox banks may be useful if the organization has multiple business units dispersed geographically over a wide area.

When dealing with deposits of checks, every business is faced with the problem of checks returned by the drawee bank for various reasons. It is preferable to develop a system that handles them efficiently, rather than to fight return items in the hope they will disappear.

A funds concentration system is a necessary cash management device for those institutions that collect funds at various geographic locations or within various separate corporate entities.

Knowledge of how checks work in the banking and check-clearing system can enable the financial manager to design a system that helps to extend disbursement float and offers greater control over payment of funds.

One of the keys to accomplishing an effective and efficient cash management system is to design the architecture of bank accounts to facilitate the inflow of funds, without any overt act by management or staff, and to control and monitor the outflow of funds.

Chapter 5

Electronic Payment Systems

INTRODUCTION

For more than 25 years, bankers and futurists have talked about a checkless society where all payments are made electronically. Electronic mechanisms have been developed and refined over the years, and indeed there are a number of business-to-business trade payment arrangements being used; but electronic payments are still a future consideration for most people and organizations. Electronic trade payments are increasing in the United States, and their use is retarding the growth rate of checks. However, the checkless society may never arrive.

As health care institutions continue to adopt electronic data interchange (EDI) as the preferred method for purchasing operations, the use of electronic payments to settle these transactions will grow as well. Also, insurance companies and health care providers alike are discovering the sharply reduced costs involved in processing claims, effecting payments, and applying cash to patient accounts through the use of EDI and electronic payments. While checks will never go away, the use of electronic payments will grow rapidly for all types and sizes of health care institutions as the industry enters the 1990s. The health care financial manager must anticipate this growth and know how to utilize new developments.

An electronic payment is the transmission of an electronic message consisting of payment instructions to a depository institution. In the banking industry, such payments are called electronic funds transfer (EFT). As with paper checks, EFT does not move money but transmits instructions to make bookkeeping entries on the bank's books. These entries affect funds, or deposit liabilities, on the depository institution's books. In reality, funds transfers are transfers of value from one depositor to another. Although in use for many years, EFT still maintains an air of the exotic. Its goal, however, can be simply stated: to settle payment transactions between payors and payees faster, more accurately, and less expensively than by means of paper checks.

There are two reasons why financial managers must understand the EFT mechanisms. First, in many business situations, EFT is the most appropriate and cost-effective method for moving funds. Second, financial managers must ensure that electronic funds transfers are used properly so that the timeliness, accuracy, and reliability of the transactions are not compromised. As the number of companies transacting business electronically increases, it will be even more important that financial managers understand EFT.

The means by which an EFT message moves varies by payee—it can use a public or private telecommunications system. The form of the message and its payment advice also vary. They can be highly structured or unstructured, encrypted or readable, and authenticated or untested.

The baseline for EFT systems is the Federal Reserve's wire transfer system (Fedwire). Other systems that have come and gone over the years have attempted to improve on the Fedwire system, and the Federal Reserve System (Fed) itself has made major improvements over the years. Bankwire, Bankwire II, and Cashwire tried to improve upon Fedwire, and all are now out of business. Cashwire ceased operations in 1986. Today, Fedwire and the automated clearing house (ACH) systems are the only EFT systems generally available to the public, although some proprietary systems serve specific constituencies. These systems include the Clearing House Interbank Payments System (CHIPS), operated by the New York Clearing House Association, and industry-specific settlement systems such as Petroclear, operated by a Houston bank, that enables large oil companies to settle bulk petroleum transactions.

SETTLEMENT SYSTEMS

It can be argued that CHIPS and Petroclear are not EFT systems but settlement systems; however, the distinction is academic. An EFT system is nothing more than a settlement system in which transactions are initiated and received electronically. The important considerations for financial managers are the speed and cost of electronic systems. Speed traditionally increases cost, but an electronic transaction that can be completed in a matter of hours may be more useful under some circumstances than one that is not settled until the end of the day. It is also more expensive to process single transactions than to process multiple transactions of the same type.

Whether a financial manager chooses low cost or high speed depends on the particular business situation and transaction requirements. To initiate an EFT transaction, a financial manager must determine the speed with which a transaction must be settled and the type of EFT transaction that is most appropriate.

Settlement Methods and Timing

Because an EFT transaction is the electronic notification of the parties concerning a transaction on the books of an intermediary, usually a bank, settlement occurs only when both sides of the transaction have been completed, which is normally simultaneous. Unlike a check, where first the payee is credited and then the payor is charged, EFT settlement is not effected until both the payor's account has been charged and the payee's account has been credited. Different EFT methods provide different settlement times. Three EFT settlement methods are available:

1. Fedwire transfer, which provides for immediate simultaneous settlement.
2. CHIPS, which provides delayed settlement on the same day.
3. Automated Clearing House, which is a value-dated settlement system in the automated clearing house system.

Fedwire

Using the Federal Reserve's Fedwire system, banks are able to reduce the balance in the payor's account and increase the balance in the payee's account virtually simultaneously. In a Fedwire transaction, the depository institution in this transaction is the Federal Reserve district bank that holds the reserve accounts of the payor's bank.

In a Fedwire transfer, which is usually called a "wire transfer," the payor instructs its bank to move money to a payee, whose account is at a certain bank. The payor's bank then instructs its Federal Reserve district bank to charge the originating bank's account and credit the receiving bank's account. The receiving bank is also notified of the party whose account is to be credited so it can carry out the instruction. When the Fed receives electronic instructions and makes entries to the books of the payor's and payee's banks, these entries are irrevocable from the moment they are made, making settlement final. Financial managers who need to make payments that must take effect immediately, such as payments for real estate transactions, debts, and corporate acquisitions, usually use a Fedwire transfer. (See Figure 5-1.)

CHIPS Transfer

Under this settlement method, payments between pairs of organizations are accumulated throughout a day. At the end of the day, the net position of each organization against the CHIPS system is calculated, and the New York Fed effects settlement for each CHIPS member. The Fed will either charge or credit each

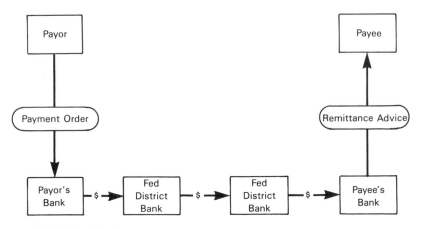

Figure 5-1 Fedwire Transfer

organization's account so that the total amount of debits equals the total amount of credits.

CHIPS is an example of a delayed settlement system. CHIPS participants are banks with offices in New York City; the central depository is the New York Federal Reserve Bank. Corporate financial managers usually do not have direct access to CHIPS, though many business-to-business payments are routed through CHIPS by the payors' banks.

From the financial manager's point of view, the disadvantage of using a delayed settlement system is not knowing when the transaction's settlement becomes final. The financial manager can only assume that settlement has occurred by the end of the day. If delayed settlement is acceptable and there is a lower charge for CHIPS transfers, a company may request its bank to use CHIPS rather than Fedwire.

ACH Transfers

The "value date" in a payment message specifies the date on which financial institutions are to transfer the value by making bookkeeping entries relating to an electronic funds transfer. When paying funds, it is wise for the health care financial manager to specify a value date to avoid an incorrect presumption, even when making transactions through same-day settlement systems such as Fedwire and CHIPS.

Action Advice. In most cases, such as funding payrolls and servicing debt, health care financial managers know they will have to transfer funds at least one day before the transaction is to take place. Because of this, financial managers should consider using value-dated transfer systems, such as ACH, for these types of transactions. Charges for value-dated ACH transfers are usually much less than for immediate-settlement systems (approximately $.50 compared with $7 to $20 per wire transfer). Payments where uncertainty of settlement rules out checks but payment dates are known beforehand, such as pension and dividend payments, are also good candidates for value-dated settlement systems.

SWIFT Transfers

The Society for Worldwide Interbank Financial Telecommunications (SWIFT), is often erroneously thought of as an international payment system. SWIFT, as its name implies, is a message system using telecommunications. Banks use it for nonpayment messages as well as for instructing each other to make payments internationally by charging and crediting correspondent bank accounts. SWIFT (unlike CHIPS) is not a settlement system for its member banks; it merely facilitates bilateral funds transfers by handling structure messages.

EFT TRANSMISSIONS

Two types of EFT transmission modes, batch transmission and single-instruction transmission, are used in EFT systems. Fedwire, CHIPS, and SWIFT move instructions one at a time. The ACH system moves multiple payments—or batches of payments—at one time. Health care financial managers must realize that batch file transfers cost much less per transaction, but single-instruction transmissions have better-defined settlements.

The Federal Reserve's fee for handling a Fedwire transfer is nominal for both the sending and receiving banks. The sending and receiving banks mark up this charge to approximately $7 to $20 to cover the banks' handling costs and profit factors. Each transaction moves separately. The transaction carries a trace number and is settled when the receiving bank accepts the Fed's notice that its reserve account is being credited.

In the ACH system, on the other hand, although both the originating and receiving financial institutions settle the same day, the settlements probably occur at different moments. As a result, the question about the precise time of final settlement is always open. The moment of finality is important because of the possibility that one of the financial institutions, the payor, or the payee could fail during the transaction. Fortunately, the question has not been tested, but Fed and industry observers recognize the potential problems that a failure could cause.

Wire Transfer Systems

The primary characteristic of a wire transfer system is that it electronically moves payment instructions one payment at a time. Three EFT systems handle most corporate-to-corporate payment instructions, in terms of dollar amounts: Fedwire, CHIPS, and SWIFT. The automated clearing house (ACH) system also utilizes EFT and handles a large volume, but it is not a wire transfer system since it moves funds in batches, not one at a time.

Fedwire

Health care organizations, their banks, and their investment dealers and managers use Fedwire to transfer funds and U.S. government securities in book entry form. Book entry is the recording of securities transfers and balances on the books of the U.S. Treasury Department; it does not include actual physical delivery of paper certificates. Fedwire transactions move between pairs of Federal Reserve Banks and their branches and involve credits and debits to the Federal Reserve deposit accounts of depository institutions. Banks use Fedwire for settlement of bank-to-bank transactions, and they often initiate Fedwire transfers on behalf of customers. In the latter case the payor bank's instructions to the Fed must specify which customer's bank account is to be credited at the payee bank.

Any bank that has an account with the Fed, whether or not it is a Fed member, can initiate and receive Fedwire transfers. The Monetary Control Act of 1980 mandated that all depository institutions (banks, savings and loans, credit unions, and any other form of deposit-taking institution) must open and maintain accounts with the Fed. Institutions making more than 600 transfers a day often use direct computer-to-computer links to communicate with the nearest Federal Reserve Bank or branch. More than 3,500 institutions are on line with the Fed. Institutions making a smaller volume of transfers communicate with the Fed either through dial-up computer links or by telephone. A health care institution can be better served by a bank that handles wire transfers through an electronic link to the Fed than by the small bank without such a link.

Fedwire is also used to transfer ownership of U.S. government securities, a service the Fed provides to the U.S. Treasury as its fiscal agent. Since 1977, the U.S. Treasury has issued Treasury bills (T-bills) in book entry form. When a health care institution invests in T-bills, the institution or the securities custodian must have an account on the books of the U.S. Treasury that is credited or charged for each transaction. All purchases and sales of Treasury securities, with the exception of old paper certificates still held by some investors, are settled by Fedwire communications.

Indeed, the U.S. Treasury is a heavy user of EFT services. Under a program called "Treasury Direct," initiated in 1986, the Treasury Department maintains accounts for investors in U.S. Treasury securities. When securities are sold in the secondary markets, payment is effected through Fedwire. Treasury makes interest payments on notes and bonds using the ACH system.

Financial managers can initiate Fedwire transfers through several methods. Although Fedwire is an EFT system, a Fedwire transaction can be initiated by non-electronic means, including telephone calls and letters to a bank or transmission of Fedwire payment instructions via telex or electronic mail (E-Mail). Telex, other forms of E-Mail, and facsimile transmission (FAX) work electronically, but they require that humans read and process the instructions, thereby introducing the possibility of human error. Messages carried on these systems are not capable of being processed electronically by computers.

Fedwire transfers also can be made using interactive terminals or personal computers that send electronic messages in standardized machine-readable format via modem to a bank. The bank receives the message on computer, then reviews, edits, stores, and routes it without manual handling. Many cash management banks allow their corporate customers to initiate repetitive wire transfers via terminal where the destination information has been preloaded and preauthorized except for the amount. Some banks are able to accept instructions for nonrepetitive funds transfers via terminal as well. Information concerning the destination bank and the ultimate payee then must be entered into the terminal each time a funds transfer is initiated.

Action Advice. It is possible to use verbal instructions for repetitive wire transfers and still maintain security and flexibility of staffing. Financial managers can authorize the bank to accept instructions from a clerk only when the clerk references a line number. The line number refers to a preauthorized destination bank and payee account number; the clerk can move money routinely only to certain preauthorized destinations without further approval. Funding payroll accounts and moving funds from one account to another within a company are excellent uses of this technique. Mistakes are avoided, because strings of bank identification data and account numbers do not need to be repeated verbally every time a repetitive transfer is required. Moreover, referring to a line number and stating only the amount of the transaction introduces some security into the transfer and also may result in reduced transaction charges.

Repetitive Funds Transfers

Health care providers have accounts subject to frequent funds transfers, both in and out, such as local payroll, petty cash, and payments to large-volume suppliers. Repetitive funds transfer systems are generally originated by using a "line number" from a "line sheet." This is a document authorized by company officials that specifies all of the information associated with the account or multiple accounts to which the company wants to send funds routinely (see Exhibit 5-1). It is possible to build line sheets into the data base of a treasury management system so that repetitive wire transfers can be initiated by terminal. Line sheets include the name, address, and transit routing number of each receiving bank; and the name

Exhibit 5-1 Wire Transfer Line Sheet

First National Bank
Customer: ABC Health Care, Inc.
Account No. 1234567

Line No.	Destination Bank	Bank Location	TR No.*	Debit or Credit	Account Name	Account No.	Maximum Account
001	First National Bank	Chicago, IL	07100001	CR	ABC Hospital, Inc.	52379680	$ 25,000
002	Sky-High Bank	Cutenshoot, MT	10110047	CR	DEF Hospital, Inc.	2134806	$ 10,000
003	New York National Bank	New York, NY	02100946	CR	Medical Supply, Inc.	6497235	$100,000
004	New York National Bank	New York, NY	02100946	CR	Ad Agency, Inc.	6497241	$100,000
006	State Bank	Atlanta, GA	06130087	CR	JKL Hospital, Inc.	30479206	$ 30,000

*Transit routing number of destination bank.

Approved by:
ABC Health Care, Inc.

by: _____
Title:
Authorized Signer

by: _____
Title:
Authorized Signer

and account number of the payee. Each destination location is assigned a number corresponding to its line on the form. When a wire transfer is to be sent to a payee, the person initiating the transaction need refer only to the line number and the amount of the desired transfer.

Organizations are increasingly using terminals or personal computers equipped with funds transfer software to initiate repetitive funds transfers. The user makes reference to a line number programmed into the system, the amount to be transferred is entered, and a verification dialogue takes place. After the transaction has been verified, it is transmitted to the bank's computer. There, the transfer is reviewed for accuracy and entered into the bank's Fedwire terminal, either automatically or manually, according to the level of sophistication of the bank's system. With a sophisticated bank system, the user automatically receives a Fedwire number or bank trace number as confirmation of the transaction.

Initiating repetitive funds transfers through terminals or microcomputers can be economical for a health care institution. Most banks offer up to a 25 percent discount on repetitive transfers made through terminals, rather than verbally over the telephone, because bank employees do not have to handle these transactions. A low error rate is also an important factor.

Nonrepetitive Funds Transfers

Funds transfers that occur one time or too infrequently to justify setting the account up on a line sheet, or that may be too sensitive to introduce the element of automatic initiation, are usually handled through nonrepetitive wire transfers. Management can exercise more control over nonrepetitive payments. For example, a hospital may not pay a vendor in shaky financial condition by repetitive EFT payments, because an erroneous payment to the company may be difficult to recover.

Internal auditors have struggled for years with the question of how to control the initiation of nonrepetitive EFTs. Financial managers typically can give instructions over the telephone to move virtually unlimited amounts of money to any destination in the world, while a check for a few thousand dollars may require the signatures of one or more corporate officers. For this reason, many organizations are now initiating wire transfers via terminal-based systems.

Because of the substantial market demand, banks and their systems software providers have developed terminal-based systems for initiating nonrepetitive EFTs. These systems generally require two people on the customer side to operate the system; each person uses a different secret password. By requiring two people to initiate a transfer, each of whom has a separate password, security of transfer initiation is greatly enhanced compared with the telephone approach or even with subsequent confirmation by telephone call-back or letter.

CHIPS

The New York Clearing House Association operates the Clearing House Interbank Payments System (CHIPS), a computerized telecommunications network used by some 140 CHIPS member banks. Members have offices in New York; they include domestic and foreign commercial banks, as well as subsidiaries of U.S. banks engaged in international transactions (known as Edge Act companies). A delayed-settlement system, CHIPS handles settlement of approximately 90 percent of all Eurodollar and foreign exchange transactions settled in U.S. dollars. Foreign trade and domestic transactions are also settled through CHIPS, which daily handles more than 100,000 interbank transfers valued at more than $350 billion.

Banks that belong to CHIPS act for themselves and their customers and correspondent banks. CHIPS payments are initiated through special dedicated computer terminals at each member bank. After the close of business each day, the CHIPS computer reports on each member's net settlement position. Each member will have either a net debit, which is due to the clearinghouse, or a net credit, which the clearinghouse owes the member. Members with debit balances must pay the clearinghouse by Fedwire transfers to the CHIPS settlement account at the New York Fed. When all debit balances are paid, the clearinghouse transfers funds by Fedwire from the CHIPS settlement account to the members with net credit balances. Settlement is final when the receiving institution receives notice of the Fedwire transfer.

Accordingly, CHIPS transfers receive same-day availability, although settlements are delayed until the end of the day. However, this delay increases the risk of the CHIPS system. It is possible that a financially ailing institution would not be discovered until it fails to cover its net debit position at the end of the day. This would result in an imbalance in the settlement system. Weak institutions, suddenly plunged into debt because they did not receive their credit transfers, could also fail. Because the daily volume of transactions is so large, it is not inconceivable for an organization's capital to be impaired should the system not achieve final settlement. CHIPS has proposed several solutions to this potential problem.

AUTOMATED CLEARING HOUSE TRANSFERS

Automated clearing houses (ACHs) provide an electronic payments and collections network that links financial institutions across the country and provides an electronic alternative to the paper-based check payment system. Because ACH uses batch file transfer, companies can originate either a single ACH transaction or thousands of ACH transactions at one time. ACH was designed as a batch-processing system to keep per-transaction costs as low as possible. Consequently, many health care providers are able to offer their employees their payroll by direct deposit to their bank accounts via ACH.

ACHs are governed by operating rules of the National Automated Clearing House Association (NACHA), which was organized by banks in 1974 to provide links among the regional ACH associations existing at that time. According to NACHA, its six primary goals are to:

1. establish and publish rules and standards
2. set standards for control and security
3. market electronic payment products
4. commercialize the ACH system
5. manage NACHA's finances responsibly
6. strengthen communication between NACHA and government regulators and legislators, service providers, trade associations, and industry groups

NACHA has chartered 29 regional ACHs and 13 additional private ACHs as of 1988 that are owned by banks making a high volume of ACH transactions. The 29 regional ACHs represent approximately 17,500 financial institutions (commercial banks and thrifts) serving about 40,000 companies and government agencies, as well as millions of consumers. The most influential ACH user is the federal Social Security Administration. It led the way in converting payments from paper check to direct electronic deposits using the ACH system. ACH transaction volumes have consistently increased (see Table 5-1).

Despite such impressive growth in ACH use, ACH volumes do not approach check volumes. An estimated 45 billion checks are written annually in the United States, compared with approximately 1 billion ACH payments. Growth in the volume of checks is slowing, however, while growth rates for the various forms of electronic payments continue to increase. Financial managers who are not using

Table 5-1 Annual Volume of Automated Clearing House Associations

	No. of Transactions (in millions)	Percent Increase
1983	399.2	12.7
1984	486.5	21.9
1985	586.0	20.5
1986	743.4	26.9
1987	936.0	25.9

Source: American Banker, March 16, 1987, and March 21, 1988, American Banker, Inc.

EFT ultimately will have to face the question of making and receiving electronic payments.

The ACH Payment Process

The terms and methods of making and receiving ACH payments require financial managers to invest time in learning about the operation of the ACH system.

NACHA requires every ACH to use standardized payment formats for the transfer of value and information. The Federal Reserve Banks and their branches process almost all ACH activities, except those of the Calwestern and New York ACHs. The Calwestern ACH, which serves financial institutions in California, Nevada, Utah, Idaho, and Hawaii, contracts with a private processor. The New York Clearing House Association operates its own ACH processing facility.

In the ACH environment, the terms "payor" and "payee" generally are not used. Instead, the parties to the payment transaction are referred to as "originator" and "receiver" of the transaction. Transactions are termed "credit transfers" or "debit transfers," because an ACH transfer can move funds in either direction between the originator and receiver. In a credit transfer, the originator's account with the bank that originated the transfer is charged, and the receiver's account with the bank that received the transfer is credited. In a debit transfer the opposite occurs at settlement. The financial institutions settle with their respective ACHs through their Federal Reserve clearing accounts.

ACH transactions use different terms than paper-based transactions because the routing sequence of the electronic message and the direction of funds flow are of critical importance in ACH processing. The terms originator and receiver describe the roles of the parties to the transaction, and the terms debit transfer and credit transfer describe the direction in which the funds travel. For example, if Insurance Company A wants to initiate a payment to Hospital B using the ACH system, Insurance Company A is the originator, the transaction type is a credit transfer, and Hospital B is the receiver. Insurance Company A, as originator, asks its bank (Bank A) to pay Bank B a certain amount for deposit into the account of Hospital B. The banks, too, are indicated by different names in the ACH environment. In this example, Bank A is the Originating Depository Financial Institution (ODFI), and Bank B is the Receiving Depository Financial Institution (RDFI). When the ODFI and the RDFI use different ACHs, the ODFI's ACH is called the originating ACH, and the RDFI's ACH is the receiving ACH (see Figure 5-2).

Credit Transfers

Originators initiate ACH credit transfers to be sent through the banking system "for credit" to the receiver's account. Credit transfers include direct deposit of

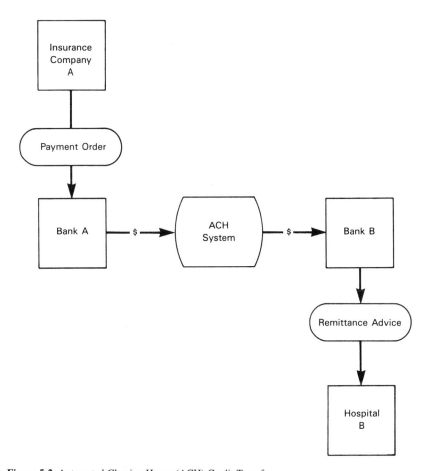

Figure 5-2 Automated Clearing House (ACH) Credit Transfer

payroll, dividends, annuities, pensions, and payment of trade accounts payable. ACH credit transfers thus act as a substitute for paper-based payments (checks).

Debit Transfers

ACH debit transfers are initiated by the recipient of the funds; funds are sent through the ACH system from the originator's (recipient's) bank to the receiver's (payor's) bank. Debit transfers are frequently used for consumer payments, such as insurance, utility, mortgage, and rent, as well as business payments, such as cash concentration transfers, preauthorized dealer or distributor payments, and an increasing number of corporate-to-corporate trade payments.

Data Formats

A critical element of ACH processing is the series of data formats used to move payment instructions. Formats used in ACH transactions are developed and maintained by NACHA to enable originators to assemble and transmit data so that computers can process it. For computer processing, the data must be organized in strict accordance with a system of rules and syntax. Data must be organized into discrete data fields, called data records, that all organizations following the same rules and syntax will be able to read. Noncompliance with the rules will prevent one organization's computer from being able to read data sent from another organization's computer.

If two data processors agree between themselves to use a certain data format, it is called a "proprietary" format and cannot be used by other processors. However, if an entire community agrees to use a certain data format and the format is available to any user, it is then called a "standardized" format. NACHA data formats are standardized; they are developed under the auspices of NACHA for use by all organizations that want to originate, process, and receive payments through the ACH system. Because of the number of participants involved in a single ACH transaction—the originator, receiver, and as many as two banks, two ACHs, and two Federal Reserve Banks—the system could not function without standardized data formats.

To originate an ACH payment, therefore, a company (the "originator") sets up the transaction details in a data format prescribed by NACHA. The originator then communicates the data to the ODFI, either by data transmission or by physical delivery of a computer medium such as a magnetic tape or a disk.

There are five NACHA formats for business payments:

1. Prearranged Payments and Deposits (PPD)
2. Cash Concentration or Disbursements (CCD)
3. Corporate Trade Payments (CTP)
4. Corporate Trade Exchange (CTX)
5. CCD Plus Addendum

Prearranged Payments and Deposits (PPD) Format

The PPD format is used for ACH transfers, both credit and debit, involving consumers. Health care organizations use the ACH for two primary purposes in consumer-oriented transactions: direct deposit of employee payrolls and "automatic bill paying" services for collections, such as health maintenance organization (HMO) payments and settlement of patient accounts through regularly scheduled payments. Unlike other ACH transactions, which are settled on the day after initiation, NACHA rules governing consumer transactions require settlement two days (or more) after initiation.

Cash Concentration or Disbursements (CCD) Format

The CCD format was designed as an electronic means of concentrating funds by debit transfer. It is a substitute for the paper depository transfer check. However, the CCD format is being increasingly used as a credit transfer for business-to-business trade payment transactions. In fact, most companies that make trade payments electronically—a small but growing minority of companies—use the CCD format. It is a relatively simple format that carries a very limited amount of remittance information, and virtually all financial institutions can receive it. The CCD transfer normally receives next-day availability.

Corporate Trade Payments (CTP) Format

The CTP format was designed specifically for companies to use in making trade payments electronically. A few large companies that made payments among themselves tested the format when NACHA introduced it in 1983. The format has been released for general use since then, although not many companies have adopted it. The CTP format was designed for trade payments covering multiple invoices and adjustments. Each invoice and each adjustment is a separate record, called an "addendum," and the CTP format can carry up to 4,990 addenda records. An addendum structures the details of a payment, such as the invoice number being paid, its amount, credits, and other adjustments. In addition, the header records in the CTP format disclose the identities of the transaction originator and receiver. The originator is usually the payor, but since the CTP can be used for either credit transfers or debit transfers, the identities of both parties and their respective banks (as well as the receiver's bank account number) must be fully detailed in the transmission. CTP transactions are settled on a next-day basis.

The CTP has not met with resounding success; the volume has remained low compared with PPD and CCD volumes. The reasons include:

- Few banks can originate the CTP format.
- Security over CTP payments is lacking; they can be neither encrypted nor authenticated under the present state of the format. These are security measures that corporations and government agencies appear to desire.
- The CTP format uses fixed-length data fields that make it inefficient for storing and transmitting data.
- To use CTP, corporate users must develop the interface and format translation facilities that CTP requires. These facilities can be used only with banks and are not compatible with the other translation facilities and data formats

that companies use for electronic communications in standardized formats with trading partners.

Corporate Trade Exchange (CTX) Format

The CTX format, released by NACHA in 1987, was designed to resolve objections to the CTP format. The CTX format, a modification of CTP, is compatible with other standardized formats for electronic communication and thus overcomes some of the objections to CTP. A number of banks implemented CTX almost immediately after its release because they felt it would be more acceptable to companies than CTP.

CTX should be helpful to health care institutions because it is compatible with the standardized formats used by the institutions in electronic data interchange (EDI) for procurement and billing. Use of these standardized formats allows the exchange of data contained in common business documents between customers (e.g., hospitals) and suppliers. While retaining the communications elements of the NACHA format that enable the message to travel through the banking system, CTX replaces the remittance information message with a format compatible with EDI. Security through authentication and encryption is also available in the CTX payment format through the use of standardized EDI security structures.

The standardized formats used in EDI are developed by Accredited Standards Committee (ASC) X12 of the American National Standards Institute. In creating the CTX format, NACHA used the ASC X12 standard format called the ''Payment Order/Remittance Advice'' (transaction set 820). This electronic document was incorporated into NACHA's standard communications electronic ''envelope,'' enabling the CTX to move money through the banking system. Inclusion of the X12 format results in several advantages of CTX over CTP:

- An increasing number of companies can read and translate between the X12 format and their own internal formats for electronic data processing.
- The X12 format uses variable-length data fields that are more efficient in terms of data storage and transmission than fixed-length fields.
- Data fields that a company does not need to use in a particular transaction can easily be suppressed in X12.
- The X12 format can be encrypted and authenticated.

CCD Plus Addendum (CCD +) Format

The CCD Plus Addendum format, not a true NACHA format, was designed by the U.S. Treasury to disburse payments to vendors, including hospitals and other health care institutions, on behalf of numerous federal bureaus, departments, and agencies. Treasury has made large vendor payments by EFT, principally Fedwire, since 1983. In 1987, when it decided to expand its EFT program for vendor payments, Treasury announced a program called "Vendor Express" to pay vendors through low-cost ACH transfers. Treasury selected the CCD format, even though it was not specifically designed for trade payments, because almost all financial institutions can accept it, in contrast to the CTP format that few can receive. Many health care companies that provide materials, supplies, and services to civilian branches of the U.S. government may be paid electronically via CCD Plus.

The standard CCD payment format uses an 80-character free-form structure to describe the transaction with no limitation on how the 80 characters are put to use (80 "free-form" characters, in standards lingo). Treasury realized, however, that free-form characters cannot be processed by computers. To overcome this problem, Treasury borrowed an ASC X12 structured data segment and inserted it into the free-form space of the CCD data format. It christened the new format "CCD Plus Addendum," or "CCD + " for short.

Treasury's addendum borrowed the RMR (which stands for "remittance") data segment from the X12 payment order/remittance advice. Treasury then advised its vendors that after July 1987 it would send payments through the ACH system using the CCD format, with an addendum record consisting of the 80-character RMR data segment. This allows up to 80 characters in the addendum that can be read by a computer capable of processing EDI transactions. Accordingly, the remittance information contained in the addendum can be read by the bank's computer and transmitted to the company for updating its accounts receivable records.

The introduction of CCD + caused considerable controversy, because Treasury made it clear that banks and corporations would have to work out the mechanisms for passing on remittance data. Many banks complained that they did not want to be in the data translation business. Government vendors complained that the government was being cavalier about providing remittance data. However, banks are developing the capabilities to capture and pass on the remittance data from the RMR data segment contained in the CCD + , and companies are developing the capabilities to interpret the data and use it for automatic cash application.

Since the introduction of the CCD + and CTX formats, many companies that previously never thought about using EFT have been encouraged by their trading partners (including the U.S. government) to consider receiving electronic payments. These considerations are being converted into reality as more corporations and banks embrace EFT. An increasing number of companies have begun to ask their suppliers to receive payments through the ACH system for several valid business reasons:

- reduced disbursing float in the paper-based check payment system since 1980
- increased postage costs, making it more expensive to mail checks and reconcile bank accounts

- rapid spread of EDI by businesses in procurement that drives the accounts payable functions

Data Processing of EFT

Data processing departments generally build or buy the computer hardware and software systems required to generate files in NACHA formats. Software in the systems typically takes data from the internal payroll, accounts payable, accounts receivable, and funds concentration applications and converts them into NACHA formatted data files appropriate for the payments in question. After conversion into NACHA formats, the files are transmitted to the bank via telecommunications. Some companies fear that telecommunications will breach confidentiality, and therefore hand deliver magnetic tapes or disks containing sensitive data. These companies, however, risk delay and failure in meeting delivery deadlines.

Prenotification

Before a company starts to use the ACH system, it must ensure that data files are formatted correctly and that the ODFI, ACH, and RDFI can read and accept its files. NACHA built into its rules for certain transactions a requirement that the originator must "prenotify" the receiver at least 10 days before the first "live" transaction using certain formats. Transactions requiring prenotification are PPD credits and debits, CTP debits, and CTX debits; certain point-of-sale transactions that use the ACH also require prenotification. Prenotification involves initiating the transaction that the company intends to use with a zero dollar amount. Any party (ODFI, ACH, or RDFI) that cannot process the transaction must notify the originator.

Bank Processing of ACH Transfers

After it receives an ACH transmission from the company, the ODFI verifies the file header and control records. It then removes from the file any "on-us" payments, which are payments made to parties that have accounts with that bank. These payments are held by the bank until the settlement date. The bank transmits the remaining payments to the regional ACH serving the bank. The regional ACH sorts the payments into files destined for RDFIs in its region and for other ACHs. It then transmits the files to their respective destinations. All sorting and routing generally occur within hours after the originator delivers or transmits the payment files to the OFDI.

NACHA Consumer Rules

Under NACHA's consumer rules, users must originate PPD credit transfers at least two business days before the settlement date; all parties to the transaction must complete their processing in time to provide the payment data to the receiver by the morning of the settlement date. For example, in a situation involving direct deposit of payroll for a Friday payday, the employer must transmit the payroll payment file to the ODFI by Wednesday. The ODFI may further require that the company deliver the file no later than noon or 1 P.M. Wednesday. This enables the ODFI to read and process the file, to contact the originator if it finds errors, and to remove any "on-us" payments before the close of business Wednesday. On Wednesday night, the ODFI transmits the file to its ACH. By Thursday, the ACH has processed the file and transmitted payment data files to the RDFIs it serves and to other ACHs that, in turn, have processed and transmitted payment data files to the RDFIs they serve.

NACHA's consumer rules also specify that a PPD credit transfer must reach the RDFI the night before settlement. The RDFI then has time to credit the deposit to the receiver's account so that the consumer/payee can withdraw the payroll amount at the opening of business on the settlement date. Whether the bank wants to credit the employee's account on the night before the settlement date, rather than at the end of the day as it would with other deposits, is a marketing issue, not a technical issue, and every bank faces it. The rule that PPD payments must arrive the night before settlement is NACHA's attempt to create a "level playing field." It is the receiving depository financial institution's responsibility to take advantage of the rule.

Indeed, the RDFI can "memo post" the credit the night before to inform tellers and ATMs that the funds will be in the account shortly. If the RDFI actually credits the funds to the receiver's account the night before settlement date, the bank is technically making an advance. Many banks do that, however, because installing system software to handle the memo post can cost the RDFI more than posting funds one day before value date. Moreover, to force customers to wait until the evening of the value date to withdraw funds will anger customers wanting access to their pay on payday.

Action Advice. The failure or refusal of a bank to give the customer access to funds is an issue between the customer and the bank. When the funds in question are payroll funds, however, the employer becomes involved because employees will complain about late paychecks. It is prudent for health care financial managers, when setting up direct deposit of payroll service, to warn employees that small banks and thrifts may not reflect the deposits to their accounts until after the close of business on payday. The company should make sure employees understand that the inability of their banks to reflect deposits on payday is the responsibility of their banks and beyond the control of the employer and its bank.

NACHA Business Rules

NACHA rules on business-to-business transfers are less stringent than on business-to-consumer transfers. Transactions that use the CCD, CTP, CTX, and CCD Plus Addendum business payment formats may settle as early as the next day; the ODFI may also "warehouse" such payments for up to 30 days. In order to settle ACH payments on the next day, the ODFI sets an early afternoon deadline for receiving payment files from the originator. It uses the rest of the afternoon to strip "on-us" transactions from the files and then send the remainder of the payment files to the regional ACH by that evening. The ACH sends payment data files to its members and other ACHs during the night. Early the next day the receiving ACHs process the files and transmit them to the RDFIs. The RDFIs receive their respective payment files and post the credits and debits to the receivers' accounts that evening.

Pricing

ODFIs are free to set their own prices for originating ACH transfers, at least within certain constraints. First, an ODFI must pay a minimum charge for each payment file it transmits through its regional ACH. An ODFI also has internal processing costs that act as constraints on pricing decisions. Prices charged by banks for ACH transactions are generally broken down into two parts: (1) a fee for each transaction and (2) a fee for the transmission of the group of payment files each day. It can cost more than $1 million for a bank to buy and install sophisticated ACH processing systems. This investment encourages banks to recoup their cost by processing high volumes of transactions. To attract high volumes, banks often price ACH transactions very competitively at less than 10 cents per transaction.

The cost a bank bears in processing ACH transactions depends on its share of the market and its internal processing efficiency. Even so, pricing differences between competing banks do not amount to much. ACH transactions are priced in pennies, and banks seeking high volumes will generally meet a competitor's lower price. For example, a price difference of one cent between banks will amount to only about $25 for a hospital that makes 2,500 ACH transactions per month. Price considerations, therefore, pale in comparison to the more substantive concerns of bank service, accuracy, and reliability. A health care financial manager, however, should understand the basic economics of ACH processing.

Settlement

ACH funds transfers are settled on the value date which, at the earliest, is either the day after origination for business-to-business payments or two days after origination for consumer payments. Because all transactions are settled at a future date, there is considerable payment risk in the ACH system. It is conceivable, in a credit transfer, that either the originator or the ODFI could fail to pay on the value date. For example, Hospital A gives its ODFI the payroll file at noon on Wednesday so that it can meet a Friday payroll. After the ODFI strips the ''on-us'' items from the file on Wednesday night, it transmits the remaining payments to its ACH. By contract, it is required to pay the ACH with available funds on Friday. The RDFIs accept the payment orders on Thursday and prepare to credit their customers, (the hospital's employees) on Friday, the settlement date.

Meanwhile, the employer, Hospital A, files a petition for bankruptcy on Thursday, while the payment orders are moving through the ACH system, and fails to pay the ODFI on Friday. By that time, it is probably too late to recall the payments, especially if the hospital has many employees. ODFIs attempt to protect themselves from such scenarios by reviewing the financial conditions of their ACH customers and approving the credit of those who want to originate payments. Some ODFIs may take the precaution to insist on receiving payment or cash collateral before they originate ACH transfers.

The problem would be solved if the ACH could settle payments on the day of origination. NACHA and the Fed have been working on rules and technology for same-day settlement, but its implementation does not appear to be on the horizon. However, same-day settlement would present a threat to the volume of transfers made via Fedwire, which is now the only wire transfer system that provides immediate settlement. The Fed performs almost all ACH processing, but it has yet to announce its intention on same-day ACH settlement.

Action Advice. Health care financial managers should beware when the ODFI requires funding of an ACH credit transfer before it is effected. Financial managers of organizations with good credit should avoid such situations altogether. A bank is entitled to be satisfied that it does not face undue credit risk. However, a bank is not entitled to require prefunding of ACH transactions unless its transaction pricing reflects the interest benefit the bank derives from the prefunding. Hospitals that prefund ACH credit transfers should try to negotiate interest payments on the funds available to the bank during the time the credit transfer is being processed.

Receiving ACH Transfers

There are no NACHA rules requiring an RDFI to notify its receiver/customer that an ACH credit transfer has been received on its behalf. Lack of notice may cause problems. The computer systems used by most banks, including major cash management banks, have had some difficulty in moving the remittance data associated with an incoming ACH payment automatically from the ACH system into the bank's balance reporting system. In the late 1980s, many of the larger banks began to make the substantial investments needed to reprogram their systems so they can notify customers of incoming ACH transactions in a timely fashion.

Consumers receiving Social Security payments generally do not need timely notification of payment receipt. They know when the payments will arrive and what the amounts will be. That is not the case, of course, for businesses, such as hospitals and other health care providers, that require timely notification of payments credited to their accounts. They also need to know who the payments are from, what billings they cover, and what discounts and adjustments, if any, payors have deducted from the payments. Accordingly, many of the large banks are developing systems that will provide same-day notification of both payments and remittance advices. EFT programs, such as the Treasury's Vendor Express, will accelerate these developments.

SECURITY

Security is always of utmost importance in any type of funds transfer. It has been a particularly difficult problem, however, in the area of EFT. Banks have tried various means of securing funds transfers, including recording verbal instructions for wire transfers on tape, using "line numbers" for repetitive wire transfers, and placing callbacks to other persons at the customers' places of business who are authorized to verify wire transfer instructions. None of these methods has been particularly effective. A tape recording will not prevent errors or fraud and provides no positive identification of the person ordering the transfer, though a tape recording will verify that errors or fraud occurred. The callback technique does not work well, because the other authorized person often is unavailable or is not aware of every legitimate transfer.

In addition to any security measures the bank may use, companies themselves usually employ their own security measures on wire transfers. Companies normally restrict the number of persons who are authorized to order wire transfers. They also restrict the number and amount of wire transfers that any one person can make in a day. These restrictions are usually put into writing, signed by a senior manager who is also authorized to sign checks on the account involved, and communicated to the bank. The senior manager should obtain from the bank a written acknowledgement that the instructions have been accepted.

Even with written restrictions, however, there are still security risks, especially when wire transfer instructions are made verbally. Verbal communication does not offer much protection against errors or fraud. Bankers and financial managers have invested considerable time and money in seeking security measures that are equally reliable and flexible. As in other instances involving financial management, the computer and telecommunications equipment such as FAX have proved useful in resolving the issue of wire transfer security.

In many transactions that require the movement of funds, written instructions signed by an authorized person are slow and subject to human error. Companies and banks, therefore, have turned to interactive terminals and personal computers to speed transactions. These have worked quite well, especially when used for nonrepetitive funds transfers where all destination bank and payee account information must be supplied with the payment instructions. Under such systems, banks will not act on instructions unless two authorized company people, each having a distinctive secret password, initiate and verify funds transfer instructions.

The system follows an established procedure. For example, the first authorized person uses his secret password to gain access to the bank's funds transfer system through a terminal or microcomputer. Details of the transaction are entered by typing in the name, address, and transit routing number of the destination bank; the name and account number of the receiver; and the amount of the transfer. The transaction is accepted by the bank's computer and stored in a queue. The transaction remains in the queue until a second person with a different password verifies it. This person, who is authorized to verify funds transfers, then enters his or her secret password into the system, checks all aspects of the transfer, and gives the computer instructions about the transfer. Options are approval, rejection/cancellation, or deferral for later action.

This type of procedure provides security because two people are independently involved in the transaction, yet it is flexible because both people can work on the transaction at their convenience. The procedure can be adjusted by the company, such as authorizing two groups of people to make transactions. For example, a group of junior employees could be authorized only to set up payments, while people in the senior group are authorized to approve and release payments. Of course, security is compromised when people tape their passwords to the sides of the terminals; this occurs frequently. It is also a good idea to change passwords periodically. Security experts suggest they should be changed monthly. Passwords should be changed immediately when a person's authorization to transfer funds is rescinded.

Security Techniques

A primary complaint about electronic funds transfer has been the difficulty of controlling security during transmission. However, two "high-tech" methods are effective in securing data transmissions, encryption and authentication.

Encryption

Encryption protects the confidentiality of messages by scrambling the messages so they cannot be read by unauthorized parties. The sender uses a predetermined algorithm to scramble the message before transmission. The receiver must have the encryption key or algorithm to decrypt the message upon receipt. A personal computer can be outfitted with an electronic circuit board to operate an encryption algorithm. When an encrypted message travels through a telecommunications network such as Fedwire, however, the message must carry the unencrypted name and address of the receiver. Some parties, particularly the military, may even want to keep the destination of the message confidential.

Authentication

Authentication protects the integrity of messages. It assures the receiver that the message originated with an authorized party and that the contents of the message were not altered during transmission. To authenticate messages, senders and receivers must exchange "test keys." A test key is an algorithm that prepares a code number, called a message authentication code (MAC). The originator places the MAC into the contents of the message. Using its test key, the receiver reconstructs the MAC. If the receiver can successfully reconstruct the MAC contained in the message, the message is considered to be authentic.

An authenticated message is not necessarily an encrypted message; if not encrypted it can be read by unauthorized persons. If the date or amount of a transaction was changed, either by an unauthorized person or through a telecommunications error, the receiver will not be able to reconstruct the same MAC as the one contained in the message. Some companies concerned about security insist that EFT messages be both encrypted and authenticated.

Legal Issues

Financial managers must be aware of the legal issues that involve electronic funds transfer. These issues frequently relate to (1) a bank's acceptance of verbal instructions to disburse funds from a customer's account and (2) an EFT system's failure to complete a transaction in a timely and accurate manner. Any uncertain business situation should be clarified with a legal agreement. Obviously, EFT can be defined as an uncertain business situation. No statutory law governs funds transfers, and case law in this area is spotty at best.

The Uniform Commercial Code (Articles 3 and 4) only addresses paper-based payments. Federal Reserve Regulation J only concerns Fedwire payments. The National Conference on Uniform State Laws, recognizing that existing laws regarding EFT are inadequate, has developed a new Article 4A of the Uniform Commercial Code titled "Wire Transfers."

Development of Article 4A could become statutory law by 1990. The main issue to be resolved is liability. As UCC 4A has been proposed, banks would be absolved of most damages resulting from a delay or failure to execute a funds transfer. Rather, damages would be the responsibility of the company initiating the transaction, even though that company has no control over what happens to a transfer in the banking system.

Because there is no clear legal framework, a written agreement between a company and its bank covering funds transfers is the only way to define each party's legal responsibilities and liability. Banks generally have a business customer sign two separate agreements, one for wire transfers and one for ACH transfers.

The wire transfer agreement generally absolves the bank of any liability in the event that a transaction is not executed properly. Sometimes a bank will accept liability in the event of gross negligence on its part, but simple negligence will generally not suffice to convict a bank.

Banks are wary of accepting liability for consequential damages; these are damages that indirectly stem from the primary cause. Consequential damages, however, are not necessarily inconsequential, as demonstrated by a 1982 legal settlement. This settlement also shows why banks try to limit their legal exposure in wire transfer agreements. The case involved a Chicago corporation that asked its Chicago bank to transfer $27,000 by wire to a Swiss bank. The wire transfer was to cover an installment payment on a ship charter. The company gave the instructions to the bank properly and in a timely manner, two days before the payment was due. The bank sent the message via telex to its Swiss correspondent bank. The Swiss bank acknowledged the message but failed to pay the ship owner, who cancelled the charter. Because ship charter rates rose dramatically after the original charter contract was signed, the Chicago company suffered damages when the charter was cancelled.

Based on the amount it cost to recharter the ship at current rates, the court agreed that damages amounted to $2.1 million. Failure to complete a $27,000 wire transfer, for which the Chicago bank charged about $5, resulted in consequential damages of more than $2 million. It seems even more absurd when the apparent reason for the Swiss bank's failure to notify its customer is taken into account. Its telex machine had run out of paper, so a hard copy of the message was not created. The damage award was later reversed after the court determined that both banks had acted properly, with the exception of the telex machine not having any paper. Because that was judged to be an unusual situation, the Swiss bank was not held liable.

Bank ACH agreements generally cover everything that wire transfer agreements cover, in addition to other clauses relating to the ACH system. Most ACH contracts, for instance, require that the customer acknowledge that it has received a copy of NACHA's operating rules and understands them. (NACHA rules are available from the bank, the regional ACH, or NACHA.) Customers must further state that they understand the rules of the regional ACH and the bank's rules and operating procedures. As with any legal agreement, agreements covering EFT should be reviewed by legal counsel and discussed or negotiated with the bank before they are executed.

SUMMARY

Making payments electronically is an important business tool for health care institutions. Electronic funds transfer (EFT) is gaining in volume at the expense of the growth rate of paper checks, as the automated clearing house (ACH) system becomes more well-known and float associated with paper checks continues to be reduced. Financial managers should allocate resources carefully in choosing the payment mechanism suitable for each type of payment. Factors that financial managers must consider include the requirement for speed of payment, affirmative notification of settlement, and finality of settlement.

Fedwire transfers are the fastest form of EFT, and the most expensive. ACH transfers make a viable substitute, especially in situations where the amount of the transfer is known a day or more in advance and knowledge of the moment of final settlement by the payor and payee is not essential. The cost to send each payment via ACH is measured in pennies when payments are sent in bulk. This cost compares very favorably with the cost of a Fedwire transfer. Each Fedwire is sent separately at a cost measured in several dollars per transaction.

Chapter 6

Short-Term Borrowing

INTRODUCTION

Planning for short-term borrowing must take place within the context of the organization's overall strategic planning process. Otherwise, borrowings may cost more than they should or funds will be borrowed on the wrong terms, or both.

Financial managers have two different ways with which to plan and manage an organization's debt and capital structure: (1) the at-whatever-price theory and (2) the strategic-planning theory. The at-whatever-price theory is related to the traditional supply-and-demand concept and is based on the belief that any financial manager can raise enough capital to do business if there is sufficient pressure. Under the at-whatever-price theory, capital is like any other commodity: the greater the need, the higher the cost.

Unfortunately, the at-whatever-price theory suggests that the most advantageous time for an organization to borrow money is when it does not need to borrow money, the most advantageous time being when borrowing is least expensive. In some cases, such blind financing can be attractive. It can be less expensive and less restrictive than financing under more pressing circumstances, for instance, when the organization has an acquisition target in mind or has committed to a major construction project or needs to purchase a major piece of equipment. Bankers are then aware of the urgency of the need to obtain money and may be inclined to dictate stiffer terms.

The more advantageous financial approach is to make capital and debt management crucial parts of the organization's strategic planning process. In fact, capital and debt management should be accorded as important a place in strategic planning as revenue projections, cost containment programs, community marketing programs, and expansion plans. If capital and debt management is part of an organization's strategic planning process, its long-range goals and objectives can be considered under all types of financing options.

THE STRATEGIC FINANCIAL PLAN

A strategic plan for financing should be a specific statement of an organization's financing goals. A debt manager must become a team member when it is time to establish a plan for the organization's capital and debt strategy. By assisting in this aspect of the strategic plan in advance, a financial manager can ensure that the organization obtains financing on the most favorable terms.

Most importantly, when setting a strategic plan, the organization must ensure that the plan dictates financing requirements; financing requirements should not determine the plan. The plan must include considerations of the organization's present assets and debt, internal funding sources, and management's expansion goals. Other pertinent factors to consider are the institution's

- mission or charter
- financial and operational goals
- market and competitive analyses
- strategies for achieving goals and objectives

No financial plan can answer every question. There is always uncertainty about future business conditions, government regulations, technological advances, and new medical techniques. A good strategic plan, however, will include various scenarios, thus adding a degree of flexibility.

Borrower's Strategic Financial Objectives

One of the most important steps toward creating a strategic plan is to understand the health care institution's strategic financial objectives. Health care institutions come in many forms of ownership and organization, including for-profit and not-for-profit, corporations and partnerships, publicly owned and private. Regardless of the form, answers to the following questions will begin the process of identifying the institution's strategic financial objectives.

- Who owns the business?
- What plans do the owners have for its future?
- Are the owners planning to sell or to add partners?
- Is the institution public or private?
- How much risk is management willing to take for various financing alternatives?
- How much interest can the institution afford?

- Does the institution intend to provide collateral to the lender, such as assets or stock?

- If privately owned, will the institution's principals sign a personal guarantee to secure a loan?

- What type of covenants and restrictions is management willing to allow?

- How much control does management want to retain?

- What limitations in other agreements must the institution consider when pledging assets?

By answering these questions, a financial manager can help to clarify the organization's current financial status and to determine the direction in which management is moving or wants to move the organization. The answers also help to specify financing sources and keep short-term strategy consistent with long-term capital management objectives. For instance, in a publicly owned for-profit company, the interests of shareholders must be treated with the highest priority. Consequently, there will be an emphasis on consistent growth, no matter how small.

In a privately held institution, by contrast, strategic objectives can be more flexible and include nonfinancial and eleemosynary goals, if desired. The primary shareholders may be willing to forgo the reassurance of consistent growth in favor of a long-term payoff of their investment.

Even the not-for-profit health care institution must develop a strategic financial plan to assure its long-term fiscal health. The absence of identifiable shareholders does not relieve the financial manager from operating the company as a business and strategically planning the fiscal health of the organization. After all, a not-for-profit organization exists to serve members of the public, who are its very real, although anonymous, shareholders. Failure to maintain fiscal health over the long term is the death knell of all businesses, public or private.

Borrowing Requirements

A strategic plan should evaluate short-term borrowing requirements. Lean periods never can be fully anticipated, so an institution always requires a contingency plan that includes short-term borrowing to tide it over until cash flow resumes. Before a plan can be developed, however, the financial manager must monitor and understand the elements of the institution's cash flow. Cash flow should be forecasted and monitored on monthly, weekly, and daily bases. When studying cash flow, the following factors should be considered:

- seasonality of revenues
- collection periods and timeliness of disbursements
- regulatory changes and economic trends
- contingency plans

Seasonality of revenues can have a tremendous impact on a health care institution's short-term borrowing requirements. By looking at historic seasonal revenue patterns, a financial manager can obtain part of the picture needed to plan borrowing strategy. For example, when patient census historically drops during the holiday season from Thanksgiving through New Year's Day, cash flow will be negatively impacted later when the insurance carriers and Medicare fiscal intermediaries otherwise would be making their payments. Cash flow also may hold up well during the summer months but drop off in September and October due to reduced occupancy during the summer. In other words, the financial manager must monitor and measure the lag time between the provision of services and the collection of revenues, as well as predict the amount to be collected. Fewer receivables and more payables may dictate that the institution borrow money to see it through the winter months. By analyzing the institution's cash flow, the financial manager can anticipate this situation and plan accordingly.

STEPS TO SUCCESSFUL BORROWING

Management will be ready to approach potential financing sources after determining strategic objectives and developing a cash flow forecast that indicates the amount of money needed, when it must be borrowed, and when it can be repaid. Before any financial source is approached, however, financial managers must understand:

1. debt
2. loan approval process
3. various short-term borrowing alternatives
4. suitability of financing sources versus strategic objectives
5. preparation and presentation of a loan request

Understanding Debt

Debt is a way of life for most consumers and business organizations. It is interesting to note that borrowing and investing are two sides of the same coin. "Capital" can be defined as the resources that an organization needs to attain a financial objective. There are two broad categories of capital: (1) equity and (2) debt. Equity is money belonging to the business owner, and debt is money belonging to another person or organization. Because borrowed funds carry the borrower's obligation to repay the debt and lenders furnish money for the sole purpose of earning more money, the only differences between debt and equity appear to rest with the person who provides the capital and the return that person seeks.

Risk/Reward Trade-Offs

Although similarities between debt and equity capital exist, the returns that accrue on each type of funding are very different. Debt capital, in the form of financing received from a lender, generally is priced in terms of an interest rate. Equity capital is "priced" in terms of appreciation of a company's stock or assets. Entrepreneurs often are willing to receive little monetary return in the short run in order to develop a business idea. A lender financing the entrepreneur's dream, however, sees the opportunity quite differently. As a financing source for a risky venture, the lender will expect a large return to compensate for the risk.

An important element in the pricing of debt and equity is the relationship between risk and reward: the greater the risk, the greater the reward. Whether that reward is garnered in terms of equity or in terms of debt depends on the perspective of the person providing the funds. The entrepreneur is willing to risk his or her time in return for a high-equity reward, while the lender is willing to risk only money in return for monetary rewards. The "junk," or high-yield, bond market that developed in the 1980s illustrates the lender's perspective. A company that wants to issue long-term bonds, but that does not have an investment grade rating, must issue noninvestment grade bonds and pay a higher return to attract the needed funds than would an investment grade company. When managing debt, a financial manager must assess the level of risk that the firm presents to a financing source, the resulting availability of financing, and the cost that the financing will carry.

Leverage

Leverage is defined as the use of another person's or organization's financial resources. The more leverage, that is, the greater the proportion of debt to equity that an organization has, the greater the risk to the company and to the lender that the organization will be vulnerable to the impact of external factors. The effects of external factors, such as business conditions and interest rates, are magnified by leverage, sometimes positively and sometimes negatively.

The amount of leverage varies that a health care institution can take on without risking future loss of control to the institution's lenders. In the health care industry, markets must be served; lenders can be instrumental in forcing changes where existing management demonstrates lack of ability. Where the market already is well-served, lenders are usually inclined to limit their losses by simply closing down an inefficient or ineffective business. Financial managers can get a good idea of where they stand in the eyes of a lender familiar with the health care industry by studying the financial statements of other companies in similar health care lines and markets. This will also assist financial managers in determining the financial alternatives available.

The Loan Approval Process

It is essential that financial managers understand what lenders and bankers consider important in making decisions to provide financing. The decision to lend capital often is an emotional one based on the personalities of the lender and the borrowing company's officers. Before the financial manager attempts to make a presentation to a lender, he or she should have some idea of the type of personality that will be sitting across the table. Although the stereotype of the banker-lender is not a totally accurate gauge, it does point out some common traits that lenders share. Lenders tend to be conservative, cautious, and pessimistic. They will look at what is wrong with a borrowing proposal and appear to exclude what is right.

Basic Preparation for a Loan Presentation

In order to be successful in obtaining financing, a financial manager must distinguish the institution's presentation from all others that lenders evaluate. The financial manager also should try to discern what the lender already emotionally believes about the deal. The financial manager must attempt to reinforce a positive belief and reverse a negative one. To be effective a financial manager should be aware that lenders, too, think in stereotypes about companies that seek financing. They perceive company officers who make financial presentations as generally unprepared, hopelessly optimistic, and out of touch with economic reality. When presenting a loan proposal, therefore, the successful financial manager will demonstrate better preparation, greater knowledge about the company and its business prospects, and better capability of repayment than any other customer that approaches the lender.

The financial manager can assess the level of preparedness to make a loan proposal by addressing the following questions:

- Why would a health care institution borrow money?
- What does a lender want to know immediately?
- How does a lender evaluate a loan proposal?

- How does a borrower generate funds to repay a loan?
- Under what reasonable circumstances would a lender agree to refinance a loan?

None of these questions is particularly easy, but the right answers may very well predict the success of a loan proposal.

Reasons for Borrowing

The reasons why a person or organization does something are important. Knowing the reasons and, more importantly, explaining them quickly are crucial when a financial manager must persuade a lender that the health care institution deserves a loan. The three essential reasons for borrowing are

1. to buy an asset
2. to pay an expense
3. to make an acquisition

Knowing those reasons, however, is not sufficient. Financial managers also must know how different lenders view these reasons. For instance, leasing firms financing equipment purchases have no interest in funding other investments. Venture capital firms seeking to invest in companies with high potential for great future equity returns seek highly leveraged transactions that will pay handsomely if the borrower is successful; but they have little interest in lending money to pay an expense. Banks are more interested in providing short-term working capital financing for seasonal needs and modest longer-term financing for equipment and construction.

Immediate Concerns of Lenders

The immediate concerns of a lender are important because they generally dictate the terms and conditions of the loan. Those concerns are:

1. How much money do you need to borrow?
2. How long do you need to keep the money?
3. What do you need the money for?
4. How do you plan to repay both the principal and the interest?
5. What contingency plans do you have in case your intended source of repayment does not work?

The most important of these questions, of course, are the last two, the repayment method and the contingency plan. Above all, a financial manager must be able to show a lender how the loan will be paid back, in scenarios of both expected conditions and unexpectedly negative circumstances.

Evaluating the Application

All lending decisions are based on the same classic set of factors known as the "5 C's of credit:"

1. character of management
2. capital available to the business
3. capacity to earn cash flow to repay the loan
4. conditions of the market
5. collateral that the borrower has available to pledge

Of these factors, the two more critical are the character of management, which may account for as much as 80 percent of a lender's evaluation, and cash flow. If one of the other factors is inadequate, a borrower can usually obtain the loan, although the source of financing, the approach to obtaining it, and its interest rate may be altered. The borrower will not be able to raise external capital, however, if the character of management or cash flow are deficient.

How Lenders Are Repaid

There are four ways to repay lenders:

1. use earnings and cash flow
2. borrow more money
3. find another lender
4. sell existing assets

Borrowing more to repay a loan is often acceptable, but can be an expensive proposition. Selling assets also can be acceptable, especially as part of a contingency plan, but the best way to repay a loan is to generate cash flow. Consequently, a financial manager is wise to keep borrowing plans confined to the capacity of the organization to generate sufficient cash flow to repay the loan within a reasonable period. Lenders prefer this method of repayment.

Refinancing

Barring a decision to restructure a borrower's total debt, a borrower seeks to refinance loans for either of two reasons: (1) the original plan did not work or (2) the borrower did not use the money for the intended purpose.

No lender is sympathetic to a borrower who did not use the money for the purpose stated in the loan proposal. Most lenders, however, understand that not all business plans work as intended. The fact is that most business plans do not work as originally intended, but they do work after they have been modified. Lenders understand that planning is a dynamic process and flexibility is part of it. Business plans that do not work, therefore, are generally considered valid reasons for lending more capital.

Alternative Sources of Short-Term Funds

Before a health care institution commits itself to borrowing money, it should look within. Often there are internal sources of funding that are not immediately apparent. Indeed, one of the objectives of making debt and capital management part of the institution's strategic plan is to ferret out such internal sources of funds before management seeks funding from outside. Four primary internal financing sources, along with methods to use them, are listed below.

1. Aggressive working capital management:
   - improve collection practices
   - extend terms of payables
   - sell nonproductive assets
2. Existing operations:
   - increase service rates
   - charge for services previously provided free
   - increase community marketing effort
   - reduce operating costs
3. Overfunded pension plans:
   - seek to recapture assets in the plans for the institution's use
4. Change in business structure:
   - offer ownership to the public or additional public owners
   - seek partnerships and joint ventures with other health care providers
   - establish employee participation programs

These internal alternatives will not meet the needs of all health care companies. The financial manager is then faced with a long list of prosaic and creative financing alternatives. Consider, for instance, the following financing possibilities. A health care company could

- obtain a bank loan, either secured by assets or unsecured
- sell accounts receivable without recourse
- sell accounts receivable with recourse
- securitize accounts receivable for offering in public or private markets

The differences among these short-term financing alternatives lie in the source rather than the particular use of the funds, and they are based on the criteria that a lender considers when making a loan decision. The three basic criteria are

1. How much debt capital must be raised?
2. How long a term does the borrower need to repay the loan?
3. What return will the lender receive for the loan?

MATCHING FINANCIAL SOURCES TO STRATEGIC OBJECTIVES

It is difficult to match the best capital source to the strategic objectives of a health care institution; few financial alternatives provide perfect matches. When attempting to match financial sources to strategic objectives, however, financial managers should

- list the strategic objectives in the order of their apparent levels of priority
- summarize in writing the alternative choices
- seek advice from consultants or others who are involved in matching strategic planning and financial sources
- consider the decision carefully and preferably without pressure of time

The first two items on the list force the financial manager to focus on the organization's critical issues, because they involve ranking objectives. By reducing these issues to a one-page summary, the financial manager can identify the major financing alternatives. This requires that the major advantages and disadvantages of each alternative be considered. It can be helpful to develop a scoring system to rate financial alternatives, although a scoring system is only as good as the thought that conceived it.

The time criterion is also particularly important. Making a final decision a day or a week after completing the list of alternatives is generally a good idea. This provides the financial manager time to reflect on the institution's strategic objectives and whether the alternative choices meet them. All alternatives should be thoroughly evaluated before a decision is made. On the other hand, delay in the name of perfection can be counterproductive. A financial manager can delay a deal so long that interest rates rise before a choice is made. Financial markets also lose interest when they believe that management is only shopping around and is not serious about a deal. It is good to generate competition among financing sources, but not to the point that it paralyzes the borrower and prevents it from meeting its objectives in the most effective manner.

PREPARING THE FINANCING PROPOSAL

After the financial manager has determined what type of financial source is best to meet the institution's particular short-term capital needs, it is time to obtain the financing. The basic tool for this task is the financing proposal package. The financial manager uses this document to present the institution's "story" as well as to anticipate and answer all questions posed by the lender. Of utmost importance in telling that story are the five criteria essential to all lenders, beginning with the character of company management (see the previous section, "Steps to Successful Borrowing").

Term Sheet

One of the most important parts of the proposal is called the term sheet. In this part of the plan, the financial manager must answer the five basic questions a lender will ask: how much, how long, what for, repayment plan, and contingent repayment plan.

Plan Overview

A financing proposal must contain a brief overview of the plan. Bankers and other lenders tend to make decisions quickly. Review committees, for instance, generally rely on a subordinate's summary and recommendation when evaluating loan requests. A review committee may spend only two or three minutes looking at what took weeks, even months, for a financial manager to assemble. As a result, when a business plan is turned into a proposal, it must include an "executive summary." This should be the most sparkling part of the package.

The overview must describe the essential nature of the health care institution's business, list its major services, and characterize its management people. The overview focuses on facts, but the facts should be presented in such a way that a potential investor—and that is, after all, what a lender is—gets a positive emotional feeling about the institution.

Presentation Contents

The overview can be supplemented with marketing brochures, testimonials, and perhaps even a video presentation to enhance the written word. A full set of financial statements for three years is essential. The financial statements will be used to evelute the risk of the proposed loan and determine the terms and conditions of any financing deal. The statements should be supplemented with explanations wherever appropriate. The statements of some health care institutions contain quirks that may confuse a lender unless they are explained. For instance, when dealing with a lender who is basically unfamiliar with the health care field, some explanation of reimbursement methods and the handling of unreimbursed charges is desirable so the lender can understand the inevitable write-offs of receivables. This explanation should extend to both the balance sheet and the income statement.

Business plans also need to cover the basics of an organization's business: delivery of health care service, marketing, and accounting. The plan should show how the desired financing will enhance these areas. However, the projections should be realistic. Lenders often believe that a borrower is hopelessly optimistic, and aggressive revenue projections will make the lender even more skeptical. In fact, it is always better for management's position if actual operating results are higher than anticipated in the projections, rather than using forecast figures that are too rosy. If management really does believe that revenues will grow by 200 percent, however, then substantiating information should be included in the plan along with documentation showing why the projections are realistic. Detail is crucial in a business plan. Any error in calculations, for instance, can threaten a plan's credibility; it gives the impression of sloppy management.

MAKING THE PRESENTATION

Even more important than a detailed business plan is the ability to communicate it with confidence and verve to potential investors. Financial managers may not think of themselves as salespeople, but that is exactly what they are when they represent the institution that requires financing. They must sell the entire organization, its business, plans, and creditworthiness. Asking questions throughout the presentation is an excellent technique as it focuses the presentation on the needs of the audience. A pointed presentation is important, because it shows that the company has thought out its financing needs. This distinguishes it from other organizations competing for the same scarce financing dollars.

The Importance of Questions

Questions can be the most effective tool for the financial manager in preparing and making the presentation. They provide valuable information and allow the financial manager to focus the presentation. Close scrutiny is avoided until the financial manager has all the necessary information to test assumptions regarding the audience, confirm suspicions, and figure out what the lender considers important before making the actual request for financing. Consequently, the financial manager is better able to handle objections. It is surprising how good questions will keep the mood relaxed and the conversation flowing.

Financial managers should not feel inadequate when they ask about the lending and loan approval process. Each lender does things a little differently. A financial manager should also ask for a copy of the financial analysis the lender performed on the institution. The analysis can provide valuable information the next time financing must be sought. Asking questions about the process will also show that the borrower is more sophisticated and thus a better credit risk.

Answering Objections

No matter how controlled and tightly organized the presentation may be, objections will arise and the financial manager will have to answer the lender's questions. Further questions by the borrower can be excellent answers to questions. For instance, if the lender's major objection focuses on collateral, the financial manager might ask, "Isn't it the case in bankruptcy that legal fees cause liabilities to increase while the value of collateral generally decreases?" The financial manager might further ask, "Doesn't the organization's real value lie in its ability to generate cash flow rather than its present holdings of assets?" And, "In a bad loan situation, does the amount of collateral really make much of a difference?"

Almost any objection can be handled by turning it around with a simple question. By understanding the motive of the investor in making an objection, the financial manager can gauge what response will be most appropriate.

The importance of questions does not end with the presentation and objections. Questions are even more important when a loan has been turned down; they may even be able to salvage a rejection or make it easier to obtain financing from the same source the next time around. Potential questions should be designed to discover why the proposal was declined, where such financing could be obtained, what would make this financing more attractive, and how would the lender who turned down the proposal respond to inquiries from other lenders. As with the other questions, this information can provide feedback that will help in the next presentation.

Personalizing the Presentation

Finally, anything that will personalize the presentation will usually work to a borrower's benefit. It is also helpful for the financial manager to invite a representative of the potential lender to tour the health care institution's facilities before the presentation. This will get the lender more emotionally involved with the institution and more concerned about its future success. It also provides a more personal and relaxed atmosphere to make initial contact with a lender. As noted, the key to obtaining a loan is to connect emotionally with the lender—to persuade the lender that the institution's success is the lender's success as well.

OTHER FACTORS IN BORROWING/LENDING DECISIONS

Borrowing and lending decisions would be easy if the loan criteria listed above were as straightforward as they sound. A financial manager would then choose the alternative that raises the most capital at the least cost over the longest term. Unfortunately, however, one alternative generally raises the most funds, while another has the longest term, and yet a third costs the least. The lender's decisions also would be more mechanical if each element to be considered were based merely on its own merits.

Intangible factors, however, often complicate borrowing and lending decisions. These factors include the following questions involved in loan evaluation:

- Is the transaction flexible enough to be structured to meet the institution's financial needs?
- Does the borrower have confidence that the lender will be able to complete the transaction?
- Can the deal be documented and negotiated within the borrower's time frame?
- How complex is the legal documentation?
- Can the borrower afford the front-end fees associated with the transaction?
- Will the borrower be able to cancel the deal if circumstances dictate, and how much it will cost to do so?
- What requirements does the investor have for credit support?

SUMMARY

Borrowers come in all shapes and sizes, and the astute lender must seek a way to differentiate between good loans and potentially unsuccessful loans. The financial manager must assist the lender to discern the differences between the good loan represented by the financial manager's organization and all others.

The process begins with the preparation of a strategic financing plan that is part of the institution's overall strategic business plan. Then, the financial manager must garner all the relevant facts and information that the lender will require, anticipate the lender's questions, and assemble a presentation to the lender. The presentation is a combination of written information and oral discussion, including an on-site tour of the health care facilities.

To be successful in the borrowing process, the financial manager must ensure that the selected lender matches the intended use of the funds and the duration of the loan. Banks, leasing companies, insurance companies, and venture capitalists all have different objectives. The financial manager must recognize these differences and play to the lender's interests.

Chapter 7

Introduction to Short-Term Investing

INTRODUCTION

The principles of investing are the same, whether one is investing the liquidity reserves or strategic reserves of an organization, its endowment funds, or dedicated proceeds of a bond issue. Sound investing requires setting clear investing objectives and an appropriate set of investing guidelines and determining the investment requirements dictated by the particular situation.

Investing opportunities occur when the institution operates with a residual of surplus cash flow or long-term capital, or when it has segregated funds earmarked for investment in fixed assets. In order to invest appropriately, management should develop an investing strategy that recognizes both the source of the funds and their use. Endowment funds are invested very differently from liquidity reserves; dedicated bond funds are invested differently from each of these.

For example, if the funds represent a temporary excess of receipts over disbursements, with the expectation that the funds will be used in the working capital of the institution in the very near future, the investing strategy should recognize a very short-term time horizon. On the other hand, if the funds represent the proceeds of a long-term bond issue, with the funds earmarked for a major construction project that will not take place for another 12 to 18 months, then the strategy should reflect this timing and dictate the employment of somewhat different tactics. Endowment funds, alternatively, are expected to be permanently employed in the capital structure of the organization and are invested with long-term growth and income in mind.

The investing objectives and guidelines should be in written form and approved by operating management and by the board of trustees or directors. All authority emanates from the board; when approved, the objectives and guidelines document becomes, in effect, a contract between the board and the members of management who carry out the investing program.

In the absence of a written and approved policy document, the financial manager may find it difficult, if not impossible, to invest funds confidently. The financial manager also risks his or her job every time an investment is made, because senior officials or members of the board have the opportunity to second-guess the investment action if there are no accepted investing standards. Accordingly, in the absence of an existing written policy statement and guidelines, the financial manager should initiate the development of such a document.

MANAGING LIQUIDITY FUNDS

Managing a liquidity portfolio is very different from managing a permanent portfolio of endowment funds. Endowment funds exist for the purpose of producing income on a total return basis over the long run. Endowment funds frequently are invested in long-term bonds, preferred stocks, and common stock, as well as in illiquid investments such as real estate and occasionally in high-yield/high-risk investments. Liquidity funds, on the other hand, serve a totally different purpose. They provide a liquidity buffer for the day-to-day operations of the organization.

Primary goals of managing liquidity funds usually are the preservation of principal and the maintenance of liquidity. Generating a yield on the funds is often a third objective. In managing a business, whether a health care institution or a manufacturer, the maintenance of the firm's liquidity is crucial to its short- and long-term success. Even in financially successful firms, there are periods in which disbursements exceed receipts, and the well-managed organization must be prepared for this occurrence. An entity that manages its cash properly will not maintain sufficient cash in its checking account to clear short-term hurdles. Rather, it will keep all of its immediately excess cash in the form of liquid investments composed almost exclusively of short-term, fixed-income money-market instruments that are convertible to cash on virtually a moment's notice with little risk of loss of principal.

MONEY MARKET INSTRUMENTS—AN OVERVIEW

The ideal money market investment medium is a debt instrument that does not fluctuate substantially in value, that carries no risk of default by the issuer, and that may be converted to cash at any time without loss of principal. The instrument that most closely approaches this standard is a Short-Maturity (90 Days or Less) Treasury bill, a short-term debt obligation of the United States government. In this imperfect world, the U.S. government is considered to carry the highest domestic credit rating, which means that the risk of default on its debt obligations is the lowest in the United States. As a result, credit ratings, as well as yields, of all other domestic instruments of any maturity are based on spreads (yield variations) from U.S. government securities by comparing similar maturities.

Other short-term debt instruments commonly used as money market investments are the negotiable bank certificate of deposit, the time draft called a banker's acceptance (the payment of which is an obligation of a bank), and the short-term promissory note of a corporation known as commercial paper.

The latter half of the 1980s saw many significant changes in the marketplace for money market instruments. During the same period the nature of commercial banking changed significantly as well, and this contributed to the alteration of the money markets. Historically, when a firm needed to borrow for its short-term working capital needs, it went to a bank and borrowed on a 90-day promissory note that the bank traditionally held until maturity. In the 1980s, however, the banking industry encountered its own liquidity crisis as well as an industrywide shortage of permanent capital in relation to assets. When these elements were combined with the severe economic stresses resulting from the collapse of the energy, real estate, and agriculture industries, in addition to loans to less developed countries that went sour, banks became pressed to find methods of improving their ratio of permanent capital to total assets. In fact, the regulatory authorities mandated higher capital levels for banks to be met by the end of 1992.

There are two ways, of course, to improve a capital ratio: (1) increase the amount of capital or (2) reduce the amount of assets. Because the cost of capital was exceptionally expensive for banks during this period, many banks took the easier path and sought ways to reduce their assets without impairing earning capacity. It was not long before banks discovered that they could originate loans and sell them to investors, while retaining an interest rate spread for servicing the loan. This device of selling loans helped the banks to restore their own capital ratios for regulatory purposes, but it had a direct impact on borrowers. Many borrowers now were required to execute standardized loan documentation and to face the possibility that someone other than their bank—even perhaps a competitor—would be the holder of the borrower's debt.

Very large companies in the United States have been borrowing in the public money markets for many years via commercial paper, but companies smaller than Fortune 500 firms were not accustomed to this kind of treatment. In the late 1980s, it has become increasingly customary for companies of even modest size to be required to borrow under documentation hinting that the bank may not hold the debt until maturity.

Perhaps the most significant effect of these developments is the recognition that an investment instrument is merely the reverse side of the borrowing instrument. In the latter half of the 1980s, it has become obvious to commercial bankers and investment bankers that their respective pools of borrowers and investors had interests in common. Consequently, the bankers have designed new instruments that simultaneously serve the needs of both the borrower and the investor. This has brought some very creative thinking to the game. The traditional short-term investment instruments—certificates of deposit, commercial paper, bankers' acceptances, and Treasury bills—have now become rather pedestrian. With the proliferation of new instruments in the money markets, the typical investor is hard-pressed to discern between those instruments that are truly safe and liquid and those that present hidden risks. While there have been no major disasters in this regard yet, many investors of institutional liquidity funds remain somewhat skeptical about instruments with names such as DARTS, CATS, and Low Floaters. Other investors, often seeking new, more unusual investments, forge ahead and usually enjoy a somewhat higher yield than their friends who remain with the traditional money market investment instruments. It is questionable, however, whether these more adventuresome investors truly understand the issues surrounding potential liquidity and credit problems, even though there is little or no documented evidence of failures in these areas to date.

One can wonder what would have happened if the economy had entered a recession during this time instead of a continual growth pattern since about 1983. If a financial manager knowingly enters into a risky investment transaction and that risk is realized with loss of principal, the loss can be much more acceptable if the manager's actions have been in accordance with board-approved policy and guidelines. Along with the variety of new instruments, the minefields also have expanded to the potential detriment of the well-being and job security of financial managers responsible for investing their institutions' liquidity funds without board direction.

CASH FLOW FORECASTING

The manager of a successful investing program must have an effective cash flow forecasting system in place. The forecasting system is necessary to give the manager an idea of the amount of funds available for investment and the time period that the funds will be available.

Risk of loss in short-term investing is not confined to credit risk alone. Loss of principal can also occur by investing in an instrument that must be sold prior to maturity, if interest rates have risen in the meantime. This phenomenon is usually referred to as "market risk" or "interest rate risk" and it can result in loss to investors, even to those who invest only in U.S. Treasury bills.

Because of market risk, the financial manager should purchase instruments with maturities that approximately coincide with the firm's need for the funds. If the cash flow forecast indicates that the funds should be available for 45 days, for example, the financial manager is well-advised to purchase instruments maturing in approximately 45 days. Purchasing a six-month security under these circumstances could result in loss of principal if interest rates rise, thereby forcing the value of the instrument down. Of course, the opposite situation may occur. Declining interest rates during the period could result in a gain on the early sale of the instrument. However, most financial managers are willing to forgo that possibility in order to avoid risking their liquidity funds.

DEVELOPING AN INVESTING STRATEGY

The financial manager is ready to begin development of a strategic plan for investing liquidity funds after the necessary tools are in place for producing forecasts. These include a short-term cash flow forecast and an intermediate-term forecast for several months. A long-range forecast is also helpful to determine the amount and duration, if any, of funds available for longer-term investing. The strategic plan should be established in concert with development of the investing policy and guidelines to ensure that the guidelines are compatible with, and indeed support, the investing strategy.

At this point, the financial manager may begin to think in terms of managing two different segments of portfolios. One segment would be the liquidity portfolio containing only short-term, fixed-income securities with high-grade credit quality and liquidity. It is this portion that will be used tactically on a daily basis to absorb temporarily excess funds generated from operations and to provide liquidity to the institution when there is a shortfall of funds. The other portion of the portfolio, for longer-term strategic use, could be invested in intermediate-term, fixed-income securities.

Before investing any funds, however, the financial manager will want to assess the institution's tolerance for risk. Typically, when asked about tolerance for risk, management will say that it has absolutely no tolerance for it. However, when faced with the low yields of risk-free, short-term Treasury bills, management will frequently inquire about other securities that offer a higher yield.

This dilemma between no tolerance for risk and a desire for high yield can be resolved if the financial manager and senior management explore in detail the nature and extent of various risks and decide how much risk they are willing to tolerate. If, in fact, they are unwilling to accept any risk greater than short-term U.S. Treasury bills, they must be willing to accept the rock-bottom yields that Treasury bills offer. On the other hand, if they wish to obtain higher yields, they must be willing to accept the reasonable credit risk of top credit-rated United States and foreign banks and top credit-rated industrial corporations and their captive finance company subsidiaries. This decision will address only the question of credit risk; the issue of market risk still has not been considered.

If management really wishes to have yield take a front seat, it should be willing to accept other investing possibilities. These include banks of less than top quality (although many are nevertheless sound) and commercial paper of industrial and financial companies that are rated in the second tier of credit ratings. The matter of market risk, or the risk that interest rates will rise, thereby forcing a decline in the market value of fixed-income securities, also must be considered. This is particularly important in a liquidity portfolio where safety of principal is of paramount importance. Management must be willing to accept market risk, even from Treasury bills, unless it is prepared to keep maturities as short as 90 days or less.

There are two ways to protect against market risk. The customary method most companies use is simply to maintain short maturities ranging between 30 and 60 days. If interest rates rise (causing the value of the instrument to fall), the investor has to wait only a short period until maturity. The other method, which is far from perfect, is to invest in interest rate futures contracts and options as hedges. When interest rates move upward, a hedge position should generate a profit to offset the loss in the value of the investment instrument.

The use of futures and options, however, is a very sophisticated practice. It should be used only by investors, with very large portfolios, who can observe all the markets virtually on a full-time basis. Futures and options could be equally beneficial for the investor with a modest-sized portfolio, but these investors typically do not have the time or the expertise to become involved with the sophisticated hedging techniques that futures and options represent.

Another strategy for managing short-term investment funds exists where the funds have been earmarked for a specific project, such as construction of a building. In this type of situation, market risk impact can be reduced by purchasing investment instruments with maturities that coincide with the projected need dates for the funds. For example, if construction plans call for a milestone construction payment on a certain date four months from now, the financial manager can invest in an instrument maturing just prior to the payment date. The institution will be assured of receiving 100 cents on the invested dollar, plus interest, at maturity, rather than risking possible loss in a sale prior to maturity. The entire investment portfolio for the project can be assembled with maturities to coincide with estimated payment dates and amounts required for the project, thereby immunizing the portfolio from any market value changes due to interest rate swings. However, if construction is ahead of schedule and funds are required sooner than expected, an instrument may have to be sold prior to maturity. This may result in a possible loss of principal (see Chapter 13 for more details about investing construction funds).

PROFESSIONAL INVESTMENT ADVISERS

The health care financial manager, because of other duties, may find the operation, supervision, and management of the institution's investment portfolio unduly burdensome. Proper investment management requires hands-on experience in the securities marketplace. It is also necessary to maintain complete records that account for portfolio transactions, provide reports, stay abreast of changes and trends in the securities markets, and continually remain within the bounds prescribed by the firm's investing guidelines and the overall context of an investing strategy.

These responsibilities, which are further explained in the following chapters, may be impossible for the health care financial manager to handle along with other duties. Therefore, many financial managers turn to outside professional investment advisers for assistance in managing their firms' investment portfolios. Professional advisers with the necessary qualifications and investment expertise constitute a useful resource for the health care institution.

Reasons for Using Outside Investment Advisers

Outside investment advisers are used by firms with portfolios of all sizes. There are usually two major reasons for employing an outside investment adviser. (1) The organization does not have a sufficiently large portfolio to support a full-time, in-house investment manager nor does it have research and information services necessary to enable an in-house investment manager to function properly. Often institutions with small portfolios are in the greatest need of outside advisers. With the small portfolio, the financial manager probably is not attuned to the fast-paced securities markets. Consequently, the overall knowledge of markets and investment securities is at a relatively low level, and the financial manager can easily make a misstep that would cost the organization dearly. (2) The portfolio is large but not permanent. This effectively prevents the investor from hiring permanent staff to manage the portfolio and makes it desirable to retain outside professional investment management. When the investment funds are no longer available, the relationship with the investment adviser can be terminated.

Professional investment advisers outside the health care institution can be particularly helpful in monitoring changes and trends in the marketplace, including fluctuating yield spreads, changes in credit quality, and new investment instruments. A competent adviser usually can enhance the profitability of the health care institution's portfolio sufficiently to offset his or her fee. The adviser provides an additional service by reducing the risk of loss due to inadequate evaluation of credit risk and market risk, as well as reducing the risk of loss of employment by the financial manager when principal losses occur. The financial manager's time is also more available for other responsibilities.

Types of Outside Investment Advisers

Two types of outside professional investment advisers work with financial managers in managing investment portfolios: investment managers and investment consultants.

Investment managers' services range from simple advisory consultation (closely akin to investment consultants) to full management control over investment activities. The latter use their own discretion in the selection of particular instruments and maturities within board-approved guidelines. Investment managers typically specialize in one particular area of investments, such as stocks or fixed-income instruments. Within the fixed-income arena, they may specialize in short-term, intermediate-term, or long-term maturities. Generally, health care institutions seek investment managers who specialize in short-term to intermediate-term maturities of fixed-income securities.

Investment consultants, on the other hand, do not manage any funds; rather, they supplement the financial manager's skills in reviewing the institution's investment operations and assess the suitability of investment instruments available in the marketplace. The investment consultant, interestingly, often is instrumental in selecting and monitoring an outside investment manager. The consultant helps to develop the firm's investing guidelines, periodically reviews current strategies, and makes recommendations for adjustments.

Selecting an Outside Investment Manager

The selection process for an investment manager should include careful attention to all appropriate details. Frequently, an investment consultant is enlisted to assist in the selection. The process begins with the consultant's review of the existing guidelines to ensure that they adequately address the client's investing objectives and provide for the necessary amount of flexibility. For example, it hardly would be worthwhile to retain an investment manager if the guidelines restricted the portfolio to U.S. Treasury bills maturing in 90 days or less.

When a well-crafted set of investing guidelines is in hand, the consultant searches a proprietary data base of investment managers to identify those who appear to meet the criteria for the type of investments, credit quality, and maturity required by the investor. After reviewing the results of the initial search, the consultant trims the list to three to five of the most attractive candidates. Meanwhile, the institution's financial manager prepares a request for proposal (RFP) describing the nature and size of the portfolio, the investment objectives and existing guidelines, and the requirements for the investment manager. The RFP should also describe any unusual features or requirements pertaining to operation of the portfolio. Investment managers have widely varying approaches to the management of funds; the institution's financial manager will want assurance that the investment manager will use compatible methods of operation, goals, and objectives.

After receiving written proposals from the chosen candidates, the consultant and the financial manager, as representatives of the investor, conduct in-person interviews. Each candidate is given an opportunity to discuss past performance and method of operation and to respond directly to the investor's questions. The interview process should include discussion of investing goals and differing assumptions and criteria on which they are based. There usually is more than one way to state an investing goal; experienced investment managers often provide guidance in this area. In any event, the investment manager must fully understand and accept the investor's goals before a meeting of the minds can occur.

Other important considerations brought to the surface through the candidates' formal proposals and the interviews are

- the candidate's willingness to engage in discussion, to demonstrate flexibility regarding the client's investing program, and to utilize the client's own investing guidelines
- other clients of the investment manager with similar investing goals and guidelines
- the investor's portfolio size in comparison with the portfolios of the investment manager's other clients
- the registration of the investment manager with the U.S. Securities and Exchange Commission (SEC), under the Investment Advisors Act of 1940, and with the state of the investment manager's domicile
- any past censures by the SEC or other regulatory authority of the investment management firm or its principals for misconduct
- the turnover rate among the investment management firm's portfolio managers, key support staff, and supervisory personnel
- the experience and background of the investment management firm's principals and portfolio managers
- the ease with which the client may communicate directly with the investment management firm's portfolio manager
- the use of a written investment management contract and the inclusion of the following three elements:
  1. clear description of how fees are calculated
  2. additional charges above the basic fee
  3. reasons for termination of the contract by either the client or the investment manager
- the capabilities of the investment manager to handle the type of portfolio involved, as indicated by the specific computerized information and analytical resources and the specific credit review services that are utilized
- the format and frequency of reports and to what extent the investment manager can customize reports to meet the investor's particular needs

When the investment manager is selected, the institution may retain the consultant to provide assistance in reviewing the manager's performance.

Compensating Outside Investment Advisers

Investment managers usually receive compensation based on the size of the portfolio that they manage. Investment consultants typically are compensated with a flat fee. Compensation may be made in either soft dollars or hard dollars.

Soft dollar compensation is involved when the investment adviser shares in the commissions generated by the execution of investment transactions. Payment via soft dollars superficially saves the investor the additional fee; however, the use of soft-dollar compensation can discourage the investment manager from seeking the most competitive prices on the execution of transactions. Instead, the investment manager may seek to execute transactions where soft-dollar compensation is available rather than where the best prices are obtainable. The client may be well-advised to pay the investment manager on a hard-dollar basis and demand the best execution possible.

Consultants, on the other hand, may be paid in hard dollars if they are independent consultants, or soft dollars if they are associated with the investment manager or an investment dealer or brokerage firm. If the investment consultant is not independent and is compensated in soft dollars, the health care financial manager should be aware that the advice and counsel received from the consultant may not be independent as well. It is possible the affiliated consultant may better serve his or her own firm than the client firm.

There are two principal aspects to the evaluation of an investment manager's fee: (1) the fee should be competitive with those of other qualified investment managers dealing with similar investment instruments and maturities, and (2) the fee should not exceed what it would cost to establish the investment management function internally with an acceptable level of sophistication and quality.

Working with an Investment Manager

The investment manager needs to become familiar with the investor's objectives, liquidity requirements, and relative risk-aversion tendencies of the health care institution's financial and administrative managers. After meeting with the institution's managers, the investment manager reviews the existing investing guidelines. If they do not appear adequate or sufficiently comprehensive, the investment manager should propose revisions.

In addition to refining the investing guidelines, the investment manager assists in developing operating arrangements necessary to execute investment transactions and facilitate delivery of investment management and advisory services to the client. In this process, the investment custodian must be selected for the safekeeping of securities, and appropriate documentation must be executed authorizing the investment manager to conduct business with securities dealers and the custodian. Finally, regular contacts with the health care institution's financial staff must be established, including a meeting schedule for regular review of the investment manager's performance, usually quarterly.

With all these details attended to, the health care financial manager will be able to utilize a structured, methodical, full-time, and hopefully professional approach to the task of managing the institution's investment portfolio. The financial manager thereby assumes the role of manager of the investment manager and becomes insulated from the minutiae of daily investment tasks.

SUMMARY

Developing an investment program for the liquidity portfolio and other funds of a health care institution has many facets. These include the concept of managing the funds to meet their respective purposes and the aspect of providing a meaningful forecast of receipts and disbursements of funds. The latter enables estimations regarding the size of the remaining pool of funds and the time horizon for its usefulness. When the physical aspects of the investment portfolio are determined, management can begin to develop a strategy for investing the funds to meet goals and maintain appropriate levels of liquidity and safety of principal. Finally, the organization must develop an operating plan for executing, verifying, and settling transactions and ensuring the safety of the instruments while they repose in the portfolio.

Unfortunately, many financial managers barge ahead and begin investing surplus funds without giving conscious thought to each of these elements. Usually there are no material adverse consequences other than perhaps confusion or lapses in record keeping. However, too often the absence of a well-thought-out and structured program leads to losses caused by either acute sloppiness or by working with unscrupulous investment dealers who take advantage of an unsuspecting investor.

There are many sources of investment advice, advisers, and managers available to assist health care financial managers in developing an informed approach to investing. Operation of an investment portfolio requires careful attention to the details of executing investment transactions and monitoring the resulting inventories. A feasible approach may utilize the services of an outside professional investment adviser to guide the institution through the thicket of the details or to manage the investments according to the institution's investing policy and guidelines. After a review of the investment information discussed in the following chapters, the health care financial manager will be better able to decide whether to manage funds internally or to seek the assistance of an outside professional.

Chapter 8

Determining Investment Requirements

INTRODUCTION

The task of managing a pool of investable funds should be approached with care and caution; not all funds require the same kind of handling. The treatment of a particular pool is determined by its source and the ultimate use to which the funds will be placed.

If the pool of funds represents the temporary liquidity pool of the health care institution, the investment of funds must be handled in a highly liquid and safe manner to reflect the fact that the pool can and probably will be tapped on a moment's notice. On the other hand, if the pool of funds represents endowment contributions to be used for production of income over a long period of time, the rather permanent nature of this pool would dictate that the funds be invested for long-term growth and income. Safety of the principal should remain a primary investment objective in any case.

Many health care institutions have various pools of funds, the source and purpose of which may fall between the extremes of excess working capital (liquidity) and endowment. For example, the proceeds of a bond issue awaiting the commitment to a construction project can be invested in instruments having a longer term (not to exceed need dates) than the liquidity pool. But investments for this purpose cannot use the long-term, capital-growth type of securities that the endowment fund can accept. A depreciation fund intended for the replacement of the physical plant also will be used within a certain time frame (measured in years); while it is a continuously replenished fund, it may not be a permanent or long-term fund.

It is important to make the distinction between the source and the ultimate use of the funds in order to be guided properly as to the appropriate investment instruments and investment terms for the respective pools.

CRITERIA FOR INVESTING

In evaluating the various avenues used to approach the investment of a particular pool of funds, the financial manager must consider a number of criteria and alternatives available with respect to each criterion. The criteria to be evaluated include

- safety of principal
- liquidity
- cash flow management
- timing of the use of funds
- reinvestment requirements
- income taxes
- management's (directors or trustees) special attitude toward such items as supporting local banks with deposits, risk sensitivity, and degree of participation in investment activities (these attitudes should be addressed in the investing guidelines)

Safety of Principal

Although discussed in Chapter 7, this point cannot be overemphasized. Ask a business executive or administrative manager about his or her tolerance for risk in making investments, and the response undoubtedly will be that there is no tolerance for risk. Then ask that same person whether he or she finds short-term U.S. Treasury bills to have an acceptable rate of return, and the response undoubtedly will be negative as well. Obviously, there is a conflict in these responses, because one cannot have a total absence of risk and reap high returns at the same time. The earning of a "normal rate of return" is related to the acceptance of a level of risk. Every investment policy must address and specify that level of risk which the organization is willing to accept. The statement of risk tolerance is the number one element in a written set of investing policy and guidelines. There are essentially two forms of risks: (1) credit risk and (2) market, or interest rate, risk.

Credit Risk

Credit risk is also known as default risk and refers to the possibility that the obligor of a debt instrument will fail to repay principal or pay interest on a timely basis in accordance with the terms of the instrument. Credit risk can be analyzed and measured by the investor prior to investing in a particular debt instrument, or the investor can rely on a credit analysis performed by a credit rating agency (see

Table 8-1). It is generally assumed that the credit risk represented by debt of the government of the United States is the highest form of credit and that all other issuers' credit ratings are measured against the benchmark of the U.S. government. Many investors mistakenly believe that the debt markets are rational and that differences in credit risk are quickly reflected in differences of yield among similar instruments of different issuers. For example, a commercial paper note due in 90 days issued by a corporation of medium creditworthiness will yield the investor a greater return than will a 90-day U.S. Treasury bill. Similarly, the yield on commercial paper issued by a very creditworthy corporation will yield somewhat less return than the rate of return on commercial paper of a medium quality issuer.

Table 8-1 Credit Review Services

Rating Service	Address and Phone Number
BankWatch by Keefe, Bruyette & Woods	2 World Trade Center Suite 8566 New York, N.Y. 10048 1-800-221-3246
McCarthy, Crisanti & Maffei, Inc.	71 Broadway New York, N.Y. 10006 (212) 509-5800
Moody's Investors Service	99 Church Street New York, N.Y. 10007 (212) 553-0300
Standard & Poor's Corporation	25 Broadway New York, N.Y. 10004 (212) 208-8000
Duff & Phelps, Inc.	5 East Monroe Street Suite 400 Chicago, Ill. 60603 (312) 263-2610
Fitch Investors Service, Inc.	5 Hanover Square New York, N.Y. 10004 (212) 668-8300
Cates Consulting Analysis	40 Broad Street 23rd Floor New York, N.Y. 10004 (212) 968-9200
Sheshunoff and Co., Inc.	P.O. Box 13203 Capital Station, Austin, Tex. 78711 (512) 472-2244
Bank Valuation	37 South Drive Plandome, N.Y. 11030 (516) 627-7470

However, markets are imperfect and sometimes very much so. It is important that the financial manager be aware of the respective "normal" relative levels of credit quality and yields among the issuers in whose securities and instruments the organization is investing. To do this, the financial manager must maintain current information about issuers and changes in their credit ratings.

In the management of pools of funds held for liquidity and intermediate-term purposes, investors tend to demand credit quality of the highest order; that is, they will generally invest only in instruments issued by companies of the highest credit quality or by the U.S. government. This is to ensure the greatest degree of market "saleability," or liquidity. However, the risk of such investments still must be carefully examined.

Some investors take a higher-risk approach, and apply the theory of portfolio management that expects some investments in a portfolio to pay off well while others actually incur capital losses, while the bulk of the investments in a portfolio will generate normal yields of approximately the average market rate of return. The hope, of course, is to manage a broad portfolio of investments so that the winners will exceed the losers in quantity and in magnitude with the result that the portfolio as a whole realizes a minimal amount of risk and an optimal amount of return and growth. However, this approach is suited only to highly skilled investors who can afford a higher degree of risk.

Market Risk

Market risk, or the risk of loss to principal due to changes in interest rates, is a subtle but very real form of risk, and it can be equally as devastating as credit risk. Interest rates affect the market value of a debt instrument when the interest rate, or coupon, of the instrument is fixed (nonfloating or nonmarket rate adjusting). When yields in the marketplace change, either the market value of existing instruments must change or the rate of return paid on that instrument must change in order to adjust an instrument's market yield to current market yield. If a bond has a fixed-rate coupon and interest rates in the marketplace rise, then the market value of that bond must decline to a point where the fixed-rate coupon and a change in its market value combine to reflect current market yield. Likewise, when interest rates decline, the market value of the bond must rise. When this bond is purchased by an investor, the combination of the bond's coupon rate and principal cost will put the net yield, based on the price paid versus interest received, where comparable instruments are now offered.

When investing in a fixed-rate coupon instrument, the investor realizes that the longer the term until maturity, the greater the possibility for fluctuation in market value due to interest rate changes and, therefore, the greater the market risk (see Table 8-2). Conversely, an instrument that matures in a relatively short period of time will be somewhat insulated from changes in market interest rates; the investor

Table 8-2 How Changes in Interest Rates Affect Market Prices

Maturity	1% Rise in Interest Rates Equals Approximately This Amount of Dollar Market Value Change (Per $1,000,000 of Par Value)
1 month	$ 805
3 months	2,583
6 months	5,111
1 year	9,583
2 years	17,218
5 years	36,882
10 years	56,196
20 years	78,796
30 years	81,349

will need only to hold the instrument until maturity to receive 100 cents on the dollar.

Different types of instruments bear different levels of sensitivity to the volatility of interest rates in the marketplace. Zero coupon bonds, for example, typically carry the highest level of volatility, or market risk, because there is no current income to cushion the investor's return. Consequently, a change in market interest rate levels impacts immediately, directly, and to the fullest extent the market value of a zero coupon bond. At the other end of the volatility spectrum are floating rate instruments where the coupon yields are not fixed but are reset periodically to reflect changes in market interest rates. Because the coupon on these instruments changes with the market, their market value is rather stable.

High-quality credit ratings also tend to insulate a security from market volatility to some degree. It has been shown empirically that in times of stress or increasing interest rates, investors begin a "flight to quality" by buying higher credit quality instruments. It creates a demand for the instruments, thereby further forcing their prices up and yields down. This was amply demonstrated in the well-documented stock market crash of October 19, 1987, when equity prices went into a free-fall and there was complete turmoil in both the equity and credit markets. Investors fled stocks in droves, and many placed their funds temporarily into U.S. government obligations. The yields on U.S. government securities remained inordinately low during the weeks immediately following the crash. Investors had bid up the prices as they purchased these instruments to obtain high-credit, quality investments.

Loss of principal due to market risk is *realized* only when the security must be sold prior to maturity. At that time, the market value of the instrument may be above or below what the investor paid for it and also may be different from the maturity value of the instrument. Market risk does not result in a loss if the investor holds the instrument until maturity, because at that time the investor will realize the return of 100 percent of the face value of the instrument. Market risk exists not only for corporate and bank securities but also for U.S. government securities. Therefore, it is incorrect for an investor to say that he demands that funds be invested only in U.S. government securities in order to avoid risk to principal. Credit risk, indeed, can be avoided or at least minimized, but market risk cannot be avoided (although it may be limited through hedging techniques) unless the securities are held until maturity, even for Treasury instruments.

Recognition by the financial manager of the existence of market risk, in addition to credit risk, is critically important to the management of an investment portfolio, particularly a pool of funds whose use is not anticipated for several years. The temptation in managing these funds is to invest in long-term securities and collect a possibly higher income, while knowing that the securities are sufficiently liquid to be sold on very short notice. The financial manager must recognize, however, that while the liquidity and current income will remain constant, a change in interest rates may cause the market value of the portfolio to decline. Losses could be realized if it were necessary to convert the portfolio to cash prior to maturity of the instruments. Therefore, in addition to analyzing and monitoring credit risk as represented by the potential for default by issuers of securities, the investment manager also must be cognizant of market risk and its potential capability to erode the market value of a portfolio.

Because of the potentially devastating effects of both credit risk and market risk, the institution's investment policy must be clear about how these two forms of risk are to be handled. This must be done before establishing an approach to investing and before discussing the particular issues and forms of investments that are acceptable. The decisions with regard to the level of tolerance for credit risk and market risk should be made by the most senior officials in management, if not by the directors or trustees themselves. The considerations should be made consciously and the results communicated in writing to the financial manager in such a way that there could be no mistaking the intentions of senior management.

Case Study of Risk Taking Resulting in Loss

ABC Hospital was a large organization with more than 1,000 beds serving an economically expanding middle-class (and higher) geographic area. The hospital had accumulated depreciation funds of approximately $40 million that were managed by a financial analyst reporting to the hospital's chief finance officer (CFO). The cash flow to the hospital was more than adequate to cover expenses, and no immediate needs were forecasted for the use of any depreciation funds; thus the financial analyst had relatively few constraints and little direction to keep cash available for immediate needs. Furthermore, no comprehensive written investment policy was in place to specifically limit ABC Hospital's investment activities.

Within this loose framework the financial analyst began to purchase longer-maturity (10 through 30 years) U.S. Treasury securities for the following reasons:

- The longer maturities presented a higher yield and would improve the rate of return on the hospital's investment portfolio.
- There were no immediate plans to utilize the funds; therefore short maturity dates appeared to be inappropriate for the investment.
- Because the instruments were issued and guaranteed by the U.S. Treasury, there appeared to be no risk to principal.

As the rate of return on the hospital's portfolio was better than the yield available on shorter-term investments, such as local bank certificates of deposit, the CFO and vice president of finance complimented the financial analyst on his ability to achieve an attractive rate of return. Furthermore, during this investment period, interest rates began to decline, causing the market value of the long-term securities to increase. This situation led the hospital's financial analyst to become more active in trading (actively buying and selling) these securities to capture as a capital gain their improvement in price. As interest rates continued to decline, the prices of these instruments continued to go up, and capital gains were realized from the transactions. Combined with their higher accrual rate, the gains substantially enhanced the hospital's yield and brought further praise to the financial analyst from the CFO.

Soon, the reality of interest rates began to set in as financial market conditions changed. Interest rates stopped going down and, in fact, began to rise quite rapidly. By this time the hospital's portfolio consisted entirely of long-maturity treasury bonds. Just as these instruments had gone up in price as interest rates were declining, they were now going down in price as interest rates were increasing. Accordingly, the financial analyst was no longer able to sell the instruments in his portfolio at prices higher than those he paid for them. Therefore, unrealized capital gains quickly turned into unrealized capital losses.

Compounding this situation was a substantial slowdown in cash flow to the hospital, and it needed to rely on funds from its excess cash investments, including substantial amounts from the depreciation fund. This need for cash necessitated sale of several investments which resulted in substantial realized losses to the hospital. At this time, the losses were noted by the hospital's auditors who discovered additional unrealized losses in the hospital's investment portfolio.

As a result of the speculation engaged in by ABC Hospital's financial analyst, the hospital realized approximately $2.5 million in losses. Its remaining investment portfolio, with an initial value of $40 million, had declined in value approximately 10 percent from the original principal investment.

This information, contained in the audit report, was made available to senior hospital management, and it immeditely demanded the situation be remedied. Unfortunately, with the losses in place and more cash needs ahead, the opportunities to remedy the situation were limited simply to establishing procedures to avoid a repetition in the future.

The following procedures should have been set in place before this situation originally developed:

- Comprehensive investment guidelines should have been established with specific limitations on risk, including maturities.
- Maturities should have been limited to conform strictly with the estimated cash needs at that time or limited to a maximum maturity date, as stated in the guidelines to avoid excessive interest rate, or market, risk.
- The financial analyst managing the investment portfolio should have been trained more thoroughly, or outside professional assistance should have been contracted.
- Frequent (quarterly) review or audit of investment activities should have been instituted to ensure that investment activities conformed with investment guidelines and to discover any unusual situations.

Liquidity

Liquidity refers to the capability of an investment instrument to be converted into cash prior to maturity without the investor suffering an unacceptable loss of principal. A portfolio is said to have near-perfect liquidity when it consists of extremely high credit quality instruments and it matures entirely in one day. In that case, interest rates could change overnight but would not affect market value of the portfolio. However, if maturity of the instruments in the portfolio extends beyond overnight, there is the possibility of the introduction of market risk and therefore the introduction of some illiquidity.

Another, and perhaps more obvious, dimension of liquidity relates to the depth and breadth of the market itself for the particular security involved. The good news about the huge size of the national debt is that it provides the broadest and deepest market dimensions for the debt instruments of the U.S. government. The vast breadth and depth of the market enable any investor to buy or sell virtually any amount of a current actively traded U.S. Treasury security virtually at any moment with a minimum search for buyers and sellers.

At the opposite extreme of this dimension of liquidity are debt obligations of obscure banks and corporations whose creditworthiness is not well-known and for which there are not many ready buyers or sellers in the marketplace. It would not be unusual for the holder of an instrument of an obscure company to encounter delays of days or even a week while a broker searched for a potential buyer, if one exists.

It is said that every asset has its price and that no matter how poor a credit risk or how long the instrument's maturity, there is always an investor somewhere in the marketplace who will buy that instrument. The question, however, is, "At what price?" Even for 30-year U.S. government bonds, the market price is determined by literally thousands of active buyers and sellers at any moment. This depth of the market provides the seller the ability to convert a government obligation into cash on a moment's notice. Meanwhile, the free-flowing market mechanism of continuing transactions between buyers and sellers provides constant adjustment to the market price based on current interest rates and expectations. This is the traditional concept of liquidity. The holder of the debt instrument of the obscure corporation may also find a willing buyer. In the absence of other potential buyers, however, the one buyer who is interested can probably dictate the price to the seller and that price may very well represent a loss. Therefore, while the seller can indeed convert the security to cash, it may have to suffer a loss in order to do so prior to maturity.

Liquidity is also an issue when funds are placed into instruments that are legally unredeemable until maturity. These include, for example, fixed-time deposits of banks or savings and loans where the amount is small or the investor has no legal or market ability to sell or transfer the deposit to a subsequent party. In the case of certificates of deposit of well-known and high credit-rated institutions where the investor has the legal right to sell the instrument, liquidity is considerably improved. Interest-rate risk, however, may reduce the market value of the instrument if interest rates have risen since the instrument was acquired.

Accordingly, the financial manager who seeks to ensure a high level of liquidity in the institution's portfolio should focus on investing in instruments of the highest possible credit quality and of relatively short maturities. On the other hand, where liquidity is not a large factor in the objectives of the funds the financial manager may consider matching the maturity of the investment to a particular date when the funds are believed to be needed. For example, in managing a depreciation fund portfolio, the investment manager may elect to invest in an instrument maturing when an expensive piece of equipment is expected to be replaced. In this case, the possibility of realized loss due to market risk would be diminished because the instrument would likely mature (at face value) in time to be used for the intended purpose. The only risk would be credit risk.

Cash Flow Management

Management of cash flows involves the maintenance of a pool of liquidity funds or, alternatively, a line of credit available for use on very short notice in order to accommodate momentary and short-term imbalances between aggregate cash inflows and outflows. The principal tool in managing these imbalances is the short-term cash flow forecast, or cash schedule.

The cash schedule enables an institution's financial manager to anticipate cash shortfalls or short-term cash excesses and to formulate a plan to dispose of either situation in a logical and rational manner. In the case of short-term temporary excesses of cash, the cash schedule helps the financial manager to estimate the approximate size of the excess and its expected duration. The funds then can be invested accordingly. By investing these funds in the exact amount and maturity indicated by the cash schedule, the financial manager should be able to reduce any possible realized loss resulting from market risk. However, short-term cash flow forecasts, or cash schedules, are seldom sufficiently accurate to accomplish this. Financial managers frequently invest temporarily excess funds in very short-term, or overnight, investments and then discover later that they could have invested the funds in a longer-term instrument paying a higher yield.

Consequently, it is a common technique for a financial manager to invest the available funds for a period of time slightly longer than indicated by the cash forecast and be ready to sell the investment prior to maturity if necessary. While this tends to introduce a degree of market risk, the entire time period is so short, usually up to 60 days, that the amount of interest-rate risk is actually very small. The institution often can obtain a slightly higher yield with little effect on the liquidity of the portfolio by investing for somewhat longer terms than indicated on the cash schedule. For example, if the cash schedule shows the excess funds to be available for 10 to 20 days, a term of 30 to 60 days may be acceptable.

Another technique that can effectively increase investment yields for health care institutions is consolidation of all available funds into one pool. Many medium and large institutions, particularly, operate their cash systems in a fragmented manner with collection points and disbursement points scattered throughout their organizational structures. By centralizing cash flows and cash management, as indicated by techniques discussed in Chapter 4, an institution can create a larger pool of investable funds. This gives the institution's financial manager greater bargaining power and the ability to invest more money in "round lots" in the money markets. In addition, the cash flow imbalances of various operating units in a large organization tend to average out and offset one another. The organization as a whole typically can operate on a smaller working cash balance than can the sum of its parts. The centralized liquidity pool usually can be invested for a longer duration than its separate components, which enhances the overall yield obtainable on the institution's invested funds.

Another frequent benefit of fund consolidation and a larger investment portfolio is a higher level of professionalism can be supported in the investment process. An internal professional funds manager or outside investment management firm using proper cash forecasting and cash management techniques may often bring about higher returns on available funds. The use of investment professionals also tends to reduce the institution's exposure to credit risk because they are familiar with debt issuers and instruments and can give constant attention to the market (see Chapter 7).

Timing of the Use of Funds

The financial manager must know the intended use of investment funds in order to manage maturities properly. Maturity and liquidity objectives should correspond with the purpose of the specific funds, whether it is to make an acquisition, repay bank debt, meet sinking fund obligations, pay taxes, or be used as contributions to an employee benefit plan.

Acquisitions, for example, can occur on fairly short notice and require relatively large amounts of funds. Long-term illiquid investment instruments may be inappropriate if the pool of invested funds will be used for acquisitions. Bank debt repayments are usually scheduled and known well in advance. Bank loans that are revolving credits, however, are subject to being repaid and reborrowed at the borrower's discretion. Therefore, repayments can occur virtually at any time the borrower has sufficient funds available. Bond sinking fund requirements also are known well in advance. Tax payments are due on certain scheduled dates, but the exact amounts are usually not known. Employee benefit plans, such as pensions and profit-sharing plans, are subject to contributions with fairly regular and defined payment dates, but the amounts may or may not be known.

Accordingly, the financial manager must plan the maturity dates of the investment instruments in the pool to coincide with the funding dates of the various uses of the funds. The manager must also obtain the highest possible market yield on the pool of funds and attempt to schedule the maturities so as to optimize the yield along the yield curve. The challenge occurs when the investment manager must seek the optimal trade-off between safety and liquidity of principal and rate of return on the investment.

Reinvestment Requirements

In order to operate an investment program properly, management must decide how to use the income earned on the pool of investments. Options include incorporating the income stream from investments with the other revenue streams of the institution or retaining the income stream in the investment pool where it is reinvested. This is a policy decision and its implications may be relatively important if investment income is substantial and becomes a large source of "budgeted" revenue. Another consideration involves funds invested in long-term instruments where the income is not used. The financial manager may have difficulty reinvesting the income proceeds in similar long-term investments when the amount of the income stream is small.

Income Taxes

The financial manager's choice of investment instruments should relate to whether or not the health care institution that owns the investments is subject to income taxes. The institution may be exempt from taxes, it may be a theoretical taxpayer with very low taxable income, or it may pay a ''normal rate'' of income taxes. If the institution is a normal-rate taxpayer, the financial manager should investigate carefully the use of tax-exempt instruments in its portfolio. On the other hand, if the institution is exempt from taxes or does not earn sufficient income to place it in a significant tax-paying category, the securities that generate tax-exempt income are of no advantage to the institution.

If the institution does, in fact, pay income taxes, the financial manager should determine the marginal tax rate, that is, the tax rate on the last dollar of income that the institution earns. Then, to determine the taxable equivalent yield of a tax-exempt investment instrument, the investment manager merely divides the tax-free return by the reciprocal of the institution's income tax rate. Assume, for example, a short-term, tax-exempt note yields five percent, and the institution's marginal tax rate is 35 percent. The investment manager wants to convert that yield to the equivalent yield on a taxable bond for comparison purposes. The formula is:

$$\frac{\text{Tax-Exempt Yield}}{(1 - \text{Marginal Tax Rate})} \text{ or } \frac{.05}{(1 - .35)} \text{ or } \frac{.05}{.65} = 7.69\%$$

The financial manager is now able to compare the 5 percent yield on a tax-exempt instrument with the yield on a fully taxable instrument of a similar maturity and credit quality to determine which offers the greatest return to the institution after taxes. In the above example, if taxable instruments of similar maturity and credit quality are available at a yield higher than 7.69 percent, the investment manager should seriously consider following the taxable route because it will result in a greater yield after taxes. This criterion is usually the only one that matters.

INVESTOR OR SPECULATOR?

Even in his prime, Babe Ruth struck out much more often than he hit home runs. The financial manager who seeks to hit home runs in managing the investment portfolio will undoubtedly find that the strikeout percentage is too high to be acceptable to senior management and the board of directors or trustees. Instead, the acceptable method of operation is to be a ''singles hitter'' with a very high batting average and probably never any home runs. After all, the investment manager who hits only singles has a certain degree of job security, while the investment manager who loses principal due to speculative investments may be frequently searching for a new job.

Professional institutional speculators in the investment profession are paid to risk capital in order to make considerable profits, or suffer losses, by participating continuously and aggressively in the marketplace. However, financial managers of health care institutions are, in effect, part-time investors who are involved in the investment markets only occasionally. The part-time investor is at a severe disadvantage against a speculative marketplace. Even full-time investment speculators strike out with a good degree of frequency. The part-time investor, however, never can be expected to hit a prodigious home run. On the other hand, the institution's senior management will not likely forget the strikeouts.

The cardinal rule for the small or part-time investor, therefore, is: *Be an investor and not a speculator.* When the financial manager encounters an apparently attractive instrument not normally included in the institution's portfolio, he or she should seek specific management approval of the instrument before executing the transaction. This requires thorough research and preparation of a recommendation by the financial manager for senior management to review so it can determine suitability of the instruments. If management supports the investment after examining all aspects of the recommendation, the financial manager cannot be criticized later for imprudence.

STANDARD OPERATING INVESTMENT PROCEDURES

The financial manager faces credit risk and market risk daily in the management of the investment portfolio. Additional risk from other quarters certainly is not welcome. However, insidious forms of risk exist within the financial manager's own office. These include fraud, malfeasance, and repeated errors. Fraud, of course, is the intentional misrepresentation of facts for the personal benefit of the financial manager or a staff member. Malfeasance, on the other hand, is the failure to conduct business affairs properly, resulting in poor performance. Repeated errors are usually the result of incompetence or poor training.

To avoid these forms of internal risk, the financial manager is well-advised to document fully all operating procedures relating to the management and operations of the investment process. Documentation of procedures is vital to the success of the internal control system. However, it is a time-consuming process, and too few firms actually get around to writing the procedure documents. A single instance of fraud or malfeasance, or repeated errors, however, can readily demonstrate the value of written procedure manuals and system documentation. The procedure documents should include

- a description of the operating structure
- job descriptions and statements of responsibility
- detailed descriptions of the processing of investment transactions, related funds transfers, and securities safekeeping requirements
- a description of all forms used to execute and confirm transactions
- a description of limitations on the authority of each employee
- a clear delineation of the duties and responsibilities of each employee involved in the investing process to report any perceived impropriety or errors

Portfolio Review

As part of the standard operating procedures in the management of an investment portfolio, senior management should review the portfolio periodically, at least quarterly or perhaps monthly, and attempt to discover any potential problems. There are several elements that should be examined by senior management, including an analysis of unrealized gains and losses and a trading analysis.

Unrealized Gains and Losses

An excellent way to discover potential problems in a portfolio is to analyze the gains and losses that exist on paper among the securities held in the portfolio. An accumulation of unrealized, or "paper potential losses," indicates, of course, the possibility that the institution must recognize these losses in its operating income statement even though the securities may not have been sold. Conversely, an increasing amount of unrealized gains in the portfolio may indicate success in the investing operations. Management may wish to realize these gains by selling the instruments and reinvesting the proceeds in other instruments with perhaps less future market price movement potential. Large gains today can signal speculative trading which, in the future, can result in large losses.

Trading Activity

An additional effective way to monitor the performance of the financial manager is to review the number of transactions taking place during a period of a week or a month. If new money is being added to the portfolio, or if there are significant numbers of maturing instruments, a higher than normal level of trading activity, particularly on the purchasing side, would be expected. On the other hand, if there is no unusual inflow of funds but a high level of buying and selling, the financial manager may be seeking speculative profit. The unusual activity in buying and selling should be cause to ask the financial manager to explain this action in light of the institution's investing policies.

SUMMARY

Initiation of an investment management program for a health care institution requires careful planning well in advance of making the first investment. The institution's tolerance for investment risk must be assessed, the sources and ultimate uses for the investment funds must be examined and documented, and a written set of investing objectives and guidelines must be drafted and approved by senior management.

The financial manager should not embark on an investment program until these elements have been crafted. Otherwise, the institution may incur undue risk to principal, either through unwise credit exposure or excessive exposure to the vagaries of interest rates; or it may unwittingly invest in maturities that do not suit the liquidity or income requirements of the institution.

A health care institution typically manages several forms of investment funds. These range from a pool of liquid investments used in the daily management of its receipts and disbursements streams, to proceeds of bonds awaiting investment in brick-and-mortar projects, to fixed asset replacement funds, to endowment funds, and to employee benefit and retirement funds. Each type of fund has its unique sources and purposes. The financial manager of these funds must recognize the uniqueness of each pool and invest accordingly.

Chapter 9

Investment Policy and Guidelines

INTRODUCTION

A written document containing a statement of investment policy and a set of guidelines are absolutely essential for the successful investing of a health care institution's funds. Individuals who invest their employer's funds function almost in a fiduciary capacity on behalf of the beneficiaries or owners of those funds. The beneficiaries or owners are represented by a board of directors or trustees. The written investment policy and guidelines document forms the bridge of understanding between the board and the person executing the investment program. In a very real sense, the document should be an agreement between the board and the financial manager. It should describe the parameters that the board wishes to maintain and authorize the financial manager to operate the investing program within these parameters.

POSSIBLE LEGAL RESTRICTIONS ON HOSPITAL INVESTMENTS

The nature of a hospital's charter (i.e., community hospital, for-profit hospital, sponsored by a municipal entity) may impose certain limitations on the investment of its funds. For example, if a hospital is a subentity of the state, county, or city government or another political subdivision, it may be faced with the same legal limitations on investments as the city, county, or state.

In this case, it is imperative that all investment activities, from the creation of comprehensive investment guidelines through daily investment activity, as well as auditing for adherence to investment restrictions, fall strictly within the guidelines of the legally approved investment requirements.

These requirements normally include restrictions as to the types of investments, such as U.S. Treasury securities, government agency securities, and bank obligations. They may also include more specific requirements as to the percentage of funds that may be invested in various types of instruments, as well as their credit quality. In any case, a thorough review of all legal limitations is warranted prior to the continuation of the entity's investment activities.

INVESTMENT POLICY

A statement of investment objectives should be the first element contained in a written investment policy. The objectives should be stated clearly and concisely and should set forth the order of priorities of multiple objectives.

Investors typically have three objectives in operating a liquidity portfolio: (1) preservation of capital, (2) maintenance of liquidity, and (3) yield. When defining an investment policy, it is important to state these goals and then place them into the order of preference. In a short-term liquidity portfolio, companies invariably opt first for safety and liquidity, with yield relegated to the third position. It is often unclear whether preservation of capital should predominate over maintenance of liquidity, or vice versa. The issue is not too important as long as both of these objectives take precedence over taking risks to obtain a higher yield.

A typical investment policy statement for a liquidity portfolio might read:

It shall be the policy of this organization to invest its temporarily surplus cash in short-term and intermediate-term, fixed-income instruments to earn a market rate of interest without assuming undue risk to principal. The primary objectives of making such investments shall be, in their order of importance, preservation of capital, maintenance of liquidity, and yield.

These two sentences clearly lay out the organization's objectives in priority order.

INVESTMENT GUIDELINES

Investing Authority and Responsibility

In creating an investing program, it is necessary for the board of directors or trustees of a health care institution to lodge continuing responsibility and authority for the conduct of the program with a particular person or a specific committee.

It is customary to establish an investment committee and to charge that committee with responsibility for managing all aspects of the investing program. The committee is normally composed of senior financial and administrative executives of the organization and may include representation from the board. The investment committee normally drafts the investment policy and guidelines and presents it to the board for its approval; the board then delegates authority and responsibility back to the investment committee.

The investment policy and guidelines should clearly identify the individuals responsible for managing the investing program and the limitations on their respective levels of authority. The responsibilities that are delegated should include the opening of accounts with brokers, dealers, and banks; the establishment of safekeeping accounts; arrangements for ongoing securities safekeeping; and authority to execute documents and agreements that may be necessary to implement the program. The guidelines should also provide for the investment committee to select and employ independent investment advisors, if deemed advisable.

The guidelines should clearly delegate operating authority and responsibility to perhaps three financial officers who will actually execute transactions. Commonly, such authority for entering into agreements is granted to the financial vice president or chief financial officer, the treasurer or controller, and the assistant treasurer or assistant controller. It may provide, for example, for the chief financial officer (CFO) to act together with either the treasurer or the assistant treasurer, but for neither of the latter two individuals to operate alone.

It is essential, however, that one qualified individual be available at all times to execute investment transactions. That authority should be strictly and clearly delegated within the limitations defined in the investing guidelines. Typically, such authority is granted to the CFO, who, in turn, may redelegate the authority to subordinates within the treasury function. It is a good idea to notify banks and securities dealers in writing of the scope of authority granted to each authorized person.

Reporting

Operating an investing program is one of those activities that can, if left to its own devices, create a nightmare of reports and paperwork. Therefore, it is essential that the investment committee, if not the board, specify the type and frequency of reports that it desires to see. Otherwise, the financial manager who actually executes the transactions may feel compelled to furnish too much information to too many people.

A practical approach is to establish tiers of reports, as in a pyramid. Proceeding upward in an organization, the volume of reported data gets smaller. The financial manager who executes the transactions maintains the bottom tier and must be responsible for total detail concerning these transactions. The financial manager also must be responsible for ensuring that appropriate information is fed to the accounting department to record the transactions properly in the company's books and records.

For the financial manager's own use, it is generally necessary to have a daily or weekly report of securities held and the instruments listed in maturity date order, with the earliest maturity listed first. The manager may also need to have the same information sorted (1) by issuer, to ensure that there is no undue concentration of funds invested in any one issuer; (2) by type of issuer, such as bank holding company, industrial company, finance company, domestic issuer, and foreign issuer by country; and (3) by safekeeping agent or other location where the securities are held in custody. All of this information is needed by the investment manager in order to conduct the day-to-day investing operations.

The level of detail that the financial manager needs is not necessary for his or her immediate superior, other senior management, and members of the investment committee. That is why the investment committee and the board should specify the level of detail and the frequency of reports they require. Typically, these reports contain a listing of all securities held, including maturity dates and yields, as well as a weighted-average yield of the entire portfolio. The reports are often produced on a monthly basis and may be accompanied by a schedule of transactions conducted since the last report.

By using microcomputers, data base management software, and electronic spreadsheets, much of the report data can be handled easily and sorted by different fields to produce the desired results. Microcomputer-based programs are also available to handle short-term investment portfolio reporting (see Table 9-1).

Provision for Review and Modification

Even the best-designed investing guidelines must be periodically reviewed and modified to accommodate changes in the organization's own situation and in conditions prevailing in the securities markets. The guidelines themselves should contain provision for their review and modification.

The investment committee should have the responsibility to initiate additional reviews and modifications and perhaps delegate the responsibility to the CFO to make recommendations for modification as conditions warrant. Many organizations require an annual review of the guidelines. The investment committee also often delegates authority to the CFO who may, in turn, redelegate it to the vice president of finance, so as to make the current investing program more restrictive than defined by the guidelines. For example, the guidelines may permit investment of funds in a particular area, such as obligations of foreign banks. It may come to

Table 9-1 Software Vendors of Fixed-Income Investment Management Programs

Source	Equipment	Services Offered
Technical Data Corporation 11 Farnsworth Street Boston, Mass. 02210 (617) 482-3341	Floppy disk for microcomputers (IBM, Apple)	Performs all investment management functions. Is relatively easy to use. Can perform several more tasks, including portfolio record keeping and analysis, if various modules (more floppy disks) are added at additional price.
Gifford Fong Associates 1600 Riviera Avenue Suite 285 Walnut Creek, Calif. 94596 (415) 932-1910	Floppy disk for microcomputers or terminal to mainframe	Various functions available with regard to reports and analysis.
Wismer Associates 22134 Sherman Way Canoga Park, Calif. 91303 (818) 884-5515	Floppy disk for microcomputers or time-share to mainframe	More comprehensive services. Includes investment, debt, cash management, and related accounting functions.

Note: The above information is not provided as an endorsement, but only as a list of firms that furnish these services.

the attention of the vice president of finance that the economy of a particular country has suddenly weakened. The vice president may choose to restrict investment in obligations of banks domiciled in that country as a temporary measure (see Appendix 9-A).

INVESTMENT INSTRUMENTS

The investing guidelines must describe the instruments in which the company may invest. The guidelines should further state that unless specifically permitted under the guidelines, all other investment instruments are specifically prohibited. This is a good reason to require an annual review of the guidelines, because new instruments may be introduced in which the company is prohibited from investing unless the guidelines specifically permit it. The guidelines should be modified to permit such new instruments, if and when warranted.

Investing guidelines typically permit the following kinds of fixed-income instruments:

- U.S. Treasury securities
- U.S. government agency obligations
- bank obligations
  - certificates of deposit (CDs)
  - fixed-time deposits
  - banker's acceptances (BAs)
  - Eurodollar deposits and CDs
  - Yankee CDs and BAs
- commercial paper
- loan participations
- corporate notes and bonds
- repurchase agreements involving permitted securities
- money market mutual funds

For institutions that generate income subject to income tax, certain tax-advantaged investments also are available with short- and intermediate-term maturities. These include:

- municipal notes and bonds
- variable rate demand notes
- adjustable rate preferred stocks

A detailed discussion of each type of investment instrument is given in Chapter 10. However, brief descriptions and generalizations about how each category may fit into the institution's investment guidelines are offered below.

U.S. Treasury Securities

The U.S. Treasury finances federal deficits by issuing debt instruments called Treasury bills, notes, and bonds. The credit standing of each is the same, and the sole difference is the length of maturity. Treasury bills are issued for periods of one year or less, notes are issued to mature from more than one year but less than 10 years, and bonds are issued to mature from more than 10 years up to 30 years. Because of the credit quality of U.S. Treasury securities, investors from all over the world with all forms of investment needs are attracted to these instruments. As a result, the market for these securities enjoys a depth that provides for substantial liquidity.

U.S. Government Agency Obligations

Various agencies of the U.S. government issue debt securities to finance various types of public operations. The agencies that issue the most popular securities, and probably issue the largest volume of government agency securities, are the Government National Mortgage Association (GNMA, commonly referred to as Ginnie Mae), Federal National Mortgage Association (FNMA, commonly known as Fannie Mae), Federal Home Loan Mortgage Corporation (FHLMC, commonly known as Freddie Mac), Federal Farm Credit Banks (FFCB), and Student Loan Marketing Association (called Sallie Mae).

With the exception of the Farm Credit Banks and Sallie Mae, debt instruments issued by the agencies are often in the form of certificates of participation in the ownership of pools of mortgage loans. While the certificates of participation themselves are not obligations of the United States government, the underlying mortgages that are owned by the pools usually are guaranteed by an agency of the government, such as the Federal Housing Administration (FHA) or the Veterans Administration (VA) in the case of Ginnie Mae.

Both FNMA and FFCB are privately owned organizations that perform specific functions in the public interest. They have strong ties to the federal government; however, there is only implied federal responsibility for the financial health of the institutions and protection of investors in the debt instruments issued by these institutions.

When an investor is considering a certificate of participation or a debt obligation of a federal agency, the investor should make a diligent investigation into the adequacy of the instrument for its purposes. In some cases, the cash flow emanating from certificates of participation is very good; the certificates provide current income and repayment of principal to the investor. At the same time, however, accounting considerations are complicated because of the combination of both principal and interest in the cash stream. Moreover, before making the investment, the investor in certificates of participation should understand the nature and long maturity of the mortgages or other debt contained in the investment pool.

For example, a GNMA pool of FHA mortgages may have an average maturity of 17 years, but in a period of declining interest rates, many of these loans in the pool may be prepaid by their respective homeowners/obligors as they refinance their home mortgages at lower interest rates. As a result, the investor in the GNMA pool will realize a more rapid return of capital and a smaller total income figure than had been anticipated. This situation may not fit into the investor's plans for providing cash flow over a budgeted period, or the stream of cash flow being heavier than anticipated may cause the investor problems in reinvesting the excess funds.

Bank Obligations

Bank obligations are evidenced either in the form of deposits in the bank or instruments that have been guaranteed or endorsed by a bank and offered in the secondary (resale) markets, such as banker's acceptances.

There are two basic forms of interest-bearing bank deposits: (1) negotiable time certificates of deposit, known as certificates of deposit (CDs) and (2) fixed-time deposits.

Certificates of Deposit

CDs maturing in a year or less are payable to the "bearer" and therefore, if properly held by a New York custodian, are liquid in the hands of the holder, if the CD is issued for at least $1 million or larger increments of $1 million. Many banks and investment dealers establish markets in CDs of the leading banks of the world and offer to buy and sell CDs for their own account. This is known as the secondary market. An investor can purchase a CD from one of these banks or dealers in the secondary market. Alternatively, an investor may initiate the bank deposit directly, in which case the CD is known as a primary certificate of deposit. If the investor chooses to sell the primary CD prior to maturity to recoup its cash funds early, it may sell it in the secondary market to another bank or dealer. A bank is not permitted to repurchase its own CDs; this would be tantamount to early redemption of the deposit and subject to penalties. It is critical to note that a secondary market exists only for CDs issued by better-known banks and savings and loan institutions. Also, the instrument itself must be in correct negotiable form and available for prompt delivery in New York. A CD issued by a bank located offshore—usually London, Cayman Islands, Nassau—is called a Eurodollar CD.

Fixed-Time Deposits

Fixed-time deposits are similar to negotiable CDs except that a bearer certificate is not issued. Fixed-time deposits often are issued domestically for amounts a bank wishes to accept. However, amounts of $1 million and more are usually required in London branches of major banks located in London, Nassau, the Bahamas, and the Cayman Islands. These are called Eurodollar time deposits since they are placed in offshore branches. Because these deposits are not represented by negotiable certificates, they are not liquid. Therefore, they often carry a higher yield to the investor than CDs.

Banker's Acceptances

A banker's acceptance (BA), is a draft drawn by a bank customer against the bank; the instrument is then "accepted" by the bank for the purpose of extending financing to the customer. The bank's acceptance of the draft means that the bank plans to sell the instrument in the secondary market, and it also indicates the bank's unconditional willingness to pay the instrument at maturity. A BA often originates as the result of a merchandise transaction (often in international trade) when an importer requires financing.

As an investment instrument, a BA of a particular bank carries higher credit quality than the same bank's CD, because it is not only a direct obligation of the bank, like a CD, but is also an obligation of an importer and usually collateralized by the merchandise itself. However, BAs are not deposits and do not carry the $100,000 insurance coverage of the Federal Deposit Insurance Corporation. Often BAs can be purchased at a few basis points' higher yield than a CD from the same issuing bank, because many investors are not as familiar with BAs as they are with CDs.

Commercial Paper

Commercial paper is an unsecured promissory note issued by a corporation. The issuer may be an industrial corporation, the holding company parent of a bank, or a finance company that is often a captive finance company owned by an industrial corporation. Commercial paper is issued to mature for periods ranging from one to 270 days. Corporate obligations issued for longer than 270 days must be registered with the Securities and Exchange Commission; therefore, companies needing short-term financing typically restrict the maturities of this debt to 270 days or less. Commercial paper is available to the investor through many major banks, who issue the bank's holding company commercial paper or act as agent for other issuers, and through investment bankers and dealers that may underwrite the commercial paper for their clients.

Loan Participations

A loan participation as an investment medium is attractive to an investor, because it presents an opportunity to invest in a corporate obligation that is similar to commercial paper but normally carries a somewhat higher yield. Banks have invested in loan participations of other banks for decades as a means of diversifying loan portfolios. However, the use of loan participations as an investment medium for corporations is a development that was new in the latter part of the 1980s.

The loan participation investment medium begins when a bank makes a loan to a corporation using standardized loan documentation. After the loan has been made, the bank seeks investors to buy "participations" in the loan. The investor in the loan participation has the obligation to investigate the credit of the obligor, as discussed in Chapter 8, since the bank selling the participation offers no guarantee or endorsement, implied or otherwise. Many companies that are obligors of these loans are rated by the commercial paper rating agencies, such as Standard & Poor's and Moody's Investors Service. In some cases the entire short-term debt of the issuer is rated, while in other cases only the commercial paper of the company is rated. However, if the short-term debt or commercial paper is unrated and an investor must rely on its own credit analysis, the investor must use extreme caution due to the difficulty in ascertaining the credit soundness of the investment. Loan participations may have maturities ranging from one day to several months. Occasionally the investor may be able to obtain a loan participation to suit its precise maturity requirements, particularly when large amounts (in excess of $1 million) are available for investment.

The investor should be aware that a loan participation is not a negotiable instrument and, therefore, it is not a liquid investment. It does not constitute good collateral for the investor that needs to pledge part or all of its investment portfolio to secure certain obligations. A loan participation, however, may be a good investment, perhaps from the standpoint of yield, subject to appropriate credit investigation by the investor.

Corporate Notes and Bonds

Corporate debt instruments with maturities longer than 270 days are considered notes if they mature within 10 years from their original issue date. The instruments are considered bonds if they mature more then 10 years from the original issue date. Notes with maturities up to approximately three to five years can play an important role in portfolios where the objective is to increase yield over what is available from strictly short-term portfolios, and where nearly perfect liquidity is not necessarily required. Because of their longer maturity than money market instruments, corporate notes are subject to greater market risk due to changes in interest rates. However, because the maturities may be only three to five years, the instruments are not subject to swings in market values as much as bonds.

Corporate bonds are often included in investment portfolios where the time horizon is much longer than liquidity portfolios. Bonds are seldom included in liquidity portfolios unless they will mature in one year or less.

Repurchase Agreements

A repurchase agreement is an investment transaction between an investor and a bank or securities dealer, in which the bank or dealer agrees to sell a particular instrument to the investor and simultaneously agrees to repurchase that instrument at a certain date in the future. The repurchase price is designed to give the investor a yield equivalent to a rate of interest that both parties negotiate at the time that the transaction is initiated.

On its face a repurchase agreement transaction, commonly referred to as a ''repo,'' appears to place full and complete ownership of the underlying securities in the hands of the investor. However, a number of incidents of default by dealers occurred in the 1980s, resulting in court rulings that brought the fundamental nature of repos into question. Those rulings implied very strongly that a repo was not, in fact, a purchase with a simultaneous agreement to repurchase the underlying securities, but rather a loan made by the investor to the dealer secured by the pledge of the underlying instruments as collateral to the loan. This viewpoint was bolstered by the fact that in the repo business the underlying instruments always have been called ''collateral.'' Investors who were previously authorized to invest in instruments subject to repurchase were now faced with making secured loans to banks and brokers.

Because repos traditionally have been a fundamental investment medium used by institutions to invest temporarily surplus funds overnight and for periods of up to a week or so, the court rulings seriously undermined the viability of the repo for this important purpose. It was not until Congress adopted the Government Securities Act of 1986 (as supplemented by regulations issued by the Treasury Department early in 1988) that the investment community regained its confidence in the repo as an investment medium. That act, however, addressed only part of the issue. It laid out very clearly the rights, duties, and obligations of the dealer in a repurchase agreement as long as the dealer is not a bank. However, it left hanging in the wind the relationship of the dealer if the dealer is a bank. This void continues to exist.

In order to fill the void, the investor should enter into an underlying written agreement with the dealer or bank as the counterparty to the transaction. The agreement should spell out very clearly the rights, duties, and obligations of each of the parties, particularly in the event of the default of one of them. The agreement should also state clearly that the transaction is intended to be a purchase/repurchase transaction and explicitly is not a loan by the investor to the dealer or bank. The agreement should further provide that in the event of the default of the dealer, the investor has the right to take possession of the collateral, if the investor does not already have such possession, and to dispose of that collateral in order to recover its investment.

The Public Securities Association, an organization of securities dealers, prepared a model agreement in 1986 that many banks and securities dealers have adopted and which they require their repo customers to execute (see Appendix 9-B). This model agreement appears to have been drafted in an even-handed manner and supports the interests of both counterparties in the repurchase transaction. Therefore, if the bank or securities dealer does not offer such an agreement, the investor should ask for the agreement from the bank or dealer.

Because of past history involving the collapse of some investment houses that were heavily involved in repos, an investor should be forewarned that the real risk in entering into a repo is the risk of failure of the counterparty (i.e., either a dealer or a bank) to perform under the agreement. Before the spate of failures in the 1980s, the investor typically looked only to the collateral for safety of principal. The investor, however, should recognize that the success of the transaction actually depends on the viability and willingness of the dealer or bank to repurchase the securities at maturity of the transaction. Accordingly, the investor must be diligent to investigate the credit standing of the counterparty to the transaction.

As an additional protection, the investor should specify to the dealer or bank those securities that are acceptable as underlying collateral. Investing guidelines should specify that such underlying collateral may consist of only investment instruments permitted by the guidelines. Moreover, the guidelines should require that in a repo transaction the value of the underlying collateral should exceed the amount of the investment transaction by some small increment, usually stated in terms of 102 percent of the amount of the transaction. This should be monitored by the investor on a regular basis to keep current on the market value of securities used as collateral. One final point to be considered is whether the collateral is set aside for the investor and does actually exist. This point is fully covered in the repurchase agreement section in Chapter 10.

Money Market Mutual Funds

A money market mutual fund is itself a portfolio of money market instruments. It provides a reasonable vehicle for investing modest sums where the amount may be too small to manage an effective investing program. For example, in managing amounts of less than $3 million, an investor is hard-pressed to meet the objectives of preservation of capital, maintenance of liquidity, and yield because money market instruments normally trade in $1 million pieces. The portfolio loses some diversification because of the large size required. If diversification is necessary, it forces the size of any one investment to be less than $1 million, and the company will sacrifice liquidity.

One solution to this dilemma is to invest in a money market mutual fund where the amounts invested may range from a minimum of perhaps $2,000 (in a retail-oriented money market fund) to many millions of dollars. Various kinds of money market mutual funds exist. The more popular funds cater to consumers and businesses with modest amounts available, and others serve institutional investors with large amounts of investable funds. Generally, both categories of funds operate similarly, with the institutional funds requiring larger minimum investments and often taking smaller management fees.

The mutual fund affords the investor the opportunity to meet its investment objectives of safety of principal, maintenance of liquidity, and yield provided that the investor carefully selects the particular fund. Fund selection should be based on a thorough review of the prospectus, with particular attention paid to the investment objectives of the fund, the experience and investment record of the fund's management, and the quality and liquidity of the investment instruments that the fund maintains in its portfolio.

The investor should inquire about redemption privileges and requirements of the fund and the fund's "pain threshhold" for withdrawals. Most money market mutual funds allow withdrawal virtually on demand either by check (which is actually a draft drawn against the fund) or by electronic funds transfer to the investor's bank account. Electronic funds transfer may be either a wire transfer for value the same day as the withdrawal, or it may be an automated clearing house transfer with settlement the following day. The pain threshhold refers to the size of withdrawal that the fund can tolerate without incurring its own liquidity problems. For some of the very large money market mutual funds, an immediate withdrawal of $50 million can be tolerated with little pain because of the fund's size. On the other hand, a small fund of less than $500 million may have a problem meeting a withdrawal request for $5 million. The size factor should be seriously considered when selecting a money market mutual fund.

Tax-Advantaged Securities

Tax-advantaged securities are attractive to organizations that pay income taxes. The stream of cash flow from tax-advantaged securities is generally fully, or at least partially, exempt from federal income taxes. Most health care institutions are either tax-exempt institutions or, in this day and age, not very heavy taxpayers. For this reason, tax-advantaged investments present little attraction to health care providers. Nevertheless, some discussion about these types of securities may be helpful to those who are sensitive about the sheltering of taxable income.

There are two basic forms of tax-advantaged investments: (1) tax-exempt securities issued by states and municipalities and (2) preferred stocks issued by corporations, in which a major portion of the dividends are excluded from taxable income when owned by corporate investors.

Municipal Bonds and Notes

With the passage of the Tax Reform Act of 1986 and subsequent technical adjustments of the act, the overall attractiveness of municipal bonds has declined somewhat. The ability of municipalities to issue tax-exempt bonds has also declined. However, many projects are financed in the capital markets that afford the taxable investor opportunities to buy intermediate- and long-term, tax-exempt municipal bonds. Also available are short-term, tax-exempt notes that municipalities and states issue in anticipation of receiving tax collections or other forms of revenue. Investors should be cautioned, however, that as a result of the 1986 Tax Reform Act, many purposes for which municipalities had previously borrowed funds were placed in a category where the interest payments relating to debt on the project would not be exempt from federal taxes. An investor interested in purchasing particular municipal instruments should make careful inquiry to determine whether the interest income is exempt from taxes under the current law.

Investment bankers have capitalized creatively on the tax-exempt nature of municipal and state debt by creating instruments that are attractive to taxable money market investors for short-term investments. This has been accomplished mainly by bringing to market long-term, tax-exempt municipal bonds that carry floating interest rates. These rates enable the price of the bond to remain stable as interest rates change, thereby protecting the investor from interest rate risk. Interest rates on these instruments, generically called "variable rate demand notes," or "low floaters," reflect their tax-exempt status.

Preferred Stock

It has long been a principle of federal taxation that when one corporation owns stock in another corporation, a substantial portion of the dividends paid on the stock should be excluded from taxable income of the owner of the stock. This is based on the premise that failure to exclude the dividends would constitute double taxation. A provision of the Tax Reform Act of 1986 reduced the amount of the exclusion to 70 percent, leaving 30 percent of intercorporate dividends fully taxable. The 70 percent excluded from taxes however, constitutes a significant tax advantage to the taxable corporate stockholder. In recent years, many creative investment bankers have built upon the concept of tax exclusion of intercorporate dividends. They offer short-term instruments that look like debt and operate like debt, but are nevertheless qualified as preferred stock bearing tax advantage benefits for the corporate holder. These instruments go under various names, but they are generically known as money market preferred stocks (MMPS).

SECURITIES SAFEKEEPING

The prudent investor will not take delivery of securities from a dealer or bank. There is the risk of loss due to theft or damage, and it is not practical to make physical delivery upon the maturity or sale of securities.

An investor will usually select a bank to safekeep securities. Most New York City banks function as securities custodians and clearance agents for investors all over the country, either directly or through a network of correspondent banks. The investor establishes a safekeeping account either with a New York bank or one of its correspondent banks, and delivery of securities is accomplished through the account.

When the investor purchases a security from a dealer, it instructs the dealer to deliver the instrument to the safekeeping bank against payment of the amount of money due on the purchase. This ensures that the purchased instrument will be delivered exactly as ordered, because the safekeeping agent should reject the delivery if there is any discrepancy. The funds remain in the investor's account until the security is delivered. If, for some reason, the selling dealer is unable to make delivery, the funds do not leave the investor's account. The safekeeping bank renders a periodic statement showing all of the securities in the safekeeping account. This is an excellent audit tool.

Another very significant advantage of the "delivery versus payment" (DVP) system is the investor's ability to deal with any securities dealer, wherever it may be located. The transaction is agreed to by the dealer and investor over the telephone, and the dealer then makes delivery in New York as described above. The need for wire transfers of funds is eliminated because the New York agent is able to charge the investor's account directly or charge its correspondent bank who charges the investor's account. This system eliminates the control problems associated with wire transfers and allows the investor to deal with more than just one or two investment dealers.

Bank safekeeping agents charge for their services. These charges may be based on the dollar value of the portfolio held by the agent or, more likey, on the basis of a price per transaction. Generally, all securities movements incur charges. Upon the purchase of an instrument, there is a charge for accepting it and lodging it in the inventory. At its sale prior to maturity, there is also a charge for delivering the instrument out. These charges apply whether the instrument requires physical delivery of a piece of paper or only book entry delivery.

An increasing number of securities are being made subject to book entry delivery, including virtually all U.S. government securities. Book entry delivery involves the maintenance of accounts with the Treasury. The Federal Reserve acts as the clearing agent for U.S. government securities and credits the delivery of securities to the investor by credit to the investor's account. Certain other securities also settle through the Federal Reserve account. Other clearing entities, such as Depository Trust Company, handle stocks and certain other corporate securities.

The importance of using an independent safekeeping agent cannot be over-emphasized. This was demonstrated during the early 1980s when many securities dealers failed. Investors who had taken delivery of securities used as collateral for repurchase agreements or other securities purchased outright from these dealers generally did not lose any of their funds. The investors who were burned had left their securities in the custody of the dealers. Auditors discovered that many of these dealers, through either sloppy bookkeeping or outright fraud, had sold and resold securities owned by one investor to other investors simultaneously. This situation created multiple claims on the same securities and was common to virtually all of the failed investment banking houses. It makes the best case for taking possession of one's own securities through the use of a safekeeping agent.

CURRENCY DENOMINATION

The institution's investing guidelines should clearly stipulate that securities must be denominated in U.S. dollars or denominated in currencies other than U.S. dollars only with certain limitations. This is an important distinction because investments in securities denominated in foreign currencies introduce a new element of foreign exchange risk. Unless an organization is prepared to speculate on changes in the rate of exchange between the U.S. dollar and other currencies, the guidelines should stipulate that all investments be denominated in U.S. dollars.

Some attractive investments do exist in other currencies, particularly Canadian dollars, British pounds sterling, German deutsche marks, Swiss francs, and Japanese yen. The health care institution may desire to purchase securities denominated in a foreign currency but it must be willing to accept the risk. It is also important that the amount of the investment, including principal and total interest due at maturity, is hedged with a foreign exchange forward or futures contract. Even though the security is denominated in a foreign currency, this will help ensure that the ultimate proceeds will be converted into a known quantity of U.S. dollars at maturity. The institution's guidelines should specifically require that all investments be made in U.S. dollars or be fully hedged into U.S. dollars if made in foreign currencies.

DIVERSIFICATION

Several dimensions of diversification should be built into the investing guidelines. Occasionally differences in yields available in the marketplace tend to encourage an investor to concentrate funds in one issuer or geographical territory. Diversification requirements in the investing guidelines are necessary to prevent the risks associated with either type of concentration.

Diversification by Type of Issuer

There are four basic forms of debt issuers: (1) governments, (2) banks, (3) industrial companies, and (4) finance companies. Presumably the banking industry could become severely stressed, with all banks as a group suffering in credit quality. This condition probably would affect other companies functioning in the economy, but it can be assumed that the other companies would not be as directly affected as the banks. Industrial companies as a group could be impacted by a recession; the finance companies that support their sales would not be as affected, because their portfolios of receivables are very broadly based. From these examples it is apparent that diversification by type of issuer makes sense. However, some companies erroneously believe in diversification by type of instrument. The instruments are irrelevant if they are all guaranteed by the same type of issuer.

Diversification by Geography

Most investors attempt to maintain a geographical dimension to their portfolio diversification. Many factors influence the world's economies, including economic mismanagement and differentials in interest rates between countries. Investments of health care institutions in debt instruments issued by both U.S. and foreign companies and banks should not present a problem. However, quite often debt instruments issued by a particular bank or company will offer both higher yields and very good credit quality. The institution should maintain care to prevent its portfolio from being dominated by instruments of one country or one industry, or of several countries that are closely related to each other. Events could occur within a country or industry that would adversely affect investments. Civil war, severe inflation resulting in economic chaos, a natural disaster, or sudden political instability can wreak havoc on an institution's portfolio that is not well-diversified. Investing guidelines should place a dollar or percentage limit, or both, on the amount of a portfolio that may be invested in the securities of any one country, region or industry.

LIMITATIONS ON MATURITY

Because the short-term investment portfolio has primary objectives of preservation of capital and maintenance of liquidity, the investing guidelines should contain a statement that limits the maturity of the portfolio to avoid interest rate risk. The limitations can relate to both the weighted average maturity of the entire portfolio and maximum limitations on maturity of any one instrument. For example, the guidelines might restrict the maturity of any one instrument to "not more than five years from the date of purchase,'' and the weighted average maturity of the entire portfolio may be no more than three years.

Two dimensions of maturity limitation working together can prevent the occurrence of several interesting, but potentially detrimental, activities. For example, if the guidelines address only the weighted average maturity of the portfolio, the financial manager may use a "barbell" strategy. Half of the portfolio could be invested in very short-term instruments, such as 30- and 60-day maturities and the other half in relatively long-term instruments maturing in 8 to 10 years. Mathematically, the weighted average maturity of the portfolio could be within the 3-year limitation. Clearly, however, the actual deployment of funds does not meet the safety of principal and liquidity goals that management had set due to the inclusion of the longer-term securities.

On the other hand, simply limiting the length of maturity of any one instrument may not be adequate. If the guidelines restrict the maturity of any one instrument, for example, to two years, the financial manager may feel at liberty to invest virtually all of the portfolio in instruments maturing in about two years. This, too, could work in opposition to the stated objectives of preservation of capital and maintenance of liquidity.

SUMMARY

A written investing policy and set of guidelines are essential elements in the successful investing program of a health care institution. The document is a contract between the board of directors or trustees and the financial manager. The policy statement describes the parameters within which the financial manager shall perform the tasks of investment management. The guidelines can be simple or complex, they can be restrictive or liberal, and they can cover a liquidity portfolio or dedicated proceeds of a bond issue or endowment funds within a single document or in several documents.

A well-structured investment policy and guidelines document clearly places authority and responsibility for management of the investing program and enables modifications to the guidelines within reasonable bounds. The guidelines further set forth the requirements for reporting the investment activities and portfolio condition and clearly describe the types of securities that are acceptable for investment. They also address the operational issues of executing and verifying transactions and of holding the investment instruments in safekeeping for maintenance of appropriate security.

The investing policy and guidelines should be broad enough to accomplish the goals and objectives of the owner of the investment pool. They should not restrict the financial manager from responding with speed and decisiveness to an attractive investment opportunity. Investment markets are telephone markets, and successful investors must be able to make decisions in a matter of moments. In the absence of clear investing guidelines, the financial manager is unable to respond in a timely manner, particularly when presented with a somewhat unorthodox investment instrument that otherwise may seem attractive.

Sample Investment Policy and Guidelines

I. *Investment Committee*
Within the spectrum of activities of this organization, it is necessary to provide a framework for the regular and continuous management of investment funds. Because there is currently no formal investment committee, the directors will assume this responsibility.

II. *Investment Policy*
The policy shall be to invest excess cash in short-term and intermediate-term fixed-income instruments earning a market rate of interest without assuming undue risk to principal. The primary objectives of such investments in order of importance shall be preservation of capital, maintenance of liquidity, and yield.

III. *Investment Responsibility*
Investments are the responsibility of the vice president of finance. This responsibility includes the authority to select an investment adviser, open accounts with brokers, and establish safekeeping accounts or other arrangements for the custody of securities and to execute such documents as may be necessary.

Those authorized to execute transactions include: (1) The vice president of finance, (2) the director of accounting, and (3) the cash manager. The vice president of finance shall ensure that one qualified individual is always available to execute the organization's investments.

IV. *Reporting*
The treasurer shall be responsible for reporting the status of investments to the directors on a quarterly basis. Those reports should include a complete listing of securities held, and this report must be verified (audited) by parties either inside or outside this organization who have no connection with the investment activities.

Source: © The Alan G. Seidner Company, Pasadena, California.

V. *Investments*

A. *Obligations of the U.S. Government or Its Agencies, Specifically:*
U.S. Treasury, Federal Home Loan Bank, Federal Home Loan Mortgage Corporation, Federal National Mortgage Association, Federal Farm Credit Bank, Student Loan Marketing Association, and Government National Mortgage Association. Note: When-issued items must be paid for *before* they may be sold.

B. *Banks—Domestic*
The organization may invest in negotiable CDs (including Eurodollar denominated deposits), Eurodollar time deposits (with branches domiciled in Cayman, Nassau, or London), and banker's acceptances (BAs) of the 50 largest U.S. banks ranked by deposit size. Also acceptable are deposits and negotiable CDs issued by the 25 largest thrift institutions (savings and loans and savings banks), according to deposits. However, the issuing institution must have a Keefe's BankWatch rating of at least B/C. For thrift institutions, those whose parent has long-term debt rated AA by Moody's or Standard & Poor's are acceptable. Exceptions may be local banks or thrift institutions that have lent the corporation money or that would be appropriate to use for some other reason. (These banks and institutions should be listed, along with the maximum dollar amount of exposure allowable for each.)

C. *Banks—Foreign*
The organization may invest in negotiable CDs (including Eurodollar denominated deposits), Eurodollar time deposits (with branches domiciled in Cayman, Nassau, or London), and BAs of the 50 largest foreign banks ranked by deposit size. However, the issuing institution must have a Keefe's BankWatch rating of at least II/III in each category of rating analysis.

Limitations

(1) The organization's aggregate investments with foreign entities shall not exceed 50 percent of total investments, and

(2) No more than 10 percent of total investments shall be exposed to any one foreign country's obligations, or $X million per country, whichever is greater.

D. *Commercial Paper*
All commercial paper must be prime quality by both Standard & Poor's and Moody's standards (i.e., A1 by Standard & Poor's and P1 by Moody's).

E. *Corporate Notes and Bonds*
Instruments of this type are acceptable if rated at least A by both Moody's and Standard & Poor's credit rating services.

F. *Municipal*
Municipal or tax-exempt instruments (this category is suitable only if your organization pays federal income tax).

Only tax-exempt notes with a Moody's Investment Grade One rating or bonds that are rated by both Moody's Investor Service, Inc. and Standard & Poor's as A may be purchased. Not more than 30 percent of the total issue size should be purchased and issues of at least $20 million in total size must be selected.

G. *Repurchase Agreements*
Repurchase agreements (repos) are acceptable using any of the securities listed above, as long as such instruments are negotiable/marketable and do not exceed other limitations as to exposure per issuer. The firm with whom the repo is executed must be a credit acceptable bank or a primary dealer (reporting to the Federal Reserve). Collateral must equal 102 percent of the dollars invested, and the collateral must be delivered to the organization's safekeeping bank and priced to market weekly (to ensure correct collateral value coverage) if the repo has longer than a seven-day maturity.

H. *Money Market Funds*
Acceptable funds are those whose asset size place them among the 30 largest according to the Donoghue Report and that are rated at least "M2" by Standard & Poor's Corporation.

I. *Safekeeping Accounts*
Securities purchased should be delivered against payment and held in a custodian safekeeping account at the organization's safekeeping bank. An exception shall be (1) repos made with approved (see above) banks or dealers for one week or less and (2) Eurodollar time deposits, for which no instruments are created. This safekeeping account will be audited quarterly by an entity that is not related to the investment function of this organization and the results of that audit shall be provided to the vice president of finance.

J. *Denomination*
All investments shall be in United States dollars.

K. *Diversification of Investments*
In no case shall more than 30 percent of the total portfolio be invested in obligations of any particular issuer except the U.S. Treasury.

VI. *Maturity Limitations*
Overall, maximum weighted average maturity shall be three years. However, on "put" instruments, which may be redeemed (or put) at par, the put date shall be considered to be the maturity date.

VII. *Review and/or Modification*
The vice president of finance shall be responsible for reviewing and modifying investment guidelines as conditions warrant, subject to approval by the directors at least on an annual basis. However, the vice president of finance may at any time further restrict the items approved for purchase when appropriate.

Master Repurchase Agreement

Dated as of ‗‗‗‗‗‗ ‗, ‗‗‗‗

Between:

‗‗‗‗‗‗‗‗‗‗‗‗‗‗‗‗‗‗‗‗‗

and

‗‗‗‗‗‗‗‗‗‗‗‗‗‗‗‗‗‗‗‗‗

1. **Applicability**

   From time to time the parties hereto may enter into transactions in which one party ("Seller") agrees to transfer to the other ("Buyer") securities or financial instruments ("Securities") against the transfer of funds by Buyer, with a simultaneous agreement by Buyer to transfer to Seller such Securities at a date certain or on demand, against the transfer of funds by Seller. Each such transaction shall be referred to herein as a "Transaction" and shall be governed by this Agreement, including any supplemental terms or conditions contained in Annex I hereto, unless otherwise agreed in writing.

2. **Definitions**

   (a) "Act of Insolvency," with respect to any party, (i) the commencement by such party as debtor of any case or proceeding under any bankruptcy, insolvency, reorganization, liquidation, dissolution, or similar law, or such party seeking the appointment of a receiver, trustee, custodian, or similar official for such party or any substantial part of its property, or (ii) the commencement of any such case or proceeding against such party, or another seeking such an appointment, or the filing against a party of an application for a protective decree under the provisions of the Securities Investor Protection Act of 1970, which (A) is consented to or not timely

---

Source: Public Securities Association, New York. Reprinted with permission.

contested by such party, (B) results in the entry of an order for relief, such an appointment, the issuance of such a protective decree, or the entry of an order having a similar effect, or (C) is not dismissed within 15 days, (iii) the making by a party of a general assignment for the benefit of creditors, or (iv) the admission in writing by a party of such party's inability to pay such party's debts as they become due;

(b) "Additional Purchased Securities," securities provided by Seller to Buyer pursuant to Paragraph 4(a) hereof;

(c) "Buyer's Margin Amount," with respect to any Transaction as of any date, the amount obtained by application of a percentage (which may be equal to the percentage that is agreed to as the Seller's Margin Amount under subparagraph (q) of this Paragraph), agreed to by Buyer and Seller prior to entering into the Transaction, to the Repurchase Price for such Transaction as of such date;

(d) "Confirmation," the meaning specified in Paragraph 3(b) hereof;

(e) "Income," with respect to any Security at any time, any principal thereof then payable and all interest, dividends or other distributions thereon;

(f) "Margin Deficit," the meaning specified in Paragraph 4(a) hereof;

(g) "Margin Excess," the meaning specified in Paragraph 4(b) hereof;

(h) "Market Value," with respect to any Securities as of any date, the price for such Securities on such date obtained from a generally recognized source agreed to by the parties or the most recent closing bid quotation from such a source, plus accrued income to the extent not included therein (other than any income credited or transferred to, or applied to the obligations of, Seller pursuant to Paragraph 5 hereof) as of such date (unless contrary to market practice for such Securities);

(i) "Price Differential," with respect to any Transaction hereunder as of any date, the aggregate amount obtained by daily application of the Pricing Rate for such Transaction to the Purchase Price for such transaction on a 360-day-per-year basis for the actual number of days during the period commencing on (and including) the Purchase Date for such Transaction and ending on (but excluding) the date of determination (reduced by any amount of such Price Differential previously paid by Seller to Buyer with respect to such Transaction);

(j) "Pricing Rate," the per annum percentage rate for determination of the Price Differential;

(k) "Prime Rate," the prime rate of U.S. money center commercial banks as published in *The Wall Street Journal;*

(l) "Purchase Date," the date on which Purchased Securities are transferred by Seller to Buyer;

(m) "Purchase Price," (i) on the Purchase Date, the price at which Purchased Securities are transferred by Seller to Buyer, and (ii) thereafter, such price increased by the amount of any cash transferred by Buyer to Seller pursuant to Paragraph 4(b) hereof and decreased by the amount of any cash transferred by Seller to Buyer pursuant to Paragraph 4(a) hereof or applied to reduce Seller's obligations under clause (ii) of Paragraph 5 hereof;

(n) "Purchased Securities," the Securities transferred by Seller to Buyer in a Transaction hereunder, and any Securities substituted therefor in accordance with Paragraph 9 hereof. The term "Purchased Securities" with respect to any Transaction at any time also shall include Additional Purchased Securities delivered pursuant to Paragraph 4(a) and shall exclude Securities returned pursuant to Paragraph 4(b);

(o) "Repurchase Date," the date on which Seller is to repurchase the Purchased Securities from Buyer, including any date determined by application of the provisions of Paragraphs 3(c) or 11 hereof;

(p) "Repurchase Price," the price at which Purchased Securities are to be transferred from Buyer to Seller upon termination of a Transaction, which will be determined in each case (including transactions terminable upon demand) as the sum of the Purchase Price and the Price Differential as of the date of such determination, increased by any amount determined by the application of the provisions of Paragraph 11 hereof;

(q) "Seller's Margin Amount," with respect to any Transaction as of any date, the amount obtained by application of a percentage (which may be equal to the percentage that is agreed to as the Buyer's Margin Amount under subparagraph (c) of this Paragraph), agreed to by Buyer and Seller prior to entering into the Transaction, to the Repurchase Price for such Transaction as of such date.

3. **Initiation; Confirmation; Termination**

(a) An agreement to enter into a Transaction may be made orally or in writing at the initiation of either Buyer or Seller. On the Purchase Date for the Transaction, the Purchased Securities shall be transferred to Buyer or its agent against the transfer of the Purchase Price to an account of Seller.

(b) Upon agreeing to enter into a Transaction hereunder, Buyer or Seller (or both), as shall be agreed, shall promptly deliver to the other party a written confirmation of each Transaction (a "Confirmation"). The Confirmation shall describe the Purchased Securities (including CUSIP number, if any), identify Buyer and Seller and set forth (i) the Purchase Date, (ii) the Purchase Price, (iii) the Repurchase Date, unless the Transaction is to be terminable on demand, (iv) the Pricing Rate or

Repurchase Price applicable to the Transaction, and (v) any additional terms or conditions of the Transaction not inconsistent with this Agreement. The Confirmation, together with this Agreement, shall constitute conclusive evidence of the terms agreed between Buyer and Seller with respect to the Transaction to which the Confirmation relates, unless with respect to the Confirmation specific objection is made promptly after receipt thereof. In the event of any conflict between the terms of such Confirmation and this Agreement, this Agreement shall prevail.

(c) In the case of Transactions terminable upon demand, such demand shall be made by Buyer or Seller, no later than such time as is customary in accordance with market practice, by telephone or otherwise on or prior to the business day on which such termination will be effective. On the date specified in such demand, or on the date fixed for termination in the case of Transactions having a fixed term, termination of the Transaction will be effected by transfer to Seller or its agent of the Purchased Securities and any income in respect thereof received by Buyer (and not previously credited or transferred to, or applied to the obligations of, Seller pursuant to paragraph 5 hereof) against the transfer of the Repurchase Price to an account of Buyer.

4. Margin Maintenance

(a) If at any time the aggregate Market Value of all Purchased Securities subject to all Transactions in which a particular party hereto is acting as Buyer is less than the aggregate Buyer's Margin Amount for all such Transactions (a "Margin Deficit"), then Buyer may by notice to Seller require Seller in such Transactions, at Seller's option, to transfer to Buyer cash or additional Securities reasonably acceptable to Buyer ("Additional Purchased Securities"), so that the cash and aggregate Market Value of the Purchased Securities, including any such Additional Purchased Securities, will thereupon equal or exceed such aggregate Buyer's Margin Amount (decreased by the amount of any Margin Deficit as of such date arising from any Transactions in which such Buyer is acting as Seller).

(b) If at any time the aggregate Market Value of all Purchased Securities subject to all Transactions in which a particular party hereto is acting as Seller exceeds the aggregate Seller's Margin Amount for all such Transactions at such time (a "Margin Excess"), then Seller may by notice to Buyer require Buyer in such Transactions, at Buyer's option, to transfer cash or Purchased Securities to Seller, so that the aggregate Market Value of the Purchased Securities, after deduction of any such cash or any Purchased Securities so transferred, will thereupon not exceed such aggregate Seller's Margin Amount (increased by the amount of any

Margin Excess as of such date arising from any Transactions in which such Seller is acting as Buyer).

(c) Any cash transferred pursuant to this Paragraph shall be attributed to such Transactions as shall be agreed upon by Buyer and Seller.

(d) Seller and Buyer may agree, with respect to any or all Transactions hereunder, that the respective rights of Buyer or Seller (or both) under subparagraphs (a) and (b) of this Paragraph may be exercised only where a Margin Deficit or Margin Excess exceeds a specified dollar amount or a specified percentage of the Repurchase Prices for such Transactions (which amount or percentage shall be agreed to by Buyer and Seller prior to entering into any such Transactions).

(e) Seller and buyer may agree, with respect to any or all Transactions hereunder, that the respective rights of Buyer and Seller under subparagraphs (a) and (b) of this Paragraph to require the elimination of a Margin Deficit or a Margin Excess, as the case may be, may be exercised whenever such a Margin Deficit or Margin Excess exists with respect to any single Transaction hereunder (calculated without regard to any other Transaction outstanding under this Agreement).

5. **Income Payments**

Where a particular Transaction's term extends over an Income payment date on the Securities subject to that Transaction, Buyer shall, as the parties may agree with respect to such Transaction (or, in the absence of any agreement, as Buyer shall reasonably determine in its discretion), on the date such Income is payable either (i) transfer to or credit to the account of Seller an amount equal to such Income payment or payments with respect to any Purchased Securities subject to such Transaction or (ii) apply the Income payment or payments to reduce the amount to be transferred to Buyer by Seller upon termination of the Transaction. Buyer shall not be obligated to take any action pursuant to the preceding sentence to the extent that such action would result in the creation of a Margin Deficit, unless prior thereto or simultaneously therewith Seller transfers to Buyer cash or Additional Purchased Securities sufficient to eliminate such Margin Deficit.

6. **Security Interest**

Although the parties intend that all Transactions hereunder be sales and purchases and not loans, in the event any such Transactions are deemed to be loans, Seller shall be deemed to have pledged to Buyer as security for the performance by Seller of its obligations under each such Transaction, and shall be deemed to have granted to Buyer a security interest in, all of the Purchased Securities with respect to all Transactions hereunder and all proceeds thereof.

7. **Payment and Transfer**
Unless otherwise mutually agreed, all transfers of funds hereunder shall be in immediately available funds. All Securities transferred by one party hereto to the other party (i) shall be in suitable form for transfer or shall be accompanied by duly executed instruments of transfer or assignment in blank and such other documentation as the party receiving possession may reasonably request, (ii) shall be transferred on the book-entry system of a Federal Reserve Bank, or (iii) shall be transferred by any other method mutually acceptable to Seller and Buyer. As used herein with respect to Securities, ''transfer'' is intended to have the same meaning as when used in Section 8-313 of the New York Uniform Commercial Code.

8. **Segregation of Purchased Securities**
All Purchased Securities in the possession of Seller shall be segregated from other securities in its possession and shall be identified as subject to this Agreement. Segregation may be accomplished by appropriate identification on the books and records of the holder, including a financial intermediary or a clearing corporation. Title to all Purchased Securities shall pass to Buyer and, unless otherwise agreed by Buyer and Seller, nothing in this Agreement shall preclude Buyer from engaging in repurchase transactions with the Purchased Securities or otherwise pledging or hypothecating the Purchased Securities, but no such transaction shall relieve Buyer of its obligations to transfer Purchased Securities to Seller pursuant to Paragraphs 3, 4, or 11 hereof, or of Buyer's obligation to credit or pay Income to, or apply Income to the obligations of, Seller pursuant to Paragraph 5 hereof.

9. **Substitution**
Seller may, subject to agreement with and acceptance by Buyer, substitute other Securities for any purchased Securities. Such substitution shall be made by transfer to the Buyer of such other Securities against simultaneous transfer to the Seller of such Purchased Securities. After substitution, the substituted Securities shall be deemed to be Purchased Securities.

10. **Representations**
Each of Buyer and Seller represents and warrants to the other that (i) it is duly authorized to execute and deliver this Agreement, to enter into the Transactions contemplated hereunder, and to perform its obligations hereunder and has taken all necessary action to authorize such execution, delivery, and performance, (ii) it will engage in such Transactions as principal (or, if agreed in writing in advance of any Transaction by the other party hereto, as agent for a disclosed principal), (iii) the person signing this Agreement on its behalf is duly authorized to do so on its behalf (or on behalf of any such disclosed

principal), (iv) it has obtained all authorizations of any governmental body required in connection with this Agreement and the Transactions hereunder and such authorizations are in full force and effect, and (v) the execution, delivery, and performance of this Agreement and the Transactions hereunder will not violate any law, ordinance, charter, by-law, or rule applicable to it or any agreement by which it is bound or by which any of its assets are affected. On the Purchase Date for any Transaction Buyer and Seller shall each be deemed to repeat all the foregoing representations made by it.

11. **Events of Default**

In the event that (i) Seller fails to repurchase or Buyer fails to transfer Purchased Securities upon the applicable Repurchase Date, (ii) Seller or Buyer fails, after one business day's notice, to comply with Paragraph 4 hereof, (iii) Buyer fails to comply with Paragraph 5 hereof, (iv) an Act of Insolvency occurs with respect to Seller or Buyer, (v) any representation made by Seller or Buyer shall have been incorrect or untrue in any material respect when made or repeated or deemed to have been made or repeated, or (vi) Seller or Buyer shall admit to the other its inability to, or its intention not to, perform any of its obligations hereunder (each an "Event of Default"):

(a)   At the option of the nondefaulting party, exercised by written notice to the defaulting party (which option shall be deemed to have been exercised, even if no notice is given, immediately upon the occurrence of an Act of Insolvency), the Repurchase Date for each Transaction hereunder shall be deemed immediately to occur.

(b)   In all Transactions in which the defaulting party is acting as Seller, if the nondefaulting party exercises or is deemed to have exercised the option referred to in subparagraph (a) of this paragraph, (i) the defaulting party's obligations hereunder to repurchase all Purchased Securities in such Transactions shall thereupon become immediately due and payable, (ii) to the extent permitted by applicable law, the Repurchase Price with respect to each such Transaction shall be increased by the aggregate amount obtained by daily application of (x) the greater of the Pricing Rate for such Transaction or the Prime Rate to (y) the Repurchase Price for such Transaction as of the Repurchase Date as determined pursuant to subparagraph (a) of this Paragraph (decreased as of any day by (A) any amounts retained by the nondefaulting party with respect to such Repurchase Price pursuant to clause (iii) of this subparagraph, (B) any proceeds from the sale of Purchased Securities pursuant to subparagraph (d)(i) of this paragraph, and (C) any amounts credited to the account of the defaulting party pursuant to subparagraph (e) of this paragraph) on a 360-day-per-year basis for the actual number of days during the period from the date of the Event of Default giving rise to such option to the date of payment of the Repurchase Price as so increased, (iii) all Income paid after such exercise or deemed exercise shall be retained by the non-defaulting party and applied to the aggregate unpaid Repurchase Prices owed by the defaulting party, and (iv) the defaulting party shall immediately deliver to the nondefaulting party any Purchased Securities subject to such Transactions then in the defaulting party's possession.

(c) In all Transactions in which the defaulting party is acting as Buyer, upon tender by the nondefaulting Party of payment of the aggregate Repurchase Prices for all such Transactions, the defaulting party's right, title, and interest in all Purchased Securities subject to such Transaction shall be deemed transferred to the nondefaulting party, and the defaulting party shall deliver all such Purchased Securities to the nondefaulting party.

(d) After one business day's notice to the defaulting party (which notice need not be given if an Act of Insolvency shall have occurred, and which may be the notice given under subparagraph (a) of this Paragraph or the notice referred to in clause (ii) of the first sentence of this Paragraph), the nondefaulting party may:

    (i) as to Transactions in which the defaulting party is acting as Seller, (A) immediately sell, in a recognized market at such price or prices as the nondefaulting party may reasonably deem satisfactory, any or all Purchased Securities subject to such Transactions and apply the proceeds thereof to the aggregate unpaid Repurchase Prices and any other amounts owing by the defaulting party hereunder or (B) in its sole discretion elect, in lieu of selling all or a portion of such Purchased Securities, to give the defaulting party credit for such Purchased Securities in an amount equal to the price therefor on such date, obtained from a generally recognized source or the most recent closing bid quotation from such a source, against the aggregate unpaid Repurchase Prices and any other amounts owing by the defaulting party hereunder; and

    (ii) as to Transactions in which the defaulting party is acting as Buyer, (A) purchase securities ("Replacement Securities") of the same class and amount as any Purchased Securities that are not delivered by the defaulting party to the nondefaulting party as required hereunder or (B) in its sole discretion elect, in lieu of purchasing Replacement Securities, to be deemed to have purchased Replacement Securities at the price therefor on such date, obtained from a generally recognized source or the most recent closing bid quotation from such a source.

(e) As to Transactions in which the defaulting party is acting as Buyer, the defaulting party shall be liable to the nondefaulting party (i) with respect to Purchased Securities (other than Additional Purchased Securities), for any excess of the price paid (or deemed paid) by the nondefaulting party for Replacement Securities therefor over the Repurchase Price for such Purchased Securities and (ii) with respect to Additional Purchased Securities, for the price paid (or deemed paid) by the nondefaulting party for the Replacement Securities therefor. In addition, the defaulting party shall be liable to the nondefaulting party for interest on such remaining liability with respect to each such purchase (or deemed purchase) of Replacement Securities from the date of such purchase (or deemed purchase) until paid in full by Buyer. Such interest shall be at a rate equal to the greater of the Pricing Rate for such Transaction or the Prime Rate.

(f)   For purposes of this Paragraph 11, the Repurchase Price for each Transaction hereunder in respect of which the defaulting party is acting as Buyer shall not increase above the amount of such Repurchase price for such Transaction determined as of the date of the exercise or deemed exercise by the nondefaulting party of its option under subparagraph (a) of this paragraph.

(g)   The defaulting party shall be liable to the nondefaulting party for the amount of all reasonable legal or other expenses incurred by the nondefaulting party in connection with or as a consequence of an Event of Default, together with interest thereon at a rate equal to the greater of the Pricing Rate for the relevant Transaction or the Prime Rate.

(h)   The nondefaulting party shall have, in addition to its rights hereunder, any rights otherwise available to it under any other agreement or applicable law.

12. **Single Agreement**

Buyer and Seller acknowledge that, and have entered hereinto and will enter into each Transaction hereunder in consideration of and in reliance upon the fact that, all Transactions hereunder constitute a single business and contractual relationship and have been made in consideration of each other. Accordingly, each of Buyer and Seller agrees (i) to perform all of its obligations in respect of each Transaction hereunder, and that a default in the performance of any such obligations shall constitute a default by it in respect of all Transactions hereunder, (ii) that each of them shall be entitled to set off claims and apply property held by them in respect of any Transaction against obligations owing to them in respect of any other Transactions hereunder, and (iii) that payments, deliveries, and other transfers made by either of them in respect of any Transaction shall be deemed to have been made in consideration of payments, deliveries, and other Transactions hereunder, and the obligations to make any such payments, deliveries, and other transfers may be applied against each other and netted.

13. Notices and Other Communications

Unless another address is specified in writing by the respective party to whom any notice or other communication is to be given hereunder, all such notices or communications shall be in writing or confirmed in writing and delivered at the respective addresses set forth in Annex II attached hereto.

14. Entire Agreement; Severability

This Agreement shall supersede any existing agreements between the parties containing general terms and conditions for repurchase transactions. Each provision and agreement herein shall be treated as separate and independent from any other provision or agreement herein and shall be enforceable notwithstanding the unenforceability of any such other provision or agreement.

15. Nonassignability; Termination

The rights and obligations of the parties under this Agreement and under any Transaction shall not be assigned by either party without the prior written consent of the other party. Subject to the foregoing, this Agreement and any Transactions shall be binding upon and shall inure to the benefit of the parties and their respective successors and assigns. This Agreement may be cancelled by either party upon giving written notice to the other except that this Agreement shall, notwithstanding such notice, remain applicable to any Transactions then outstanding.

16. Governing Law

This Agreement shall be governed by the laws of the State of New York without giving effect to the conflict of law principles thereof.

17. No Waivers, Etc.

No express or implied waiver of any Event of Default by either party shall constitute a waiver of any other Event of Default and no exercise of any remedy hereunder by any party shall constitute a waiver of its right to exercise any other remedy hereunder. No modification or waiver of any provision of this Agreement and no consent by any party to a departure herefrom shall be effective unless and until such shall be in writing and duly executed by both of the parties hereto. Without limitation on any of the foregoing, the failure to give a notice pursuant to subparagraphs 4(a) or 4(b) hereof will not constitute a waiver of any right to do so at a later date.

18. Use of Employee Plan Assets

(a) If assets of an employee benefit plan subject to any provision of the Employee Retirement Income Security Act of 1974 ("ERISA") are intended to be used by either party hereto (the "Plan Party") in a Transaction, the Plan Party shall so notify the other party prior to the

Transaction. The Plan Party shall represent in writing to the other party that the Transaction does not constitute a prohibited transaction under ERISA or is otherwise exempt therefrom, and the other party may proceed in reliance thereon but shall not be required so to proceed.

(b) Subject to the last sentence of subparagraph (a) of this paragraph, any such Transaction shall proceed only if Seller furnishes or has furnished to Buyer its most recent available audited statement of its financial condition and its most recent subsequent unaudited statement of its financial condition.

(c) By entering into a Transaction pursuant to this paragraph, Seller shall be deemed (i) to represent to Buyer that since the date of Seller's latest such financial statements, there has been no material adverse change in Seller's financial condition which Seller has not disclosed to Buyer, and (ii) to agree to provide Buyer with future audited and unaudited statements of its financial condition as they are issued, so long as it is a Seller in an outstanding Transaction involving a Plan Party.

19. **Intent**

(a) The parties recognize that each Transaction is a "repurchase agreement" as that term is defined in Section 101(39) of Title 11 of the United States Code, as amended (except insofar as the type of Securities subject to such Transaction or the term of such Transaction would render such definition inapplicable), and a "securities contract" as that term is defined in Section 741(7) of Title 11 of the United States Code, as amended.

(b) It is understood that either party's right to liquidate securities delivered to it in connection with Transactions hereunder or to exercise any other remedies pursuant to Paragraph 11 hereof, is a contractual right to liquidate such Transaction as described in Sections 555 and 559 of Title 11 of the United States Code, as amended.

[Name of Party]   [Name of Party]

By _____   By _____

Title _____   Title _____

Date _____   Date _____

Chapter 10

Investment Instruments

INTRODUCTION

One of the more important jobs a financial manager performs is to ensure that the institution's cash is always working. Cash that lies in a checking account when it is not needed to pay bills is not working. Rather than leave cash in checking accounts, a financial manager invests it; the institution derives financial benefits from its cash surplus. Hundreds of investment vehicles may be used for excess cash, some with long terms and some with short terms, some extremely safe and some quite risky. A financial manager must match the yield objectives, level of risk, and liquidity tolerances of the institution, as stated in the investment guidelines, before making investments. As an aid in that decision-making process, this chapter describes the most common types of investment vehicles: U.S. Treasury and government agency instruments, corporate and money market instruments, and repurchase agreements.

It is apparent that many of these instruments are quite similar. In many cases, the only difference is in the length of maturity. Therefore, it is important for a financial manager to understand the importance of managing maturities in an investment program. The longer the instrument's maturity, the greater the possibility that its market value will fluctuate as interest rates change. In choosing securities for investment, a financial manager must examine and be satisfied with each of the following aspects of an investment instrument besides its maturity (see Table 10-1):

- issuer's credit quality
- instrument's liquidity
- instrument's complexity
- ease of obtaining an instrument's credit rating

194   CASH AND INVESTMENT MANAGEMENT

Table 10-1 Instruments at a Glance

Type	Instrument	Guarantee	Liquidity rating*	Interest paid	Typical maturity	State/local income tax**
U.S. Treasury securities	U.S. Treasury Bills	U.S. government	10	At maturity	3–6–12 months	Exempt
	U.S. Treasury Notes	U.S. government	9	Semiannual	2–7 years	Exempt
	U.S. Treasury Bonds	U.S. government	8+	Semiannual	7–30 years	Exempt
U.S. government agency securities	Federal Home Loan Bank discount notes	Issuing agency	9	At maturity	30–360 days	Exempt
	Federal Home Loan Bank debentures	Issuing agency	8	Semiannual	1–20 years	Exempt
	Federal National Mortgage Assn. discount notes	Issuing agency	9	At maturity	30–360 days	Not exempt
	Federal National Mortgage Assn. debentures	Issuing agency	7	Semiannual	1 year to several years	Not exempt
	Federal Home Loan Mortgage Corp. discount notes	Issuing agency	9	At maturity	5–360 days	Not exempt
	Federal Home Loan Mortgage Corp. debentures	Issuing agency	2	Semiannual	1–30 years	Not exempt
	Farm Credit Bank discount notes	Issuing agency	9	At maturity	5–360 days	Exempt
	Farm Credit Bank debentures	Issuing agency	6	Semiannual	6 months to several years	Exempt
	Student Loan Marketing Assn. discount notes	Issuing agency	9	At maturity	5–360 days	Exempt
	Student Loan Marketing Assn. debentures	Issuing agency	7	Semiannual	1–30 years	Exempt
	International Bank for Reconstruction and Development discount notes	Issuing agency	8	At maturity	30–360 days	Not exempt
	Government National Mortgage Assn.	U.S. government	7	Monthly	12–25 years	Not exempt
Municipal or tax-exempt securities	Municipal bonds	Varies by issue	7	Semiannual	5–30 years	Varies
	Municipal notes	Varies by issue	7	Semiannual	1–48 months	Varies
	Municipal (tax-exempt) commercial paper	Varies by issue	7	At maturity	5–270 days	Varies
	Municipal floating rate notes	Varies by issue	9+	Monthly	1–30 years	Varies
Banking-type obligations	Banker's acceptances	Issuing bank	8	At maturity	7–270 days	Not exempt
	Certificate of deposit: (1) U.S. bank (2) foreign bank (3) savings & loan	Issuing institution	8,7,5	At maturity or semiannual	7 days to several years	Not exempt
	Certificate of deposit-Eurodollar: (1) U.S. bank (2) foreign bank	Issuing bank	7,5	At maturity or semiannual	14 days to several years	Not exempt
	Certificate of deposit with floating rate	Issuing bank	5	Varies	Varies	Not exempt
	Eurodollar time deposit: U.S. bank or foreign bank	Issuing bank	0	At maturity	360 days	Not exempt

Corporate obligations	Commercial paper	Issuing corporation	8	At maturity	1–270 days	Not exempt
	Corporate notes	Issuing corporation	6	Semiannual	3–7 years	Not exempt
	Preferred stock	Issuing corporation	5	Quarterly	No maturity	Not exempt
Repos (bank/dealer)	Repurchase agreements	Firm accepting money	0	At maturity	1–360 days	Not exempt

*Liquidity Rating: These ratings, from 1 through 10 with 10 being the highest, represent an estimation of the ability to sell this instrument into the market under even the most adverse market environment. Although this rating does not, in every case, indicate the credit quality of the instrument, it does indicate, in the author's judgment, how market participants would view this investment as concerns its liquidity.

**Many states apply a "franchise tax" to corporate income and thus no exemptions are granted. Check with your tax counsel for specifics.

Source: © The Alan G. Seidner Company, Pasadena, California.

- instrument's sensitivity to market risk
- flexibility of the instrument's maturity ranges
- yield of the instrument
- investor's potential tax exemption
- structure of the instrument's principal and interest payments
- financial manager's ability to actively manage a portfolio containing that particular instrument

U.S. TREASURY SECURITIES

Background

The U.S. government is one of the largest economic organizations in the world; it is also one of the most indebted. In fact, the U.S. Department of the Treasury is the largest issuer of debt instruments in the world. Even so, debt instruments issued by the U.S. Treasury are considered to be the safest investments available. They are used as a means to reap investment returns from surplus cash by financial managers from all types of businesses, including health care institutions, that seek to put this cash to work. U.S. Treasury debt instruments meet their requirements of high liquidity and low credit risk and make perfect investments for this purpose. The strength of the U.S. economy, for instance, prompts dealers and investment analysts to grade Treasury securities as virtually free of credit or default risk.

Liquidity and the Market

One of the criteria for high liquidity is the existence of a large market for an investment instrument. Liquidity refers to the ability to convert a security into cash quickly and without loss of principal. Because the volume of debt issued by the Treasury is so great, the market for government securities is one of the most active—and thus most liquid—of investment markets. There is a tremendous amount of participation by both foreign and domestic investors in this market. Liquidity is further increased by the existence of a core of primary dealers that buy and sell huge quantities of government securities, both among themselves and with other investors. It is a highly competitive market, with prices varying between dealers by only one or two thirty-seconds of a point (on a par value of $1,000,000, one thirty-second of a point is $312.50). Liquidity is also increased by the existence of a huge resale market, where dealers and investors who bought securities at issuance sell them before maturity.

Treasury securities are initially sold at auctions that are conducted through regional Federal Reserve Bank offices. Dates for those auctions are announced in newspaper notices well beforehand. There are two types of bidding at Treasury auctions: (1) competitive bids for certain quantities of securities at a certain price and (2) noncompetitive bids submitted by an investor or institution that simply agrees to buy a certain amount of the security and pay a price equal to the weighted-average price of all competitive bids accepted by the Treasury. The difference between competitive and noncompetitive bids involves risk. When financial managers submit competitive bids, they take the risk of paying more than the average noncompetitive price or of bidding too low to obtain the desired securities. (After the auction's deadline, the Treasury reviews all bids and establishes the minimum price at which bids will be accepted.)

Individual and institutional investors may bid on Treasury securities at a Federal Reserve Bank or have major banks or securities dealers submit bids on their behalf. Investors may also, of course, buy Treasury securities from the many resale markets through banks or securities dealers.

Before considering Treasury securities as an investment, financial managers must be familiar with the different types of Treasury securities and their characteristics. Treasury securities fall into three categories: bills, notes and bonds.

Treasury Bills

Treasury bills (T-bills) are short-term debt instruments that are issued at a discount and repaid at full value, called par value, upon maturity. The amount of interest on a T-bill is thus the difference between the purchase price and the value of the bill's par value. T-bills are issued with maturities of three months, six months and one year. Also, when the Treasury needs funds to finance operations before a tax receipt date, it will issue "cash management bills" having odd maturities ranging from a few days to 60 days.

The advantages of T-bills for the institutional investor are the wide range of short-term maturities, their high liquidity, and an active secondary market for most denominations. The minimum denomination of a T-bill is $10,000; additional amounts are available in increments of $5,000. T-bills are sold only in book entry form (by credit to the investor's account with the Treasury).

Treasury Notes

Treasury notes (also called coupon notes) are instruments that mature from more than one year up to 10 years and bear interest. They are issued at or near face value and are redeemed at par value upon maturity. Original maturities for Treasury notes (T-notes) are two, three, four, five, seven and 10 years. Notes with a two-year maturity are issued each month, while notes of three years and longer are issued quarterly. The Treasury issues notes of other maturities if it needs to balance its maturity schedule. Like T-bills, T-notes are issued in various denominations. The minimum denomination of two- and three-year notes is $5,000, and the size increases in $5,000 increments. Notes with maturities of longer than three years are issued in minimum size of $1,000, with larger amounts in $1,000 increments. Interest on T-notes is paid semiannually and at maturity together with par value of the notes.

Treasury notes, like Treasury bills, are initially sold to investors at auctions conducted by the Federal Reserve. Investors bid on the basis of yield to maturity, and the Treasury accepts the bids that result in the lowest cost to the Treasury. Accordingly, the market itself generally determines the interest rate of Treasury notes. Also like T-bills, T-notes are highly liquid because of the existence of a vast secondary market, especially for notes in denominations of $1 million and more. The secondary market also provides a wide range of maturities and prices. Treasury notes, like all direct obligations of the U.S. government, carry no credit risk.

Treasury Bonds

Treasury bonds (T-bonds) are interest-bearing debt instruments with original maturities longer than 10 years; most original maturities are 20 or 30 years. T-bonds also have a call feature that allows the Treasury to pay off the bonds before maturity, though most of them are not callable until the last few years before maturity. T-bonds are excellent investments when interest rates have declined sharply, because the bonds are not likely to be called. Like T-notes, the bonds pay interest income semiannually. These long-term Treasury securities are issued in $1,000 denominations and are sold quarterly at auction. They have the same liquidity and credit risk characteristics as Treasury bills and Treasury notes.

U.S. GOVERNMENT AGENCY SECURITIES

Most of the departments and agencies of the U.S. government, as well as organizations and corporations chartered by Congress, issue debt securities. They are referred to collectively as government agency securities. Like Treasury securities, they are either issued at a discount and redeemed at par upon maturity, or they pay a fixed rate of interest until maturity.

Credit Quality

All agencies of the federal government are considered to be more creditworthy than private organizations. However, some government agencies are more creditworthy than others. The liquidity of government agency securities also varies by issuer. Most investors consider government agency securities to have little default risk. Even so, financial managers investing an institution's funds should keep three points in mind:

1. Not every government agency security carries the full faith and credit of the U.S. government; many actively traded government agency securities must maintain their own financial strength and security.
2. Of the major credit-rating agencies, only Moody's rates most government agency debt. Securities that carry a direct government guarantee or are backed by collateral generally receive an AAA rating. Because the rating agencies tend not to rate government agencies, however, it is difficult to find information on the financial strength and stability of many agencies.
3. Government agencies can experience financial difficulties—some so substantial that the agency must apply to the federal government for assistance. In 1986, for instance, earnings and assets of the Federal Farm Credit Banks (FFCB) began to suffer as a result of the deteriorating agricultural sector of the country's economy. The FFCB had to ask Congress for financial aid while the agency strengthened its financial position. While Congress was considering aid, the uncertain status of the FFCB's creditworthiness caused its debt instruments to trade at much higher yields than those of other government agencies.

Advantages

Safety, liquidity, and yield are the main advantages of government agency securities. Despite some credit concerns, these securities are still among the safest instruments available to an investor. In most instances, government agency debt is considered second only to Treasury securities in terms of safety. Although few agencies besides the Treasury are backed by the full faith and credit of the U.S. government, many experts contend that Congress has a "moral obligation" to bail out an agency that finds itself in fiscally dangerous waters. Indeed, Congress approved a form of aid for the FFCB when it was having loan problems. It ruled that the government could buy FFCB securities to provide the agency with a temporary source of funding, under the condition that the agency institute fiscal reforms.

The liquidity factor of most government agency securities, although generally not as high as Treasury securities, is still a major advantage. Many of these securities are more liquid than other types of financial instruments, because there is active secondary-market trading in most government agency securities. A financial manager should look carefully at liquidity, however, as not all government agency securities have active markets. Those that are not very liquid have been omitted from descriptions of government agency securities in the next section of this chapter.

The differences between government agency securities and Treasury securities regarding safety and liquidity lead to yet another major advantage of agency securities: yield. Because most government agency securities are not backed by a Treasury guarantee and are slightly less liquid, they generally trade at higher yields than Treasury securities. The amount of the yield spread for any given maturity between Treasury securities and government agency securities depends on market conditions, but the yield spread is always present. This spread is usually ⅜ percent for maturities under one year and ¼ percent beyond one year.

Methods of Sale

Government agency securities are not sold at auction like Treasury securities. They are issued through an underwriting syndicate composed of a select group of securities dealers and banks. Every dealer in the group underwrites a specific portion of the total issue. Consequently, the interest rate for government agency securities is not determined in the same manner as the rate for Treasury securities, as there is no auction in which the market can determine the rate. Instead, the coupon yield of each issue is set by the underwriting syndicate and the agency's fiscal manager on the morning of the sale date.

Before setting the interest rate, the syndicate must obtain instructions from the agency as to the amount of money it needs and the length of maturity it prefers. If the money needs of the agency are less demanding, the security will carry a rate that is below the prevailing market rate. If the agency needs money for a particular date, however, a higher rate will be set to attract investors. Yields on government agency securities thus reflect both market conditions and the needs of the borrower, much like commercial paper rates. The public learns of the amount, maturity date, and settlement date for government agency securities through the news media. Most daily newspapers carry "pre-sale" announcements of these securities. Syndicate members then take orders from investors.

"When Issued" Trading

Dealers begin to make markets to buy and sell new securities when an issue is announced, even if that instrument has not yet been issued. The period of time between announcement of a security issue and when it is paid for and delivered is called the "when issued" (WI) period. To trade in securities on a "when issued" basis requires little or no principal investment during the WI period, because payment is not due until the settlement date. This enables speculation during the

WI period; both Treasury and agency securities are heavily traded during this period. Conservative financial managers, however, should avoid the temptation to speculate by committing only to securities on a WI basis when they intend to take delivery of the securities on the settlement date.

Types of Government Agency Securities

Certain government agencies that are in the business of lending funds generally issue debt to fund lending activities. The following sections provide descriptions of the more actively traded government agency debt obligations.

Farm Credit System Securities

The nation's farmers require an enormous amount of credit and financial assistance. A constant supply of funds is maintained to meet farmers' credit needs through the Farm Credit Administration, which oversees the Federal Farm Credit System. The system, which contains 12 farm credit districts each having a Farm Credit Bank, raises funds to lend to farmers by selling notes and bonds to the public. The FFCB securities, called Consolidated Systemwide discount notes and bonds, are backed by the assets of the Farm Credit Banks. The securities are not guaranteed by the U.S. government, so their market value is subject to the credit soundness of the farm loan market. In the mid-1980s, for instance, the Farm Credit Administration suffered substantial losses as a result of the collapse of the agricultural markets. Congress temporarily bailed the system out in January 1988, but whether the reforms mandated by Congress will keep the agency solvent remains to be seen.

Consolidated Systemwide short-term debentures are issued monthly and have maturities of 180 and 270 days. They are issued at par and pay principal and interest at maturity. The system also issues longer-term notes, approximately six times a year, with maturities of up to several years and interest payable semiannually. Debentures with maturities of less than 13 months are issued in increments of $5,000, and those with longer maturities are issued in $1,000 increments. All of these securities are issued in book entry form. Under a special program, however, dealers can issue Consolidated Systemwide notes with maturities ranging from five days to a year. These notes trade at a discount from face value and are repaid at par upon maturity. They are issued in $500,000 denominations and in bearer form.

Federal Home Loan Bank Securities

The Federal Home Loan Act of 1932 created the Federal Home Loan Bank (FHLB) system. The system's two primary responsibilities are to (1) oversee its member savings and loan institutions and savings banks, and (2) lend money and provide liquidity to its members. To obtain the money that the FHLB lends to its members, it borrows money from the public by issuing bonds and notes. Debt is issued by a credit system operated by the FHLB system's 12 district banks under the supervision of a central board based in Washington, D.C.

There are two types of securities issued by the FHLB, consolidated bonds and consolidated discount notes. The debt is called "consolidated" because it is the joint obligation of all 12 Federal Home Loan Banks. These banks operate under a federal charter and are supervised by the government, but their securities do not carry a government guarantee. The banks, however, are required to maintain assets at least equal to the amount of debt that has been issued. Such assets include guaranteed mortgages, U.S. government securities, and cash.

Federal Home Loan Mortgage Corporation

Called "Freddie Mac," the Federal Home Loan Mortgage Corporation (FHLMC) is a subsidiary of the Federal Home Loan Bank. Established in 1970, the FHLMC is charged with maintaining mortgage credit for residential housing development and promoting a nationwide secondary market for conventional residential mortgages. The agency accomplishes these goals by buying mortgages from members of the FHLB system. The mortgage purchases are financed by marketing mortgage participation certificates (PCs) and guaranteed mortgage certificates (GMCs). As a supplement to its practice of obtaining all of its credit from the FHLB system, Freddie Mac also now offers discount notes and bonds under its own name.

Federal National Mortgage Association

Called "Fannie Mae," the Federal National Mortgage Association (FNMA) is a public corporation owned by nongovernment stockholders. (It was originally a government-chartered corporation that did not issue stock.) The FNMA's primary goal is to provide funding for conventional mortgages, which it finances by selling debentures and short-term securities.

FNMA debentures have maturities of up to several years and its short-term securities have up to one year. The FNMA issues a large volume of short-term securities, thereby fueling a strong secondary market that provides a good deal of liquidity to its securities. FNMA notes are unsecured obligations of the issuer and are not backed by government guarantees. As a result, they often provide high yields in relation to Treasury securities.

Student Loan Marketing Association

Called "Sallie Mae," the Student Loan Marketing Association is a private, nonprofit corporation that was created to encourage lending for higher education by guaranteeing student loans and financing the Federal Guaranteed Student Loan Program. Sallie Mae buys loans made by financial institutions under various federal and state student loan programs. Securities issued by the agency include discount notes that carry maturities ranging from a few days to one year. The agency also issues floating-rate obligations and fixed-term debentures that carry maturities of several years. (Rates on floating-rate securities vary on the basis of changes in market rates.) The federal government oversees the operations of Sallie Mae but does not guarantee its securities.

Government National Mortgage Association

Called "Ginnie Mae," the Government National Mortgage Association (GNMA) supervises and sponsors support programs for mortgages that do not qualify for private mortgage insurance and therefore cannot be sold in normal nonfederally guaranteed mortgage markets. Ginnie Mae also funds and provides liquidity for conventional mortgages. GNMA securities are called participation certificates (PCs), and they provide a pass-through (or pay out) of the interest and principal on pools of mortgages. The underlying mortgages are guaranteed by the Federal Housing Administration or the Veterans Administration. As a result, Ginnie Mae securities are considered to be backed by the full faith and credit of the U.S. government. This makes Ginnie Mae securities one of the few government agency securities carrying that high guarantee.

Because Ginnie Mae participation certificates have competitive yields and are backed by a government guarantee, many investors consider them to be an attractive investment in the intermediate- and long-term maturity areas. Maturities on Ginnie Mae pass-through certificates are 30 years. Homeowners whose mortgages have been sold to Ginnie Mae, however, may refinance them or sell their homes and repay the mortgage loans underlying the certificates. For that reason, Ginnie Mae mortgage pools actually have a much shorter average life than 30 years. Calculating the exact length of that average life is not easy; in fact, experts disagree over what method produces the most accurate results. Such disagreements are not academic, especially to investors who intend to hold Ginnie Mae or other mortgage-backed securities until maturity so that they can receive a stream of cash over the security's life.

For example, if the aggregate yield for mortgages in the pool is higher than current mortgage rates, the homeowners who are obligated on these mortgages will refinance the mortgages or repay the mortgages faster than scheduled. Homeowners have demonstrated a propensity to refinance mortgage loans as interest rates decline, with such refinancing representing repayment of the original mortgage and creation of a new mortgage. The new mortgage will not be part of the same Ginnie Mae pool as the original mortgage. On the other hand, mortgages in a Ginnie Mae pool with rates lower than the prevailing rate for mortgage financing will be paid off slower than the expected payment rate. Despite such uncertainties, a generally accepted estimate for the average life of a Ginnie Mae pool is about 12 years from its original creation.

Adverse Features of GNMA Investments. Mortgage-backed (MB) securities and participation certificates (PCs) carry several potentially adverse features of which investors should be aware. Prices for these types of securities tend to be more volatile than prices of other government securities with similar maturities. GNMA prices tend to fall faster with rising interest rates than other 12-year government agency securities and Treasury bonds. Ginnie Maes tend to trade in a manner similar to 30-year bonds (the stated maturity of Ginnie Mae certificates is 30 years). As a result, an investor who sells Ginnie Maes in a market with higher interest rates than those prevailing at the time the certificates were purchased may have to take a loss.

It also can be difficult to reinvest interest proceeds on Ginnie Mae certificates (or other pass-through securities) unless the investor holds a large portfolio of Ginnie Mae securities providing several hundreds of thousands of dollars in monthly cash flow. One problem with reinvesting the proceeds of a portfolio providing less than $100,000 in monthly cash flow is the difficulty in finding instruments that have yield, portfolio compatibility, and liquidity characteristics suitable for proper investment. A financial manager may end up with a portfolio consisting of small amounts of various instruments, rather than large blocks of securities. A large block of a security tends to be more liquid than a small block.

A second problem with these securities is the possibility of an accounting nightmare. Because the cash flow of the securities combines both principal and interest payments, delays and accounting errors can occur. It takes time to verify payment amounts and to file claims on incorrect amounts, both of which result in lost interest on funds received past their due dates. The yield advantage of the securities is thus diminished. Many investors think these securities are exempt from state income taxes, as Treasury securities are. In an increasing number of states they are not tax-exempt, however. It is important to have a tax adviser review state tax exemptions on government agency securities. It is also important to check into guarantees on the securities because not all of them carry a government guarantee.

Another potential problem with Ginnie Mae securities results from yield volatility. When interest rates drop and homeowners pay off mortgages faster than anticipated, the remaining life of the mortgage pool declines rapidly. An investor who bought a security with a high yield will find that the period of time the high yield continues to accrue shortens with falling interest rates. If the investor paid a premium to obtain the above- market yield, the income stream that was to amortize the premium could be prematurely eroded. Accordingly, market prices on the securities do not rise as fast as prices on other investments when interest rates fall.

Mortgage Pass-Through Securities. During the past several years financial innovations have been responsible for the creation of many types of securities based on pools of home mortgages. Mortgage pass-through securities guaranteed by GNMA have been quite popular, because they typically provide greater yields than Treasury securities. Some studies even suggest that GNMA pass-through securities provide higher returns than many other fixed-income securities, but those returns are partly the result of some investors' resistance to the complexity of the instruments. Before investing in mortgage pass-through securities, the financial manager must study all of the characteristics of the underlying mortgage pool, especially if the securities will be sold before maturity. Again, the guarantee status of the securities is important; those issued by Freddie Mac, for instance, do not carry a government guarantee.

Collateralized Mortgage Obligations (CMOs). CMOs are bonds backed, or collateralized, by instruments such as GNMA or FHLMC pass-through securities. They were designed to improve on simple mortgage-backed securities and provide more predictable returns by taking specific characteristics of MB securities and solving the problems of receiving repayments that combine principal and interest. In essence, investment bankers have developed computer models that estimate the payback dates of a mortgage pool. Based on this analysis specific durations, or tranches, are created. As mortgages backing the CMO pay back principal, the cash is set aside to pay off the first maturity, or tranche, on a quarterly basis. This process continues until all of the tranches are paid off. A more predictable maturity duration is thus established.

Because the actual duration of the underlying pool is not certain, however, CMOs still suffer some of the same payment problems as other MB securities. Despite the yield advantages CMOs have over other securities of comparable credit quality, financial managers should beware of the following four disadvantages:

1. CMOs have very complicated payback formulas, like other mortgage-backed securities, when interest rates are volatile.
2. Accounting is difficult because flows of principal and interest are uneven.
3. Incorrect and late payments can result from problems in bank and dealer offices.
4. Market prices are more volatile on CMOs than other fixed-income securities as a result of such problems.

CORPORATE DEBT INSTRUMENTS

Corporate debt is issued by industrial corporations, utility companies, finance companies, bank holding companies, domestic facilities of foreign institutions, and other private-sector organizations. All corporate debt is subject to default risk. Therefore, financial managers should examine the credit ratings of the organization issuing corporate debt instruments. In general, corporate debt falls into three categories: (1) commercial paper, (2) medium-term corporate notes, and (3) long-term bonds. The differences among these categories, of course, lie in varying maturity lengths.

Commercial Paper

Many large corporations in recent years have eschewed bank loans in favor of financing obtained from less expensive sources. For a large corporation with an excellent credit rating, the least expensive source of financing is to issue its own debt in the form of commercial paper that is sold to investors through the capital markets. Domestic and foreign manufacturing and industrial companies issue commercial paper, as do finance companies and bank holding companies. Paper issued by finance companies is called direct finance paper; it is generally sold directly to investors through banks acting as agents for the issuers. Paper issued by industrial companies is called dealer paper; it is usually sold through dealers who have purchased the paper themselves.

Commercial paper is a promissory note, usually unsecured, maturing on a specific date. In most cases, it is issued in bearer form in minimum denominations of $100,000. Commercial paper is liquid, because a secondary market exists. However, investors generally hold commercial paper to maturity. Issuers and dealers often will buy paper back if an investor needs cash. Maturities on most commercial paper run from 1 to 180 days. The longest maturity that commercial paper carries is 270 days, as debt issues with longer maturities must be registered with the Securities and Exchange Commission. Registration is expensive. Commercial paper provides investors with an efficient short-term investment instrument that matures on a specific date.

The yield on commercial paper depends on the issuer's credit rating, its need for money, maturity of the paper, its face value, and general money market rates. Most companies that issue commercial paper are rated by agencies such as Moody's, Standard & Poor's, Fitch, and Duff and Phelps. Commercial paper that falls into the highest rating class is called "top tier." Investing in top tier paper entails minimal credit risk, though risk is still present. Commercial paper, therefore, provides higher yields than Treasury and government agency securities of the same maturities.

Issuing Formats

In addition to the flexibility and efficiency of its maturity dates, commercial paper offers a choice of two formats, interest-bearing or discounted. An investor buying $1 million in interest-bearing commercial paper pays the $1 million face value and collects interest upon maturity. Not much interest-bearing commercial paper is issued, however, except in very short maturities. Because most interest-bearing commercial paper is held to maturity, its liquidity is decreased. Discount commercial paper, which is more common, works like U.S. Treasury bills, where an investor buys the note at a discount and receives its face value at maturity.

Types of Commercial Paper

Commercial paper is a flexible investment vehicle available in eight types:

1. Bank holding company commercial paper is issued by the parent companies of commercial banks.
2. Industrial commercial paper is issued by major industrial companies to provide short-term working capital.
3. Finance company commercial paper is issued by captive finance companies of major industrial corporations. The finance companies use the money generated by commercial paper programs to provide financing to buyers of the parent corporation's products.
4. Dealer commercial paper is issued by corporations through securities dealers, rather than through banks or the company itself. A dealer generally underwrites an issue, which means that the dealer buys the paper and resells it to investors.
5. Direct or finance commercial paper is paper distributed by banks. Until recently, banks could not act as dealers; they could act only as agents for commercial paper issuers, generally finance companies. The bank would take orders from investors but would not invest any of its own money to maintain its own inventory of an issue.
6. Foreign commercial paper is issued in the United States by domestic subsidiaries of foreign industrial and financial organizations. The paper generally is guaranteed by the foreign parent.
7. Collateralized commercial paper is usually issued to generate funds to purchase loans from an affiliated savings and loan. The collateral often takes the form of Treasury or government agency securities pledged by the institution's parent. Many investors consider collateralized commercial paper to be a secure short-term investment.
8. Letter of credit commercial paper (also called "commercial paper LOC") is, as its name suggests, supported by a bank letter of credit (LOC). A major bank or insurance company backs the credit quality of LOC commercial paper for a fee. Companies that issue LOC commercial paper tend to be smaller, are less well-known, and have less than the highest credit rating. These issuers use the LOC guarantee to enhance their credit standing to raise

short-term borrowings at a lower interest cost. The credit strength behind the paper is not the issuing company but the institution that provides the LOC. This commercial paper comes in the following varieties:

- Full-and-direct pay paper. The institution backing the issue with its LOC will pay upon maturity if the issuer cannot pay the full amount directly to the investor.
- Standby LOC commercial paper. This variety does not carry as strong a guarantee as full-and-direct pay LOC commercial paper. A standby LOC, for instance, may cover only partial payments and various types of delayed payments. This is acceptable but not preferable in the opinion of many investors.
- Irrevocable LOC commercial paper. The LOC cannot be revoked or cancelled.

Loan Participations

Major money center banks developed loan participations as a means of providing financing to bank customers in lieu of the customers issuing commercial paper. Because it had been illegal for commercial banks to underwrite commercial paper, several banks developed loan participations as a way of keeping customers from going to other institutions for financing. Under a loan participation arrangement, a bank creates a loan to one of its customers, then sells pieces of the loan to investors. It is similar to a securities dealer selling commercial paper to investors in order to provide funds for a corporate borrower.

Investors find loan participations attractive because their yields are higher than certificates of deposit and commercial paper. Yields on loan participations can be as much as 15 basis points greater than comparable investment instruments, depending on the creditworthiness of the borrower. Loan participations are attractive borrowing vehicles because they carry low administrative charges. Accordingly, finance managers can look upon loan participations as good investment alternatives, though they should be used selectively. Loan participations are not liquid investments. Before investing in a loan participation, an investor should examine the borrowing company's credit ratings.

Corporate Notes

Medium-term notes are promissory notes that pay either a fixed or variable rate of interest, with principal payable at maturity. As the name suggests, these instruments lie in the middle ranges of the yield curve. Corporate notes carry maturities ranging between nine months and 10 years; their maturities thus begin where commercial paper maturities end. Issued in much the same way as commercial paper, corporate notes are available either through underwriting or ongoing issuance programs called "medium-term notes" or "shelf registrations." Under a shelf registration, an issuer maintains a continuing registration statement with the Securities and Exchange Commission and posts rates daily for a range of maturities. This allows the issuer to control both maturity length and the overall distribution of securities. The ability to offer medium-term notes whose rates fluctuate for different maturity periods allows large corporations to plan borrowing better based on corporate needs and market rates. (Shelf registrations were made possible by changes to Securities and Exchange Commission Rule 415 that allow corporations to make certain types of amendments to debt documents without SEC review.)

For investors, on the other hand, medium-term notes allow financial managers to choose the exact maturities they need and to base investment decisions on the yield curve. Medium-term notes offer four basic advantages to institutional investors:

1. Medium-term notes are issued with a range of maturities. By choosing any maturity date within that range, financial managers can tailor the instruments somewhat to fit into a portfolio.
2. The primary and secondary market availability of medium-term notes allows investment managers to satisfy maturity, yield, and duration needs of a portfolio.
3. Yield spreads on medium-term notes are relatively stable under most market conditions, because many different issuers and maturities are available on any given day.
4. Growth in the medium-term market, since it first appeared in 1982, has resulted in excellent liquidity for the instruments. This allows financial managers to use active investment management techniques.

Corporate Bonds

Corporations seeking to borrow large sums of money over a period of time longer than 10 years issue corporate bonds. A corporate bond is essentially an IOU under which the borrower (bond issuer) agrees to pay the investor a fixed amount of interest in return for the use of the investor's money over the period of the loan (the bond's maturity). There is an active secondary market for corporate bonds of many large companies, and this enhances their liquidity. When an investor wants to sell bonds before maturity, the bond's value becomes critical, especially because the long-term bond market can fluctuate widely. Bonds offer the important advantage of high return to financial managers who can invest in longer maturities. Because an investor takes on more risk when investing in instruments with long maturities, fixed returns are greater. Bond investors also stand to gain if interest rates decline, though bonds often have call features, allowing the issuer to redeem them prior to maturity without penalty.

High-Yield (Junk) Bonds

High-yield bonds, commonly called junk bonds, are bonds that have a high default risk. They are issued by unrated borrowers or borrowers with low credit ratings. Because bonds issued by these borrowers have low perceived credit quality that portends a high default risk, they offer a high yield. In terms of credit ratings, junk bonds carry a rating of Ba and below when rated by Moody's Investors Service and BB or less when rated by Standard & Poor's, assuming they are rated at all. According to Moody's *Bond Record*, "Bonds which are rated Ba are judged to have speculative elements; their future cannot be considered as well assured. Often the protection of interest and principal payments may be very moderate and thereby not well safeguarded. . ."

Master Notes

Master notes are variable-rate demand notes that are used in ongoing borrowing programs of large companies. Master notes are made available to investors through bank trust departments by some of the same companies that issue commercial paper and medium-term notes. Master notes are generally issued in denominations of between $5 million and $10 million. They are flexible instruments that allow an investor to determine the terms under which funds are invested. Investors can stipulate such requirements as

- the amount of money the investor wants to invest initially and the ability to add or withdraw from that investment on short notice
- the length of maturity that the investor wants, as an investor can withdraw funds on short notice
- the times at which the investor wants to receive interest payments, whether monthly, quarterly, or semiannually

Accordingly, each master note has its own terms and conditions that can be discussed and set through negotiations with the dealer. The ability to deposit and withdraw funds on short notice is the primary advantage of a master note.

A master note is generally issued in two parts: (1) "A Note," a variable-term note, and (2) "B Note," a fixed-term note. The note is divided because master note investors usually keep their balances at a certain level. The bottom half of the master note (the B Note) is the half in which funds are maintained. The investor often is required to give notice of up to 12 to 15 months to withdraw funds from the B Note. Investors can withdraw funds from the top half of the master note (the A note) on demand. A master note structured in two parts should pay a higher yield than a regular master note because the borrower is able to lock up a portion of the funds for a fixed term.

Yields on master notes are generally set in relation to a well-established base rate. For instance, daily floating yields may be set on the basis of the Federal Reserve's daily Fed funds rate. Yields on master notes are about the same or slightly less than those of other money market instruments. The reason for the lower rate is that master note investments are highly liquid and flexible, as they essentially allow financial managers to determine maturities and investment amounts.

MONEY MARKET INSTRUMENTS ISSUED BY BANKS

The term "money market," as distinguished from the term "capital market," refers to borrowing and lending for periods of a year or less. Organizations issue money market instruments for a variety of reasons, one of the most common of which is the mismatched timing of their cash receipts and cash disbursements. They need financing in the short run and can obtain it by borrowing from a lender or issuing short-term, or money market, instruments. From the investor's point of view, the money market affords a way to earn interest on excess capital without tying it up for long periods of time. The more common money market instruments used by financial managers for short-term investing are discussed below.

Banker's Acceptances

Banker's acceptances (BAs) are short-term drafts whose drawee bank has accepted the obligation to pay the instrument at maturity. BAs are used primarily to finance trade transactions, frequently in international trade, and are similar to commercial paper except they entail less risk to investors. A BA is drawn on and accepted by a domestic bank and sold to an investor at a discount. The bank agrees to redeem the note at maturity for full face value. Most BAs have maturities of three months, though they can be as long as six months, and are sold in denominations of $500,000, $1,000,000, and multiples of $1,000,000. BA investments offer the following advantages:

- yield spread advantage ranging between 25 and 75 basis points higher than Treasury bills
- smaller capital investments that produce yields similar to certificates of deposit
- full negotiability
- active secondary market for BAs of $500,000 or more

The following example illustrates how BAs work to finance international trade transactions. Company A, a U.S. company, plans to import optical lenses from Company B, a West German company. Company A wants to pay for the lenses six months after shipment, hoping that the lenses will have been sold and the proceeds collected by that time. Company A is too small to issue debt in the open market, so it seeks financing from its bank. The company uses banker's acceptance financing, because it is less expensive than a normal business loan. For its part, the bank issues a letter of credit (LOC) to Company B on behalf of Company A for the purpose of importing and paying for the lenses. When the lenses are shipped, Company B draws a time draft due in six months on Company A's bank that issued that LOC, discounts the draft at its own West German bank, and receives payment. The West German bank then sends the time draft to Company A's bank, which "accepts" the draft, indicating acceptance of the liability to pay the instrument when it matures.

Company A's bank is obliged to pay the draft at maturity. Meanwhile, Company B's bank may hold the draft until maturity or sell it in the money market to investors. Ultimately, it is the responsibility of Company A's bank to pay off the acceptance at maturity even if Company A cannot. As a result, BAs are direct obligations of both the accepting bank and issuing company, and usually the goods underlying the transaction are pledged to secure the obligation. Investors have very little risk if the draft is accepted by a bank with a top credit rating (see Appendix 9-A). Very large banks long have been active in BA financing. In 73 years, no investor has lost principal except on counterfeit BAs. There are three additional varieties of BAs.

Working Capital BAs

These BAs are also called "finance bills." Unlike traditional BAs, working capital BAs are not associated with goods or collateral underlying the draft. The credit quality of the bank takes on more importance with working capital BAs, as investors have no recourse to underlying goods should the issuer fail.

Edge Act BAs

Edge Act BAs are created by an office of a bank located outside its state of domicile. These BAs are issued with or without the credit guarantee of the parent bank, even though they are created by a subsidiary located in another state. If an Edge Act BA is not guaranteed by the parent bank, it should trade at a higher yield to compensate for the additional risk.

Yankee BAs

The difference between Yankee BAs and regular BAs is that the accepting bank is the U.S. office of a foreign bank. The credit quality of the bank is of utmost importance, as is the political stability of the country in which the head office of the accepting bank is located. BAs accepted by major foreign banks generally are as liquid as BAs accepted by domestic banks.

Negotiable Certificates of Deposit and Time Deposits

The removal by the Federal Reserve system of interest rate restrictions on time deposits in the early 1980s has led to increased competition among banks. Banks now attract deposits by offering higher interest rates than their competitors, especially for deposits of more than $100,000. The result has been an active resale market for certificates of deposit (CDs) in amounts exceeding $1 million.

Corporations and other investors with large sums to invest had not used fixed-time deposits because they lacked liquidity. Consequently, negotiable time certificates of deposit were invented in 1961. Negotiable CDs thus provide institutional financial managers with the advantages of flexible maturities, an active secondary market, and some collateralization of deposits.

Marketable CDs are generally sold in units of $1 million or more. They are issued at face value and generally pay interest semiannually if issued for maturities of one year or more. Maturities on CDs range between a few days and several years, but most are less than a year. Yields on CDs are greater than Treasury and government agency securities, as investors are exposed to some credit risk. Liquidity depends on the credit quality of the issuing bank and the size of the instrument. An excellent secondary market for CDs issued by major banks does exist.

There are three sources for negotiable CDs: (1) domestic banks (Domestic CDs); (2) U.S. branches of foreign banks (Yankee CDs); and (3) thrift institutions (Thrift CDs). Thrift institutions include savings banks and savings and loan associations. There is an active secondary market for Domestic CDs; Yankee CDs; and, to a somewhat lesser degree, major thrift CDs. Domestic and Yankee CDs are sold directly to investors by banks or through dealers. These dealers also contribute to the activity of secondary CD markets. Since CD's have federal deposit insurance (FDIC or FSLIC) only up to $100,000, an investor must check the credit quality of the issuing entity for amounts over $100,000 (see Chapter 9).

Variable-Rate CDs

Variable-rate CDs are a relatively new type of negotiable CD. Two types of variable-rate CDs dominate the market: (1) six-month CDs with a 30-day roll, and (2) one-and-a-half year (or longer) CDs with a three-month roll. Interest is paid upon each roll and a new coupon set. Coupons established at issue, as well as those set on roll dates, are set at some increment above a benchmark interest rate that often is the average rate banks pay on new CDs with similar maturities. Rates range from 12.5 to 30 basis points above the benchmark, depending on the credit of the issuer and the maturity of the note. Benchmark rates are published by the Federal Reserve System. Financial managers must examine variable-rate CDs closely because of their unique features. Variable-rate CDs provide investors with some rate protection against increasing interest rates. They tend to be less liquid than other CDs, however, until their last roll period when they trade like regular CDs of similar maturity.

Eurodollar Time Deposits

Eurodollar time deposits are non-negotiable deposits made in an offshore branch of a foreign or domestic bank. They have all the protection afforded to any domestic deposit except Federal Deposit Insurance Corporation (FDIC) insurance. As their name suggests, Eurodollar time deposits are deposits; hence, no financial instrument is created. Because the deposits are not traded, they are illiquid. Some banks, however, will allow depositors to withdraw their money early with no interest penalty, although investors interested in liquidity should use Eurodollar time deposits only as short-term investments (one to 90 days).

A unique risk element of Eurodollar time deposits is sovereign or country risk. This refers to an investor's exposure when money falls under the control of the country in which it is deposited. If the foreign government decides that funds will not be transferred out of the country, investors may find their money tied up for longer periods than they had planned. Investors can minimize sovereign risk by selecting offshore sites carefully. Professional investors consider the branches of major banks in London, the Cayman Islands, and Nassau to be relatively safe locations for depositing investment dollars.

Eurodollar CDs

Because Eurodollar time deposits are not liquid and many investors desire liquidity, banks that had accepted Eurodollar time deposits in London and Nassau began to issue Eurodollar CDs. A Eurodollar CD is similar to a domestic CD, except that the liability resides with the bank's offshore branch rather than its domestic branch. Any domestic or foreign bank can issue Eurodollar CDs, though Eurodollar CDs issued in London and Nassau are the most common.

The primary advantage of Eurodollar CDs to a financial manager is their rate of return, which is higher than for most domestic CDs. However, they are also susceptible to sovereign risk and are slightly less liquid than domestic CDs. Many Eurodollar CDs are issued through dealers that maintain an active secondary market in the instruments. If the instrument is denominated in U.S. dollars, domestic investors have no foreign exchange exposure.

Yankee CDs

When foreign banks issue U.S. dollar-denominated CDs through their domestic U.S. branches, the instruments are called Yankee CDs, in contrast to Eurodollar CDs that are issued through offshore branches. Yankee CDs are not as liquid as domestic CDs, so their rates are closer to those of Eurodollar CDs and a little higher than domestic CDs but not substantially. Most of the institutional investors that buy Yankee CDs are interested primarily in yield. Changes in Federal Reserve regulations that make it more expensive for foreign banks to raise money by issuing Yankee CDs account for less attractive rates on Yankee CDs.

INVESTMENT POOLS

In a number of states investment funds are available to health care institutions from one of two sources: (1) municipal bodies, such as state treasurers' offices, and (2) hospital associations.

For example, in the state of California, district hospitals formed under municipal guidance are allowed to participate in an investment fund managed by the state. Municipal entities may invest up to a maximum of $10 million in this fund knowing that professional management and proper procedures are applied to make their investments safe. The state has placed restrictions as to the amount of deposits and withdrawals investors may make from this fund, but it is generally considered a safe and convenient investment opportunity.

Funds offered by various hospital associations generally allow greater flexibility to investors. A hospital association may contract with an investment management organization to offer a choice of two or more investment funds, such as mutual funds, to the hospital association's members. In most cases, the hospital association is paid a fee by the mutual fund management company when the association brings an investor into the fund. Unlike the state fund, the hospital association investment funds are managed by independent professional investment management companies that receive a fee based on a percentage of the fund assets for their management services. Also, certain administrative expenses are paid by the fund for all the operational and mechanical activities involved with operating a securities portfolio.

This arrangement should be examined carefully by the health care institution to determine the suitability of the funds' investment objectives to its particular needs. Furthermore, the amount of fee charged and the investment performance of the fund must be competitive.

One drawback of investment funds consisting of longer-term maturities (one year and longer) is their slow reaction to changes in market rates. As current interest rates on newly issued instruments begin to increase, prices of investments in the fund may decline. Or on some funds that are not market-price adjusted, such as the state of California Local Agency Investment Fund, yields are slow to reflect rate increases. Existing investments in the fund must mature and then be reinvested at current higher rates before the fund's return begins to match those available in newly issued instruments. Therefore, maturities of instruments in the fund should be reviewed to ensure that the fund's yield will approximate current interest rates. Also, the opposite situation may provide an advantage. In a declining interest rate environment, funds with larger maturities may have higher yields than the existing market rate of return if the fund does not adjust its market value (as in the case of the California fund mentioned above).

Money Market Mutual Funds

Pools of money invested in particular categories of instruments (i.e., stocks, bonds, and short term money market instruments) and managed by professionals are called mutual funds. Money market funds, of course, are a type of mutual fund that invests solely in short-term, fixed-income instruments. In return for investing money in a mutual fund, an investor receives shares and becomes a part owner of the mutual fund. The original purpose behind mutual funds was to allow individual investors to earn the same returns as large institutional investors. However, large institutional investors are now investing in mutual funds because they are easier to manage than some other forms of investment.

In fact, a money market mutual fund can occasionally provide higher yields than direct investments made by an experienced money market investor. When interest rates are falling, for instance, yields on money market mutual funds are slow to fall because of the time it takes for instruments to mature and be replaced with new instruments that carry the lower rate. Money market mutual funds generally invest in instruments with maturities of 60 days or less, and they generally do not penalize investors for early withdrawal.

However, there are risks associated with money market mutual funds. The primary risk is mismanagement, though the investment manager is required to keep any promises made in the prospectus. The other risk is poor investing. The fund must invest in instruments that have risk characteristics acceptable to the institution and that have performed well over time. A service providing performance and characteristics of money market funds for a fee, is the Donoghue *Money Fund Report*, P.O. Box 6640, Holliston, MA 01746, phone (800) 343-5413. There are advantages to money market mutual funds as well. Some funds allow investors to write checks or otherwise transfer money invested in the fund. Many money market mutual funds invest in municipal instruments that provide tax-exempt returns to investors in high tax brackets. These funds also may limit market risk, as most instruments carry maturities of less than 60 days and do not tend to fluctuate in price. Many newspapers carry listings of current yields and weighted average maturities on a variety of money market mutual funds. It is easy to compare yields and lengths of maturity, because most funds use standard formulas in reporting them.

Bond Funds

During the past several years, bond funds have grown in relation to the number of funds offered and the number of investors attracted to them. Marketing of all types of bond funds, from those investing in municipal bonds to those investing in government securities, has been heavy. The major advantages of bond funds are (1) reduced administrative expenses, (2) reduced research and management costs, and (3) yields equal to a broad market index for government, corporate-mortgage, or municipal securities.

However, it is recommended that institutional financial managers take particular care when investing in bond funds for the following five reasons:

1. Until recent Federal Regulations were imposed, advertisements often did not state fund income accurately. The advertised yield was the current yield of the items in the fund, not the fund's total return. The total return may have been substantially lower because of the effect of market prices on yields. Investors should make sure that fund yields, as advertised, comply with the new standards for accurate comparison.
2. Bond funds, in order to present more attractive yields to investors, often buy bonds with the longest maturities available, and these usually have the highest yields. At the same time, however, long-term bonds decline in price faster than other instruments when interest rates increase, and they are difficult to sell in unsettled markets. Bond funds, therefore, can decline in value relatively fast.
3. Investors are often under the impression that no-load funds allow them to buy shares without paying a sales charge (called a load). Fund managers can, however, charge a redemption fee that reduces an investor's total yield.
4. Bond funds sometimes have difficulty changing investment strategies to reflect changes in the bond market. This is especially true of funds that

specialize in municipal bonds, Ginnie Mae securities, and junk corporate bonds. Their markets may not be highly liquid or stable; indeed, in the highly unstable markets of May and October 1987, for example, massive redemptions by municipal bond funds contributed to market instability.
5. A bond fund can receive permission from the U.S. Securities and Exchange Commission to stop redeeming its shares in situations such as panic selling—a fact not many investors know. Such situations are rare, however.

When these five factors are considered, along with sales charges and management fees, it is often less expensive to retain a professional fixed-income investment adviser than to buy into a bond fund. This decision, however, depends on the amount of money the institution has invested in fixed-income securities.

OTHER INVESTMENT MEDIA

Dividend Capture Programs

Dividend capture plans are fixed-income investment strategies in which an investor actively trades in and out of high-yield stocks to take advantage of the low tax rates corporations receive on dividends. At the same time, a dividend capture program usually hedges its portfolio with futures and options contracts that protect the portfolio against any large decreases in stock prices. This investment strategy results in 70 percent of the income received on dividends being tax free for a corporate investor, as long as the investor has owned the stock at least 46 days. The rationale behind the tax law is that corporate profits would be subject to double taxation if a corporation's profit is taxed once before dividend distribution and the dividends are taxed a second time after they are paid to other corporations.

How long dividend capture programs will remain attractive investment alternatives is questionable. Future tax laws now being considered may reduce their advantage. The stock market crash of October 19, 1987, revealed that the level of risk associated with dividend capture programs had been understated when hedging techniques failed to protect investors. Even though dividend capture programs yield more than other instruments, the pending tax changes and market volatility are likely to make them investment dinosaurs.

Preferred Instruments

Adjustable Rate Preferreds (ARPs)

The intention behind ARPs, which are also known as "hi-point preferreds," is to provide high after-tax yields and price stability. The instruments were introduced in the early 1980s and reached their height of popularity in 1983. As with other floating-rate instruments, the yield of ARPs is determined on the basis of a pre-established index or base rate. The rate is revised quarterly to conform with current interest rates. Because they have a multiple reset option, ARPs are good investments for investors who are averse to fluctuations in the market value of the investment but still want a competitive yield. The base index often is composed of the discount rate on three-month Treasury bills and the constant yields of 20- and 30-year Treasury bonds. The name hi-point preferred comes from the fact that the rate after reset is the highest of those three yields, as reported by the Federal Reserve.

It is important for financial managers to compare effective after-tax yields on ARPs to those of other instruments. Additionally, the reset factor sometimes causes ARPs to have volatile prices, because prices can drop below par. As a result, dealers have developed new types of preferred stocks whose prices are not affected by interest rate changes quite as severely. Descriptions of these instruments follow.

Price-Adjusted Rate-Preferred Stock (PARS). This type of stock is not as volatile as traditional ARP securities, because its dividend is reset on the basis of a formula related to the bond-equivalent yield of three-month Treasury bills. As a result, dividend rates of PARS stock adjust with market changes, and the stock maintains stable value. Financial managers interested in PARS need to pay close attention to the issue's "collar." The collar consists of floor and ceiling limits within which the dividend may fluctuate. If the collar does not allow enough flexibility for the issue to adjust to changing market conditions, especially steep yield increases, the market price of a PARS stock could fall when the dividend rate reaches the ceiling and market interest rates continue to climb.

Money Market Preferred Stock (MMP). The newest type of preferred stock, MMP has the lowest risk of declining in price, it pays a competitive yield, and it has good liquidity. MMP is now the most popular type of preferred stock. It pays dividends every seven weeks, and like other types of preferred stock, its dividends are adjusted up or down according to market conditions. The process of buying MMP stocks, however, involves participating in an auction. Issuers select securities dealers to hold "dutch auctions" every 49 days. Dutch auctions are governed by the rule that the accepted bid is the one low enough to place all of the securities on the block. At auction time, new investors can buy MMP stocks. Current stockholders wanting to keep their stock can either accept whatever dividend is established at auction or they can place a bid that might allow them to buy the stock for another 49 days at a lower price and thus obtain a higher yield.

Because of the auction process, the rates on MMPs are set differently than rates on other preferred instruments. Issuers do not set rates on MMPs; investors participating in the auctions do. As a result, MMPs perform better in a volatile market, because investors can adjust their bids to keep yields high. When no bids are submitted on an issue, its rate is set at the 60-day ''AA'' commercial paper rate as quoted by the Federal Reserve System; that rate is generally higher than what the ''dutch auction'' rate would have been. Dealers say this feature ensures that the MMP market is always a liquid market. However, financial managers must consider what would happen if the credit quality of an MMP issuer suddenly fell and, as a consequence, no investors submitted bids. That issue would carry the higher commercial paper rate, but it might be difficult to sell to investors.

Remarketed Preferred Stock. Remarketed preferred stock differs from MMP stock in that rates are set by the dealers themselves rather than at auction. The dealers set rates at a level they believe investors will find attractive. Investors wanting to buy remarketed preferred stock commit for an initial period of 46 days. (An investor must hold an instrument at least 46 days to be eligible for the 70 percent federal tax exemption on dividends according to current tax law requirements.) After 46 days, investors can renew their commitments during a period of time between seven and 49 days. Commitments can be renewed for any length of time desired. When the investors decide to liquidate their stocks, they have the dealer remarket it to another investor. The financial manager, therefore, must work with dealers who are likely to find buyers. Remarketed preferred stock competes with MMP stocks.

REPURCHASE AGREEMENTS

Introduction

For many institutional financial managers, repurchase agreements, or repos, are one of the most common fixed-income investment media. Repos are short-term investments, often for one day only, that supplement a cash management or liquidity portfolio. Securities dealers use repos to finance their inventories of U.S. Treasury, government agency, and other securities. The dealer puts its inventory of securities up as collateral (see Figure 10-1). The repos allow the dealer to finance its inventory at a lower interest rate than other sources of short-term capital. The Federal Reserve System also uses repos to manage the nation's money supply. It initiates repos to add money and reverses repos to decrease the money supply. For the investor, repos can be exceptionally sound investments. Before financial managers use repos, they must understand the nature of their investment and financing uses so that funds are not lost.

Repurchase agreements became particularly popular in the 1970s when interest rates reached new heights. Interest rates were so high that banks were barred from paying interest on short-term deposits by regulations limiting interest rates. By

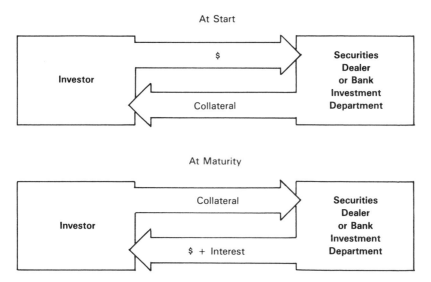

Figure 10-1 Repurchase Agreement. *Source:* © The Alan G. Seidner Company, Pasadena, California.

investing in an overnight repo, however, financial managers could effectively create demand deposits that paid interest. Financial managers were able to use repos to earn high yields but retain liquidity.

Repos can be somewhat expensive in terms of paperwork and complexity, especially overnight repos. Other instruments, such as overnight commercial paper, can provide better returns with less administration. When funds arrive late in the day, however, there is often no other investment vehicle available for the funds. Delivery transactions generally must be made before noon Eastern time. However, a repo that is executed with a local bank often can be executed later.

Definitions

The term repurchase agreement refers to the basic feature of the instrument. A repo involves the temporary sale of a security that is repurchased at a later time. To a securities dealer, the repo represents a borrowing at a fixed interest rate for a specific period of time. (Interest is payable upon maturity and rates are generally lower than those on federal funds loans or deposits because the transaction is backed by collateral.) By nature, therefore, a repo involves two simultaneous agreements, one under which the security is sold at a specified price and another under which the security is repurchased at a higher specified price on a date that can be anywhere from one to 360 days later. The interest, of course, is the difference between the sale and repurchase prices. What happens, in essence, is that investors give funds to the dealer and receive collateral (the security) in return. When the funds are returned, investors receive interest.

When entering into a repo transaction, financial managers should seek to receive securities with a slightly higher market value than the funds they are lending, especially if the agreements last for more than a few days. This is to protect the investor (lender) if the seller defaults. It also protects the investor in the event that the market value of the securities declines before the conclusion of the agreement. A repo agreement may also include a provision requiring the investor to return a portion of the securities to the borrower if they increase in market value. Some financial managers further seek to limit risk by limiting repo activities to banks that have high credit ratings and to primary dealers monitored by the New York Federal Reserve Bank.

Repos Collateralized with Mortgages

Another important element for financial managers to consider is the credit quality of the securities. It is especially important to check credit quality of repos that are backed by mortgages, a type of repo often put together by savings and loan institutions. Answers to the following questions can help financial managers judge the credit quality of mortgage-backed repos:

- What market value has been assigned to the mortgages to determine their value as collateral?
- Is the liquidation value of the mortgages the same as the investment value?
- Are mortgages physically delivered to a third party for safekeeping while the repo is in effect?
- Are the actual mortages delivered so that it is possible to sell them should a problem arise?
- Are the mortgage properties at risk to natural disaster; if so, is that risk insured?
- Do Federal Deposit Insurance Agency or Federal Home Loan Bank Board policies prevent the institution from using the mortgages as collateral?

Reverse Repurchase Agreements

A reverse repo is one viewed from the side of the counterparty, or dealer. A borrower puts up Treasury, government agency, or other securities as collateral and borrows funds against them for a specified period of time. A reverse repo, therefore, is not an investment but a loan with securities used as collateral. To a financial manager, reverse repo is a means of borrowing funds, while a repo is a means of lending them. In fact, every repurchase agreement—because it involves two agreements—consists of a repo on one side and a reverse repo on the other. When a transaction is viewed from the dealer's point of view, it is a reverse repurchase agreement when the customer delivers the securities to the dealer. An investor that needs funds for a short period of time should consider a reverse repo instead of an outright sale of a security.

An institution's financial manager can derive two benefits from reverse repos. First, they provide a relatively low-cost source of short-term debt. Second, the funds obtained through a reverse repo often can be used to make investments that will pay a higher return than the rate at which they were borrowed. (The difference between the cost of borrowing the funds and the yields received from reinvesting them is a form of interest arbitrage.)

In considering a reverse repo, a financial manager must determine the credit quality of the dealer with which the securities are placed. If it is insufficient, the dealer may not be able to return the securities upon conclusion of the agreement, even when the securities appreciate during the agreement. The amount of the loan is generally 85 percent of the value of the securities used as collateral in a reverse repo; the lender is thus protected against a decline in their value.

Brokered or Matched Repurchase Agreements

These repos are tied to reverse repurchase agreements. Rather than placing collateral directly with the lender, the borrower places the collateral with a third party, a dealer or a bank. The collateral is placed with an investor by the third party. In exchange for this service, it receives a "spread," the difference between the cost the third party charges the borrower and the return it pays the lender.

Risks of Repo Transactions

Repurchase agreements contain three sources of risk. The first involves control over the securities that are being used as collateral. The investor should seek to obtain control by using one of the custodial arrangements discussed at the end of the next section or by taking physical possession of the securities. In that way, there will be no misunderstanding of whether there are liens on the securities. Even when an investor has control over the securities, however, questions over the ability of the investor to see these securities in the event of a default by the borrower may still arise.

The second source of risk in repo agreements involves changes in market conditions. If the value of the securities used as collateral in the agreement falls, the collateral may not be of sufficient value to compensate the investor in the event of a default. The seriousness of market risk, of course, depends on the length of the agreement; an overnight repo contains very little market risk. In recognition of this risk, many repo agreements contain margin requirements. An investor lending $10 million, for instance, generally will require that the securities dealer put up securities having a market value of $10,100,000 to $10,500,000, depending on their volatility. Such agreements can also include provisions that the borrower put up additional cash if market conditions threaten the value of the securities during the agreement.

The third source of risk is the possibility that the securities dealer or bank may fail during the term of the repo. This risk was reported extensively during the early 1980s, when several securities dealers and banks failed for reasons unrelated to repos. Unless steps are taken to safeguard capital, such failures can subject an investor to losses. Examining the capital position of the securities dealer is one step an investor can take. However, it is often difficult to make that examination because many dealers are not regulated, which means they are not subject to examination by an independent agency.

The possibility that a dealer may fail should not be taken lightly. A string of failures and near failures ended with losses suffered by clients of E.S.M. Government Securities, Inc. Other failures in recent years include the 1982 failure of Lombard-Wall, the 1983 bankruptcies of RTD Securities and Lion Capital Corporation, and the collapse of Drysdale Government Securities in 1984. Drysdale, for instance, got into trouble because it used a quirk in the repo market to assemble a massive securities portfolio without having much cash. When bonds are bought or sold, the amount of accrued interest is added to their price. Drysdale ignored that accrued interest in its repo transactions. When it sold the securities, the firm profited from both the sale price and the accrued interest. The practice caught up with the company when the interest payments came due and it did not have the cash to pay them. As a result, investors no longer ignore accrued interest in repo transactions.

When Lombard-Wall filed for bankruptcy in 1982, its repo customers were left without recourse. The investors had made repo agreements with Lombard-Wall because they believed they were not really loaning money to an unstable firm but rather were purchasing government securities. The bankruptcy court ruled, however, that a repo was not a separate purchase-and-sale transaction. It ruled instead that a repo was a collateralized loan, and Lombard-Wall's collateral was millions of dollars less than it needed to cover outstanding repo loans. Even after the 1984 Drysdale failure, investors still did not examine the creditworthiness of their counterparty dealers closely enough. Congress has since amended the Bankruptcy Code so that repurchase agreements are exempt from a provision freezing a bankrupt corporation's assets, so that lenders can now liquidate the securities immediately.

The question of collateral takes on extreme importance in light of recent failures. A financial manager should realize that the institution's collateral is likely to be used by the dealer or bank as collateral on a repo with another client. The dealer will lend an organization money against its collateral at one rate and then use the same collateral to borrow in another repo transaction. The dealer thus makes interest on the spread, the difference in rates between the two transactions. Dealers are required to provide investors with written notice of the possibility that their collateral may be used in other transactions. These agreements are called substitution agreements, as the dealer is effectively substituting one group of securities for another.

Reducing Repo Risk

Because of the repurchase agreement market's history of dealer failure, it is of utmost importance that an investor not rely solely on collateral when examining the quality of a repo dealer. The dealer's creditworthiness should be the foremost consideration. Investors should also take the following seven steps to guard against the risk of exposure in a repo transaction:

1. verify that the dealer, even if it is a bank, is a creditworthy institution; it should have a high credit rating from a major investment-rating service (see Chapter 8, Table 8-1)
2. confirm that the repo's collateral is delivered to a safekeeping agent if the repo term is seven days or longer (see the following subsection)
3. monitor the collateral's market value to ensure that it is always greater than the amount invested in the repo
4. make certain when entering into the transaction that the collateral meets the organization's investment guidelines for credit quality
5. sign a written repurchase agreement before executing the transaction
6. ensure that the repo rate is in accord with the quality of the securities used as collateral
7. ascertain the dealer's substitution policy, and obtain a higher rate if the dealer retains the right to substitute collateral

Custodial Arrangements

Custodial and contractual arrangements can lessen the risks of repos. The custodian is a third-party institution that takes delivery and control over the securities used as collateral in a repo transaction (see Figure 10-2). Financial managers can choose among three types of custodial arrangements: (1) delivery repo, (2) three-party repo, and (3) letter repo.

Delivery Repo. The delivery repo is generally considered to be the most secure arrangement. The securities used as collateral in the transaction are physically delivered to the investor. In the case of "book entry" instruments, the dealer wires

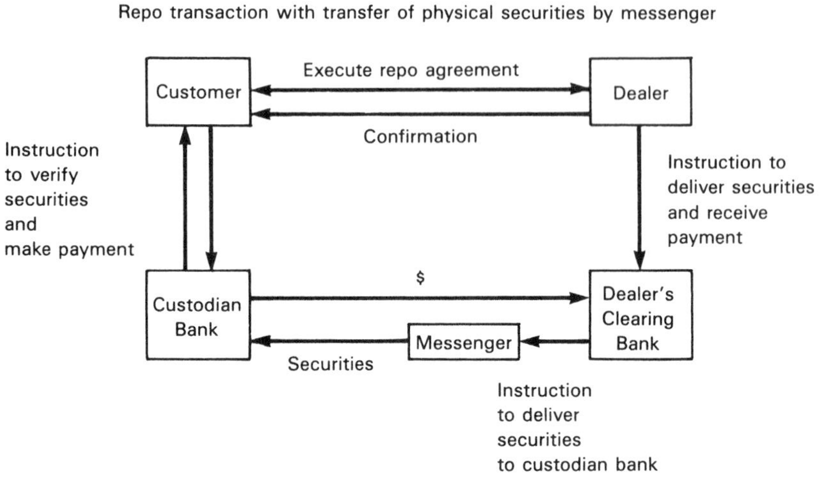

Repo transaction with transfer of physical securities by messenger

Figure 10-2 Delivery versus Payment in Repurchase Agreements. *Source:* Reprinted with permission of the Federal Reserve Bank of Atlanta, Don Ringsmuth, "Custodial Arrangements and Other Contractual Considerations," *Economic Review*, Vol. 70, No. 8, p. 44, © September 1985.

the collateral securities into the custodian bank's Federal Reserve account. If the securities are in "physical form," they are physically delivered to the investor or its custodian against payment. Despite the security of delivery repos, however, they are expensive; delivery costs can erode the investor's return on the repo unless the transaction is large or lasts more than a week.

Three-Party Repo. The original custodian of the securities retains physical possession, but it acknowledges that it is holding the securities of a three-party repo in the investor's own safekeeping account, rather than that of the securities dealer (see Figure 10-3). The entity that retains custody of the securities is the dealer's clearing bank, not the investor's. The contract among the investor, dealer, and bank stipulates that the bank must transfer securities into the investor's safekeeping account against payment to the dealer. The bank then polices the repo by monitoring the value of the securities. It will also calculate the margin to ensure that the securities meet the collateral conditions of the transaction. The advantage of a three-party repo is its lower costs, because no external transfer of securities is involved (both the investor and dealer use the same custodian). In addition, the custodian makes sure that no securities are transferred until funds are transferred as well.

Letter Repo. Under a letter repo, the securities dealer sends a letter of confirmation to the investor that it is holding the securities in the investor's account. These are risky deals, and letter repos have been nicknamed "trust-me repos." Many

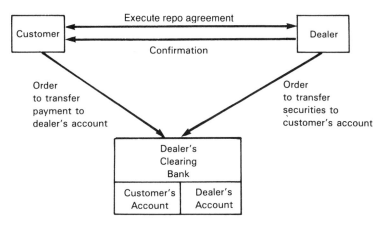

Repo transaction with transfer of securities by dealer's
clearing bank from dealer's account to customer's account

Figure 10-3 Three-Party Repurchase Agreement. *Source:* Reprinted with permission of the Federal Reserve Bank of Atlanta, Don Ringsmuth, "Custodial Arrangements and Other Contractual Considerations," *Economic Review*, Vol. 70, No. 8, p. 44, © September 1985.

investors use letter repos, however, because no transfers are involved, which means costs are minimized. The key determination a financial manager must make before entering into a letter repo is that the dealer's integrity is impeccable. Legal counsel should also approve such transactions.

Alternatives to Repos

Repurchase agreements are not the only alternative to flexible short-term investing; there are other instruments that provide a similar degree of credit quality and flexibility for investments of between one and 30 days. In fact, it is wise for financial managers to diversify investment exposure by investing funds in other instruments. The instruments, discussed in previous sections, that are alternatives to repos include government agency discount notes, commercial paper, master notes, Eurodollar time deposits, municipal floating rate notes, and money market funds.

SUMMARY

One of the jobs performed by investment bankers and securities underwriters is devising new and different investment instruments—instruments that will strike investors' fancies and cause them to part with their funds. In many cases, the creativity of investment bankers has worked to the benefit of institutional investors. At the same time, however, many innovative instruments have caused more problems than they have solved. Collateralized mortgage obligations (CMOs), for example, were designed to solve the problems inherent in the repayment of principal and interest in mortgage-backed securities. However, CMOs have disadvantages distinctively their own.

Accordingly, financial managers must weigh all of the possible problems of new and unusual securities. Such securities often have yield advantages over other types, but frequently the yield advantages are destroyed due to the following three reasons:

1. The accounting effort to maintain the securities in an investment portfolio is costly.
2. Interest income is lost because principal is not paid on time.
3. Most new instrument types have limited initial market activity. Therefore, a weak market can destroy the liquidity and further adversely affect the market price of the instruments, thus lessening the additional income they pay should they have to be sold.

Financial managers should examine all of the consequences of investing in new and exotic instruments, estimate any yield problems, and evaluate the problems against the benefits before buying the instruments.

Chapter 11

Strategies and Techniques for Short-Term Portfolio Management

INTRODUCTION

One enduring characteristic of investment markets is price volatility. Like any other activity within the U.S. economy, the market for fixed-income investments is subject to the laws of supply and demand. And like any other shopper, a financial manager seeks to make these laws work to the advantage of the institution. To do so, the financial manager must seek specific instruments that provide the best relative value among different securities with different maturities while meeting the institution's needs for safety and liquidity. Consequently, the financial manager must have tools and techniques with which to compare the various types of instruments and their differences in credit quality and maturity.

The financial manager can use two analytical tools to judge relative value, a yield curve analysis and yield spread analysis. By using a yield spread analysis, the financial manager can evaluate a fixed-income security in relation to others by comparing the yields of different securities having different risk characteristics but similar maturities. By using yield curve analysis, the financial manager can judge the best relative value of a maturity length in relation to other maturity lengths, because the analysis compares yields and maturities relative to market risk and reward. Combining yield spread and yield curve analyses should improve a financial manager's selection process and, therefore, the institution's overall yield.

YIELD CURVE ANALYSIS

Yield curve analysis provides a method for a financial manager to determine how changes in interest rates are likely to affect the value of the institution's investment portfolio. The yield curve shows the relationship between yield to maturity and time to maturity. It allows an investor to compare the returns of different types of fixed-income instruments, evaluate possible changes in interest rates, and gauge potential price movements. Yield curve analysis allows a financial manager to estimate the rates of return an investment will produce as interest rates change.

Factors Influencing the Yield Curve

Yield curves allow comparison if the securities they compare are identical in all respects except length of maturity. Yield data and yield curves are often published in the *Wall Street Journal*, most major newspapers, and publications issued by securities dealers. Each type of investment security, such as U.S. Treasury bills (T-bills), has a unique yield curve. The horizontal axis plots the security's maturity, expressed in months or years. The vertical axis plots yield levels. The yield curves in Figure 11-1 show how different economic conditions can affect the instrument's yield.

The positively sloped and the negatively sloped curves in Figure 11-1 illustrate an important generalization about yield curves. In periods of economic expansion, with positively sloped yield curves, investors find long-term rates more attractive. In a slow economy, with negatively sloped yield curves, investors are wary of tying up funds at low interest rates for long periods of time. One of the factors that influences the shape of the yield curve is interest rate, or market, risk. Investors are exposed to market risk in any investment, and market risk tends to be greater as the maturity of an instrument lengthens. As a result, yield curves tend to curve upward; that is, yields are higher at longer maturities. In curve A, a relatively flat

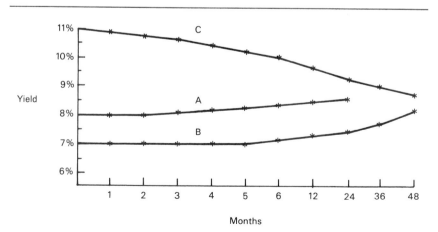

Figure 11-1 Yield Curves

yield curve, economic expectations may be described as stable to uncertain. There is not much reward for investing in longer maturities, so most investors will remain with short-term instruments.

Curve B, on the other hand, rewards the investor for taking on longer-term maturities and is more nearly like the classic positive (upward) sloping yield curve. In this scenario, the yield curve rises sharply with yields increasing as maturities lengthen. Curves such as this one typically occur when business conditions are beginning to improve after a recession and interest rates are expected to increase even further. This causes investors to be reluctant to tie up their money for long periods of time. Consequently, rates for long-term securities are relatively higher to reflect the increased risk of a long-term investment under these economic conditions.

Curve C, an inverted or negative (downward) sloping yield curve, is characteristic of interest rates in a recession, where short-term interest rates are high and the market anticipates that interest rates may soon fall. As a result, borrowers are willing to pay high interest rates to cover their short-term requirements, but they will only pay lower rates for longer-term debt.

The shape of the yield curve is influenced by factors other than the present health of the economy. Such factors include the expectations of investors (affecting demand) and a heavy or light calendar of new issues (affecting supply). For instance, if investors believe that interest rates are going to rise, they will seek to keep funds invested in short-term maturities. At the same time, borrowers seek to lengthen maturities on their debt in order to lock in low interest rates before rates rise. Both responses force short-term interest rates down and long-term interest rates up. Consequently, the upward slope of the yield curve is heightened.

Conversely, if investors expect interest rates to fall, they often invest in longer-term instruments (causing demand for these maturitries that forces prices to rise and yields to fall), because they want to lock in high yields for as long as possible. At the same time, borrowers are paying high short-term interest rates while they wait for interest rates to decline. As a result, the yield curve could be inverted, such as curve C in Figure 11-1.

Large sales of new issues also can skew the shape of a yield curve. Such sales would be reflected in the yield curve by a large upward bulge in the maturity range of the new security.

In general, then, the shape of the yield curve is influenced by the supply and demand for short-term investment maturities in relation to the supply and demand for long-term investment maturities.

A pitfall to avoid when calculating the yield curve is the different methods used to measure the yield on discount securities and interest-bearing securities. For instance, interest on Treasury notes is calculated on the basis of an actual day year, while interest on certificates of deposit is calculated on the basis of a 360-day year. Consequently, a one-year Treasury note at 8 percent, using the par value of $1,000,000, produces a return of $80,000, compared with a one-year CD, where interest is calculated on a 360-day year, that yields $81,111. Of course, the difference is partially offset because the CD pays interest only at maturity while the Treasury note pays interest twice a year.

Using the Yield Curve

There are two basic ways a financial manager can use yield curves. First, yield curves allow the investor to judge whether the price of a new issue is in line with current market trends. Second, yield curves allow a financial manager to compare securities of different maturities. Even so, it can be difficult to predict "normal" spreads between securities with different maturities, because the slope and shape of yield curves vary over time.

Despite this uncertainty, yield curve analysis can be helpful in the management of an institution's investment portfolio. Yield curves are useful in determining whether yields are more attractive in short- or long-term instruments. The duration for which an institution wants its funds invested, however, should be spelled out in a written investing policy and comprehensive set of investing guidelines (see Chapter 9) and not rest solely on yield curve analysis.

Yield curve analysis also enables a financial manager to assess market risk. The yield curve can help determine whether the potential market risk of loss on an investment is outweighed by its yield. It can also assess the effect of rising interest rates as they relate to the investor having to sell the instrument at a loss. For instance, the yield curve may shift upward as the economy heats up, with the potential increase in return outweighing the decline in value of certain securities.

Riding the Yield Curve

A financial manager can receive yield on the sales of securities before they mature, and indeed in some cases the best investment strategy is to sell securities before that time. When a financial manager buys one-year Treasury bills at 7 percent and holds them for a year, they earn 7 percent. If the bills are sold before the date of maturity, the earned rate will, of course, depend on the market rate prevailing when the bills are sold. If that rate is higher than 7 percent, the return will be less than if the bills had been held to maturity, but the proceeds can be reinvested in higher-yield securities.

As a result, it is possible for the financial manager to use yield curve analysis to time buying and selling opportunities in order to reap unanticipated profits. Using the yield curve to help determine the timing of investments is called riding the yield curve. The following example, depicted in Figure 11-2, illustrates how financial managers can ride the yield curve to profits.

Assume that an institution has $1 million that it can invest for three months. Its financial manager observes that six-month T-bills are trading at 7.5 percent and three-month T-bills are trading at 7.1 percent. The financial manager can buy either the three-month T-bills and hold them to maturity or the six-month T-bills and sell them after three months. To determine which strategy will work best, the financial manager uses break-even analysis.

The six-month T-bill would yield an additional 80 basis points, or $2,000, compared to the three-month T-bill (over three months, one basis point is worth $25). The gain is 80 basis points because the financial manager accrues interest at 40 basis points above the three month T-bills (7.50 − 7.10 = .40). The other 40 basis points arise because, assuming the yield curve remains unchanged, the financial manager will sell the six-month bill at the 7.10 level and realize a gain of 40 more basis points, bringing the total return to 80 basis points. Of course, the risk involved in this strategy lies in whether the yield curve will remain constant. If the yield curve rises during the three-month period, the investor may find that three-month T-bills yield 7.50 percent, and there would be no gain on their sale at that time.

In fact, the rate on three-month T-bills would have to rise above 7.90 percent before it would be advisable for the financial manager to buy three-month bills and hold them to maturity, assuming that interest rates remain the same. The slope of the yield curve shows that six-month T-bills should trade at 7.10 percent in three months if the yield curve remains the same. The financial manager thus has an 80 basis point cushion against increased interest rates. If he or she believes that it is unlikely that the yield curve for T-bills will rise that much, then the best bet is to buy the six-month T-bills and ride the yield curve.

YIELD SPREAD ANALYSIS

A financial manager uses yield spread analysis to ensure that the institution's investment portfolio is generating maximum profits. The yield spread is the difference between yields of various investment instruments of similar maturities. Like the yield curve, the yield spread is affected by market conditions and thus changes constantly. A financial manager should stay abreast of the spreads between different investment instruments. In fixed income instruments, the benchmark for comparison is Treasury securities, because their liquidity and credit quality are consistently high. In general, as a security's credit risk increases and its liquidity decreases, its yield in relation to Treasury securities increases.

Yield spreads are measured in basis points, which are equal to one-one hundredth of a percentage point. For example, if six-month Treasury bills are quoted

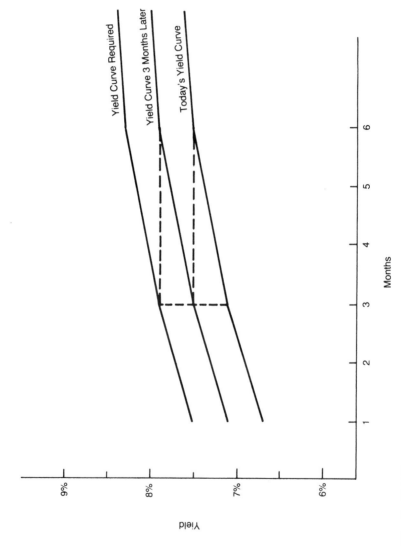

Figure 11-2 Riding the Yield Curve

at 6.45 percent and six-month commercial paper is quoted at 6.65 percent, the spread between the two types of instruments is 20 basis points. By studying the spreads between different types of securities with similar maturities, a financial manager can decide whether a riskier security carries a sufficiently larger return to justify the investment, as long as the choice is consistent with investment guidelines. Table 11-1 shows the yield spreads that generally exist among common investment instruments.

The yield spreads in Table 11-1 are estimates as of a specific moment and under specific economic conditions. These spreads change continuously, requiring constant monitoring, and do not always follow a normal pattern. Abnormal spread relationships (as in Figure 11-3) occur frequently, and such spreads can provide investment managers with profit-making opportunities.

The two bars on the left of the graph in Figure 11-3 show the normal relationship between Treasury bills and government agency discount notes of similar maturities. Normally, the government agency discount notes yield 12 basis points higher than T-bills. The two bars on the right show an abnormal yield spread, where government agency discount notes are more than 100 basis points higher than T-bills. Such a difference may be possible because of a temporary oversupply in the market for government agency discount notes and a simultaneous shortage of Treasury securities. A financial manager who monitors market conditions can use some of the institution's excess cash to make a short-term investment in the government agency notes, thus reaping an unexpected profit, in this type of situation.

Time constraints and limited personnel often prevent financial managers at health care institutions from checking yields on every investment vehicle suited to the institution's portfolio. They can obtain daily yield spread information easily, however, by developing strong relationships with securities dealers and bank investment departments. These organizations keep abreast of the markets and can be valuable sources of current information. Financial managers can obtain market

---

Table 11-1 Approximate Yield Spreads of Various Instruments in Relation to U.S. Treasury Bills

Type	Quality	Yield
Government agencies	Discount notes	0.12%
CDs	Prime quality U.S. banks	0.30%
Commercial paper	Prime rated (A1-P1)	0.40%
CDs, Euro CDs	Prime quality U.S. banks	0.50%
Time deposits, Eurodollars	Prime quality U.S. banks	0.55%
Banker's acceptances	Prime foreign banks	0.40%
CDs, Euro CDs	Prime foreign banks	0.65%
Time deposits, Eurodollars	Prime foreign banks	0.70%

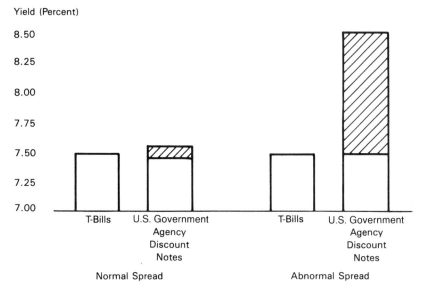

Figure 11-3 Normal and Abnormal Yield Spread Variations (Six-Month Maturities). *Source:* © The Alan G. Seidner Company, Pasadena, California.

information over the telephone. Many organizations distribute market information gratis through printed newsletters. By the time the newsletters reach the desks of financial managers, however, much of the information may be obsolete.

Securities dealers are happy to provide information to investors with whom they have done business before. Accordingly, it is of the utmost importance that financial managers carefully select their securities dealers, especially if they make only a limited number of transactions. (Dealers eagerly offer market information to investors with a large number of transactions.) The difference between valuable market information and market gossip is often difficult to discern, so financial managers, as buyers, must beware.

Finding an attractive value among a morning's investment opportunities requires a financial manager to obtain yield and maturity information quickly on an array of securities and to compare yield spread and yield curve data. Dealers and brokers readily provide this basic information for Treasury bills, government agency securities, bank instruments, and commercial paper. Rates gathered from dealers then can be plotted so that yield spreads and curves become clear. To highlight yield spreads and curves, the financial manager can use color-coded graphics to chart the yields of several instruments at various maturities. The chart should reveal the similarities and demonstrate the differences among instruments.

For instance, a financial manager may learn from yield spread analysis that T-bills are presently at yields close to those of instruments of lower credit quality.

Because the lower-quality instruments are riskier than T-bills and because yield-spread analysis shows that the yields are similar, the financial manager can invest the institution's money in T-bills. He or she does so knowing that T-bills have better credit quality and liquidity at a yield similar to lesser-quality instruments and therefore present a better value.

PRICE MOVEMENT OF FIXED-INCOME SECURITIES

The relationship between interest rates and the price of a fixed-income security is inverse; that is, as interest rates rise the price of the security falls. This ensures that the value of the fixed-income security is brought into line with market interest rates. To compensate for fluctuating interest rates and the resulting market price risk, yields on fixed-income securities are adjusted to prevailing rates after they are issued through the market price mechanism. For that reason, it is important that a financial manager use yield curve analysis to attempt to monitor interest rate changes.

As the institution's funds are invested, the financial manager must know how the investments will introduce market risk into the portfolio. A simple approach is to examine the yield curve to predict how returns may increase as maturities are extended. In that way, the financial manager can ascertain the point on the curve where rates provide the greatest return consistent with the market risk appropriate to the portfolio. The following examples illustrate how changes in interest rates affect the prices of investments.

Rise in Interest Rates

In the first example, the financial manager for Hospital A buys a new six-month certificate of deposit with a par value of $1 million, bearing interest at 10 percent. At the time the investment is made, other instruments of similar credit quality and maturity are also trading at 10 percent. One month after the purchase, however, interest rates increase. As a result, CDs maturing in five months (the term remaining on the six-month CD one month after purchase) are now yielding 11 percent. Because interest rates have increased, the value of the 10 percent CD declines so that its yield is in line with the increased market rate.

After one month, the CD has accrued interest (at 10 percent) of $8,333.33 and therefore a book value to the investor of $1,008,333.33. If the investor wants to sell the CD, the CD must fetch a price calculated to provide the new investor with a prevailing market interest rate. As a result, the financial manager must sell the CD at a loss. The buyer will pay only the amount calculated to yield an 11 percent return over the remaining five months. That amount is only $1,003,984.06, leaving the selling investor with a discount (or loss) from the accrued basis of $4,349.27. When the instrument reaches its maturity value of $1,050,000 ($1,000,000 plus interest at 10 percent for six months), the new investor will realize a return of $45,650.73 on its investment of $1,003,984.06. This results in a yield of 11 percent over the five months that the second investor owns the CD.

Decline in Interest Rates

In the second example, the financial manager at Hospital B buys a six-month CD bearing interest at 10 percent. One month later, interest rates fall to 9 percent. This increases the market value of the CD so that a new buyer must pay more than par to purchase the CD. The premium, however, will be lost at maturity when the CD is redeemed at par value plus interest; the CD thus costs the second buyer more than par. In this case, the new investor is willing to pay as much as $1,012,048.19 (compared to the first buyer's book value of $1,008,333.33) for the instrument that has a maturity value of $1,050,000 in five months. The amount of income earned, $37,951.90, represents a yield to the new investor of 9 percent over that period.

Calculating Yield

Financial managers can receive information that will lead to beneficial investments by analyzing and anticipating changes in yield. Calculating yield, however, can be difficult. The most widely used methods of calculating the yield of fixed-income securities are:

- current yield
- yield to maturity
- yield to discounted cash flow
- yield to call
- total realized compound yield

Each of these methods has specific uses for different investments, so financial managers must know which analysis is best suited to the instrument at hand and the available information.

Current Yield

Current yield relates an investment instrument's annual interest payment to its current market price. It is the rate of return (annual interest payments) divided by the current market value of the instrument. As such, current yield does not take into account other possible sources of income, including reinvestment of interest income during the life of the security, an important consideration when an investment's market price is at either a premium or discount in relation to par. Calculation of the current yield on an instrument involves multiplying its coupon rate by its face value, then dividing that by the instrument's market price, and multiplying by 100. The current yield on a note with a $1,000 face value that sells at $985.13 (a discount) and has an 8 percent coupon is thus 8.12 percent:

$$[(.08 \times 1,000) \div 985.13] \times 100 = 8.12 \text{ percent}$$

On a discount note or bond, the current yield always will be less than its yield to maturity. This is because the current yield does not include the instrument's capital gain. Conversely, the current yield on a note or bond selling at a premium always will be greater than its yield to maturity. For instance, a $1,000 instrument with an 8 percent coupon selling at $1,014.73, a premium, to yield 7.5 percent has a current yield of 7.88 percent. Because current yield does not take into account capital gain (or loss in the case of instruments selling at a premium), yield to maturity or call is the most prevalent calculation of an instrument's yield.

Yield to Maturity (YTM)

The calculation of yield to maturity takes into account the capital appreciation and depreciation of a fixed-income instrument. It also takes into account reinvestment of interest. However, the calculation assumes that the rate at which interest payments are reinvested is equal to the yield to maturity existing at the instrument's purchase date, which may or may not be the case.

Calculation of yield to maturity for nondiscounted format instruments includes two components. First, the calculation includes the coupon rate, the maturity date (to determine the holding period) and any discount or premium resulting from changes in market interest rates. Second, the yield calculation includes the accrued interest that has accumulated from the time the instrument was issued. It is important for financial managers to understand that yield to maturity is based on total dollars invested. Because that total figure includes the premium or discount plus any accrued interest, the instrument's return at maturity is a net return based on the total dollars returned and total dollars invested in the instrument.

For example, a new six-year note with an 8 percent coupon is issued at par. Six months later, the Federal Reserve tightens the money supply causing yields on comparable securities to increase to 8.5 percent. The security must now sell at less than its par value; a new investor who buys this "seasoned," or secondary issue will receive only the maturity value based on the 8 percent coupon and will want to be compensated for buying the instrument at a time when 8.5 percent returns are now available in other similar instruments. Consequently, the new investor will want to pay less than par value for it.

It is necessary to understand the concept of YTM as an effective yield in order to determine how much less than par the instrument should be priced. Again, there are two parts to the return an investor receives on a security that is bought at a discount and held to maturity. Return consists of the periodic interest payment plus a capital gain. The capital gain is the difference between the instrument's purchase price and its par or face value. Investors who buy instruments at a premium and hold them to maturity also receive a two-part return. In this case, the return consists of interest payments plus a capital loss, which is equal to the dollar value of the premium. An investment instrument's overall or effective yield takes into account both interest and capital gains or losses. When financial managers choose between securities of comparable risk and maturity, they do not make their decisions on the basis of coupon rate but on the basis of effective yield.

In the above example, then, once market interest rates increase to 8.5 percent, a security bearing interest at 8 percent must be priced at a discount if a buyer is to be found. The discount, of course, must be large enough to make the instrument's yield to maturity equal to 8.5 percent. The calculations involved in putting a dollar figure to that difference are complex. Using a bond calculator, a dealer can determine that a $1,000 note with an 8 percent coupon and three and one-half years to maturity must sell at $985.32 in order to yield 8.5 percent at maturity. The dollar discount is thus $14.68.

Yield to Discounted Cash Flow

The yield to discounted cash flow calculation allows financial managers to relate the current value of future cash flows expected from an instrument, such as periodic coupon and principal payments, to the instrument's current market price. In short, the calculation discounts each interest and principal payment and, consequently, allows cash flows from both interest and principal to be predicted and discounted back to a present value.

Yield to Call

Some fixed-income investments contain provisions that allow the issuer to redeem ("call") the issue before it matures at a predetermined price. Financial managers can calculate the yields on such issues in two ways. First, yield can be calculated by using the yield-to-maturity method; this assumes that the instrument will remain outstanding until maturity. Alternatively, the yield-to-call method can be used. This method assumes that the investment is called by the issuer at the earliest possible date, as specified in the bond's indenture. Financial managers often use both methods and base their evaluation of the investment's attractiveness on the method that provides the lower yield, thus providing a measure of conservatism to the consideration.

Like yield to maturity, the yield to call calculation assumes that all investment payments will be reinvested at a rate equal to the yield to maturity that existed at the time the instrument was purchased. Yield to call disregards how the proceeds will be invested after the investment is called.

Total Realized Compound Yield

Total realized compound yield measures the underlying fully compounded growth or accumulation rate relating to a fixed-income instrument. The measure takes varying reinvestment rates into account. Because the rate at which coupon payments will be reinvested is uncertain, the financial manager can only estimate a range of rates. Varying assumptions on interest rates determine the range used in the calculation.

EFFECT OF CHANGING INTEREST RATES ON LONGER MATURITIES

As maturity lengthens, risk increases and long-term investments thus should be compensated for the risk. The compensation is reflected in the upward sloping yield curve that says, in effect, that yield increases as maturity increases. Table 11-2 illustrates how changes in interest rates affect the market value of Treasury securities.

Although a positive yield curve suggests that yields rise steadily as maturities lengthen, this is an arguable assumption when it comes to developing an invest-

---

Table 11-2 Effect of Interest Rates on Market Value of Fixed-Income Securities

Maturity	Approximate change in market value after a 1 percent change in interest rates per $1 million par value
1 month	$ 805
3 months	2,583
6 months	5,111
1 year	9,583
2 years	17,281
5 years	36,822
10 years	56,196
20 years	78,796
30 years	81,349

ment strategy for a health care institution. A financial manager who chooses investments of long maturities must always assume that they are putting the institution's principal at a greater risk. The financial manager cannot assume that the additional yield will compensate for the increased risk.

SUMMARY

A yield curve can be used to monitor future interest rates. If the yield curve has a sharp upward slope, it often reflects the aggregate perceptions of investors that interest rates will continue to rise. As a result, investors will demand higher rates for investments with longer maturities.

The best protection against fluctuating interest rates is to distribute maturities in the institution's portfolio among short-, intermediate-, and long-term maturities. This strategy will ensure that the institution's portfolio is protected even against rates dictated by a positive yield curve.

Chapter 12

Investment Operations

INTRODUCTION

Managing an investing program has many facets and considerations, but the financial manager should have three key elements in place before embarking on an investing program:

1. written investing policy and set of guidelines
2. safekeeping arrangements for the securities
3. defined operating procedures

The first element, the written investing policy and guidelines, is discussed in Chapter 9. The elements of a custodian for safekeeping of securities and appropriate operating procedures are explained in this chapter.

SELECTING A CUSTODIAN

Traditional custom and practice dictate that settlement of money market securities transactions occurs by delivery of the securities in New York City against payment to the seller of the amount due. Therefore, it behooves the investor organization to maintain a custodian account in New York for the clearance and safekeeping of its portfolio of securities. An investor organization that does not have a banking relationship in New York usually can work through a local or regional bank's New York correspondent bank to provide the custodian service. Many banks throughout the United States offer custodial and safekeeping services, but they typically act as investors' agents and make arrangements with New York City banks to handle the actual securities clearance and safekeeping operations.

It is not a good idea for delivery to occur outside of New York City. Taking delivery of securities in another city entails additional costs for delivery, as well as additional costs for redelivery upon redemption or early sale. Also, it is not wise for an investor to accept physical delivery of investment instruments because of security considerations.

Selection of the securities clearance/custodian bank may be as simple as merely approving the use of the correspondent bank of the organization's principal depository bank or as complicated as an elaborate selection process that includes requests for proposals and personal visits. In any event, the investor's fundamental interest is to ensure (1) safety of the portfolio holdings, (2) integrity of information concerning the investment instruments, (3) accuracy and accountability of the custodian, and (4) reliability of the custodian to execute instructions concerning receipt and delivery of securities in settlement of investment transactions.

Using a New York correspondent bank introduces an extra layer of administrative bureaucracy into the picture, and the financial manager should be satisfied that this extra layer provides value. The financial manager also should inquire as to where in the New York bank and the local bank the securities clearance and safekeeping services are performed. For example, many banks offer similar services out of both their trust departments and investment departments. Experience has shown that securities clearance services provided by an investment department tend to be expedited because of that department's own requirement for handling transactions swiftly and accurately.

The securities clearance service offered by a trust department, on the other hand, is not often geared to the fast-paced settlements required in money market securities transactions. This difference simply reflects the nature of the business handled by the respective departments. Trust department investments are more heavily weighted toward equity securities that settle in five business days rather than same- or next-day settlements of most money market transactions. Consequently, trust departments tend not to function with the speed and cost effectiveness required when dealing with money market instruments.

Banks that offer custodian services are willing to hold in safekeeping virtually all types of fixed or variable income or equity securities for the customer regardless of where they were purchased. Banks usually base their charges for the service on the volume of transactions conducted in an account; however, some banks base charges on the value of the portfolio held in safekeeping or a combination of the two bases.

The concept of delivery versus payment (DVP) is fundamental to the operation of an investment portfolio because it is an important safeguard against the risk of loss for the health care institution. The alternative to DVP is to pay for the purchase of securities by wire transfer and to allow the selling investment dealer to retain possession of the instruments. This presents a risk, however, that the selling dealer may fail to segregate properly the customer's securities from the dealer's own inventory of securities, or fail to segregate the securities owned by each customer. Securities dealers, of course, welcome the opportunity to hold customers' securities free of charge, while banks charge fees for this service. However, an independent custodian does add value in the form of assurance that the specific asset actually exists.

The use of an independent custodian is very important in the investing process for the following five reasons:

1. It provides securities clearance service in New York City, that makes it possible for the investing organization to deal with virtually all brokers and dealers in the country.
2. It eliminates the need for expensive wire transfers.
3. It eliminates the possible commingling of securities owned by multiple clients and the investment dealer itself.
4. It provides independent verification of the receipt and holding of securities and facilitates the investor's audit process.
5. It ensures the safety of the investing organization's funds in the event of the failure of a dealer from which the investor has purchased securities, because the DVP method of settlement involves an independent third-party safekeeping agent.

The importance of the last point is illustrated by the failure of ESM Government Securities, Inc., as well as several other securities dealers that failed in the mid-1980s. While ESM's failure was caused by a number of factors, not the least of which were alleged mismanagement and fraud, dozens of investing institutions lost hundreds of millions of dollars because they had not insisted on delivery against payment of the purchased securities to an independent custodian. Therefore, ESM was able to resell the securities, or borrow further, by using their customers' securities as collateral.

One investor, a municipality, initially, lost more than $14 million (before recovering $10 million after spending $1 million in legal fees) when ESM failed. In the aftermath of this debacle, auditors discovered that ESM apparently had sold the same securities not only to the municipality but to other investors as well. Had the municipality insisted that ESM deliver the securities to an independent custodian against payment, there would have been no question about the safety of the municipality's funds and the integrity of its investment portfolio. The municipality would have had either the funds or the investment securities; however, in the absence of actual delivery, the municipality had neither the funds nor the investment instruments.

BEARER VERSUS REGISTERED (AND BOOK ENTRY) FORM

Many years ago all securities were issued in physical form as certificates. The burden of storing and moving all of this paper became too great, however, and a number of securities markets changed their method of operation to maintenance of ownership records in electronic form. When a security changes ownership, the transaction and resulting ownership registration records are changed in the central computer. Today, many markets utilize the electronic "book entry" form of registration; some markets offer a combination of physical and book entry forms. Stocks listed on the New York Stock Exchange, for example, are generally held in book entry form at a central depository, but any investor who wishes to hold a physical stock certificate may do so upon request.

The U.S. Treasury, on the other hand, has been phasing out physical certificates completely. Certain issues of Treasury bills (T-bills) were issued in book entry form beginning in 1977, and since 1987 all T-bills have been issued in book entry form. The T-bill investor maintains an account with the Treasury at the Federal Reserve Bank and all transactions involving Treasury securities are handled through this account. It is no longer possible to hold a T-bill in physical form in one's hand.

To accommodate the use of book entry delivery through independent bank custodians, settlement systems have been developed that enable the electronic delivery of a security against electronic payment. The accuracy of using an electronic system is at least as great as the accuracy of the clerk reviewing the physical characteristics of the paper certificate and authorizing the issuance of a paper check for payment. Moreover, the maintenance of inventory and transaction records is greatly enhanced by the use of the book entry form of transactions. Finally, institutions are able to retard the escalating costs of manually handling these transactions and can pass along savings in administrative costs to their investing clients.

The paper certificate is negotiable only when payable to "bearer" or when payable to an individual whose signature accompanies the certificate on a separate form, called a "Bond Power," and has been guaranteed by a bank, trust company, or stockbroker. To negotiate, or transfer, a certificate registered in the name of a corporation, on the other hand, requires that a certified copy of a corporate resolution authorizing the transfer of the security be attached to the certificate. This process is cumbersome and subject to legal review. Consequently, delivery of a security registered to a corporation is viewed with caution. Accordingly, corporate investors are encouraged to accept physical delivery of securities payable to "bearer" or, if registration is required for some reason, to accept delivery in negotiable form and to reregister the security in the name of a nominee of the custodian. A nominee is a fictitious name properly and appropriately registered for use by the custodian whereby the custodian is able to execute transfers without the necessity of obtaining corporate board resolutions.

OPERATING AN INVESTMENT PROGRAM

Having selected a custodian to hold the portfolio of securities in safekeeping, and having become familiar with the registration requirements of particular securities, the health care financial manager still must establish the operating procedures for the execution of transactions. In this connection, certain documentation needs to be created or borrowed from other sources. These documents are designed to (1) record the transactions as they are made, (2) control those transactions for research and follow-up, (3) provide the means by which an investment manager is reminded of the maturing securities in the portfolio, and (4) provide an audit trail.

The financial manager requires a systematic approach to investing. The basic elements of the system include:

- execution of transactions
- verification of transactions
- delivery and safekeeping of instruments (previously discussed in this chapter)
- reporting of transactions, portfolio inventory, and yield earned

A properly constructed set of documentation and procedures will facilitate the swift verification of transactions and the maintenance of appropriate records for reporting and research. The following pages describe many of the details of the procedures and documents that are used in some well designed investing programs.

Executing Transactions

It is very important that the person authorized to execute investment transactions is fully aware of the internal rules and regulations contained in the written investing policy and guidelines. This document constitutes the ''contract'' between the manager who handles the investing program and the organization's senior management and board of directors or trustees.

Money market investment transactions are executed on the telephone between the financial manager (or other authorized person) of the investor organization and the salesperson of the securities dealer. The financial manager may talk with salespeople of several dealers before agreeing to buy or sell a particular instrument at a certain price. Although the aggregate dollar volume of money market transactions each day is huge, there is no central marketplace and each dealer quotes its own prices to buy and sell particular securities. Therefore, the financial manager should shop among several dealers for a competitive price (yield) value on their investment.

Transaction Memos

The financial manager generally utilizes a form, called a transaction memo or ticket, that indicates the basic information, as depicted in Exhibit 12-1. Upon completing a transaction on the telephone, the financial manager fills out the transaction memo and sends a copy of it to the accounting department. Another copy should be sent to a person responsible for independently verifying the transaction.

Exhibit 12-1 Transaction Memo

Transaction No.: (1)	Name of Issuer: (2)		Par Value: (3)
Type: (4)	Cost: (5)	Purchase Date: (6)	Settlement Date: (7)
Maturity Date: (8)	Coupon: (9)	Yield: (10)	Guarantor: (11)
Rating: (12)	Custodian: (13)	Delivery: (14)	Call Provisions: (15)
Executed by: _____	Dealer: _____		
	Sales Representative: _____		

The following is a description of each numbered component of the transaction memo illustrated in Exhibit 12-1:

1. Transaction Number—a unique internal trace number assigned to each trade that identifies the particular transaction
2. Name of Issuer—the party whose indebtedness is evidenced by the investment instrument
3. Par Value—the stated value of the instrument; the amount that will be paid at maturity
4. Type—type of security, such as T-bills, CDs, BAs, commercial paper
5. Cost—the amount paid by the investor to acquire the instrument
6. Purchase Date—the date on which the investor and dealer agree to make the transaction
7. Settlement Date—the date on which ownership of the instrument and payment will change hands
8. Maturity Date—the date on which the instrument is scheduled to be paid
9. Coupon—the rate of interest paid on the instrument as stated on the face of the instrument
10. Yield—the rate of return to the investor, based on the coupon *and* the cost
11. Guarantor (if not the issuer)—the name and form of guaranty (such as letter of credit) attached to the instrument, if any
12. Rating—the rating assigned by a credit rating agency that predicts the degree of certainty applicable to the full and timely payment of principal and interest on the instrument
13. Custodian—the name of the safekeeping custodian
14. Delivery—description of method of delivery (such as DVP, dealer hold)
15. Call Provisions—the date and price at which the instrument may be prepaid by the issuer, if any

Maturity Ticklers

A cardinal error in managing an investment portfolio is to lose track of maturing investments and unintentionally to leave the proceeds uninvested, even for a day. The financial manager, therefore, needs a foolproof system to signal maturing investments. If the portfolio inventory is maintained in a data base, the data base usually can be sorted by maturity date showing the earliest maturities first. As a backup procedure, the financial manager may also maintain a file of transaction memos in maturity date order and have an assistant check the file daily. It is a good idea to mark on the maturity file copy the ultimate disposition of the instrument, such as "matured," or "sold on (date) to (name of dealer)."

Transaction Log

To facilitate the tracking of inventory and the conduct of audits, each security purchase should be assigned a unique identification number. The simplest method is to assign consecutive transaction numbers by prenumbering the transaction memos in serial order. Another method is to incorporate the Gregorian or Julian date of the transaction together with a one- or two-digit number that recycles each day. As transactions are executed, they are recorded in a log, either paper or electronic, to show at a glance the transactions that have been conducted. Exhibit 12-2 depicts a sample transaction log sheet.

Exhibit 12-2 Transaction Log

Transaction No.	Cost	Issuer	Type	Settlement Date	Maturity	Yield	Dealer

Verifying Transactions

To ensure the integrity of the investment operation, each transaction should be verified soon after execution by a person other than the person who executed the transaction. Verification takes the form of both verbal (immediately after the trade) and subsequently written confirmation from the broker or dealer and from the custodian. The verifications are matched to the transaction memo (see Exhibit 12-1) that the financial manager prepared at the time of executing the transaction. If the three "tickets" (dealer, custodian, and the financial manager's transaction memo) match in all respects, they are then marked with the transaction number, stapled together, and filed, usually by transaction number. If there are any discrepancies, the verifier should be instructed to bring them to the attention of either the financial manager or that person's immediate superior, who should discuss the situation promptly with the financial manager. Responsibility for resolution of the discrepancy usually lies with the financial manager.

Reporting Transactions

The financial manager is responsible for reporting transactions, the inventory, and yield of the portfolio. Management should determine the frequency and extent to which reports are prepared and the distribution of these reports; however, the financial manager needs most of these reports for the internal operations and management of the portfolio.

For example, the financial manager must have a continually updated listing of the inventory of investment instruments in order to conduct portfolio transactions. The inventory listing is often maintained in a data base or electronic spreadsheet system. It should have the capability to sort by various data fields in order to give the financial manager immediate access to the portfolio on the basis of maturity date, issuer, type of security, yield, investment dealer, or custodian (if there is more than one).

Incorporated into the inventory listing can be a program that calculates and reports the weighted average maturity and the weighted average yield of the portfolio as of any moment in time. These two characteristics, maturity and yield, can be plotted periodically to show trends in yield and maturity length. In the management of the portfolio, there should be a close correlation between changes in cash need forecasts and average maturity of the portfolio. Again, it is important to remember that maturity date decisions should not be made on the basis of anticipated changes in interest rates, since this is sheer speculation by the financial manager.

Delivery and Safekeeping

Upon executing a purchase transaction, the financial manager issues DVP instructions. The investment dealer is instructed to deliver the instrument to the New York custodian against payment of the precise amount of funds required to settle the transaction. Immediately upon executing the transaction on the telephone, the financial manager covers the other leg of the transaction by instructing the custodian to accept delivery of the particular security and to make payment of the required amount of funds upon delivery by charging the investor's bank account. When the investment dealer makes delivery of the instrument to the custodian, the custodian inspects the instrument to make sure that it conforms with the investor's instructions. If the instrument does not conform, the custodian rejects the transaction and keeps the investor's funds in its checking account. If the instrument conforms with the investor's instructions, the DVP occurs: the investor's checking account is charged, payment is made to the delivering dealer, and the instrument is accepted for safekeeping by the custodian.

A sale transaction operates in a similar, but reverse, manner. After arranging the sale of an instrument to a dealer, the investment manager instructs the custodian to deliver the particular instrument to the dealer against payment. Upon completing the delivery, the proceeds are credited to the investor's bank account. Note that the party holding the security is required to make the delivery, and safekeeping fees are charged for every transaction.

Upon completing the DVP transaction, the custodian sends a safekeeping receipt (or delivery advice, in the case of a sale) to the investor that is used in the verification process by matching it with the dealer's advice and financial manager's transaction memo. Periodically, usually at the end of each month, the custodian prepares and sends a report of instruments held in safekeeping to the company for its records and verification. If this report is not offered, it should be requested. Immediately prior to the maturity of each instrument, the custodian withdraws the instrument from safekeeping and submits it for collection to the paying agent for payment of principal and interest on the instrument at its maturity date.

OPERATIONS USING AN OUTSIDE INVESTMENT MANAGER

Use of an outside investment manager need not compromise the security of an investor's system. There are many ways in which outside investment managers operate, ranging from the mutual fund approach, to investors' separate accounts under complete control of the investment manager, to investors' separate funds with no access by the investment manager. Each outside manager has its own preference for the method of operation, and the investor's management should determine for itself the degree of control, if any, that it is willing to relinquish to an outside investment manager.

If management prefers not to relinquish control over its assets, then the investor's bank account configuration can include a separate "investments" bank account. The investment manager would be authorized to operate this account for DVP transactions only. An important advantage of this method is that all investment transactions, including purchases, sales, maturing investments, and dividend and interest collections, are run through this account and can be easily audited. Further, by isolating only investment transactions in the account, the investment manager can be in control of the full balance without that balance being disturbed by other noninvestment transactions. This permits reinvestment of income as well as principal and places the burden on the investment manager to remain as fully invested as possible.

In addition, the institution also authorizes the investment manager to give DVP instructions to the custodian. In this way, the investor's assets are protected; they are always in the form of either funds in the bank account or securities in the custodian account. They can never be used for other purposes.

SUMMARY

Operation of an investment portfolio requires careful attention to the details of executing investment transactions and monitoring the resulting inventories. Systems and procedures must be established ensuring that all necessary information about transactions and inventories is readily available and that controls are in place to highlight promptly any errors that occur. The system also must be capable of producing reports of inventory and transactions in multiple versions to enable management to monitor compliance with guidelines and to audit the portfolio holdings.

Whether the portfolio is large or small, appropriate procedures and controls must be in place and made effective. Otherwise the financial manager may jeopardize the safety and liquidity of the investment portfolio.

Chapter 13

Borrowing and Investing Tax-Exempt Bond Proceeds

INTRODUCTION

In the fall of 1987, many large municipal bond underwriting firms either curtailed or completely eliminated their activities in the municipal bond market. Salomon Brothers, Kidder Peabody, L.F. Rothchild, and E.F. Hutton (now part of Shearson, Lehman) were among these firms. The turmoil occurred as a result of two specific changes in the municipal bond market during the preceding two years:

1. Fewer municipal bonds could be issued due to recent tax law changes. Therefore, municipal bond firms had much less "product" to sell and the reduced volume made dealing in municipal bonds less profitable. In those sections marked with *, readers should verify current laws with their tax or bond counsel. Tax law changes included the following:

   • the loss of "arbitrage" profit opportunities (discussed later in this chapter*)

   • loss of the 25 percent in "minor portion" ability to finance medical office buildings (presently 5 percent), including the 2 percent issuance cost maintained*

   • a limit of 2 percent on the cost of issuance related to initiating new bond issues*

2. Most securities dealers, in addition to carrying an inventory of bonds that they sell to investors, trade or speculate in bonds for their own profit. Many dealers had misjudged the market and consequently suffered substantial losses from their speculative trading. These losses added to their desire to leave the municipal bond area.

These changes were rather substantial and obvious, but there have been other, more subtle effects on the municipal bond market. However, this chapter will discuss primarily the impact of the changes mentioned above on health care institutions that borrow in the debt markets through the issuance of municipal bonds. Overall, the declining number of investment banking firms participating in the municipal bond market has reduced the choices of an institution in selecting a firm to underwrite, or sell, to the public, a municipal bond issue on its behalf.

SELECTION OF AN UNDERWRITING FIRM

Because of the limited choice available, a health care institution must be particularly careful in its selection of a capable and experienced underwriting firm. The health care financial manager must first determine that the underwriting firm plans to continue in the municipal bond business for at least a sufficient period of time to market the bond issue. A firm that knows its bond operations soon will be terminating is simply interested in getting the issue sold as quickly as possible without the attention necessary to present it in the market in a proper and competitive fashion, and make a market in the bond issue until it becomes seasoned.

If the bond issue is a floating rate, put-option bond and the investor has the right to redeem it for the return of principal on a one-day or one-week notice, what is known as a "remarketing agent" is required. This agent provides the vital function of accepting bonds tendered, or put, by investors and immediately finding other investors to purchase the bonds. A continuing underwriting responsibility exists to accomodate both investors and the borrower, whose interest it is to see that the issue continually remains in the hands of investors. At present, however, this situation is not a problem. The remarketing responsibility is usually assumed quickly and efficiently by other institutions.

Although most issues, once sold, do not trade actively in the secondary market, it is important to the health care institution that its bonds receive reasonable secondary market activity, particularly if it expects to sell bond issues in the future. The institution does not want to lose potential investors because they had purchased its previous bonds and had been unable to sell them due to a weak or, worst yet, "no bid" situation.

After a municipal bond issue has been sold, securities dealers frequently buy the bonds from investors who sell them before maturity or sell them to investors who are looking for secondary (or already-issued) bonds. It is important to maintain a relatively stable market price for the bond issue after its initial sale to the public. Therefore, the underwriting firm or group of firms that brought the issue to the public market should continue to participate actively in buying and selling the bonds in the secondary or resale market.

PREPARATION OF BOND DOCUMENTS

After selecting a bond underwriter and other professionals necessary to complete the financing task, including bond counsel, the actual indenture or disclosure statement is one of several documents that must be prepared. Of particular importance is the segment of the borrowing indenture that lists the instruments considered acceptable for investment of the bond issue proceeds prior to their disbursement or ultimate use. In many cases, the credit rating agencies, such as Moody's Investors Service and Standard & Poor's Inc., have their own rating criteria that include specific information about the instruments in which bond proceeds may be invested. However, very often the bond counsel for the underwriters uses a file form for the compilation of indenture clauses, including one listing acceptable investments. This file is often outdated and inappropirate for the listing of acceptable investment instruments.

It is very important for the health care financial manager to submit to the underwriter a list of investments that the health care institution considers safe and appropriate. The list should be broad enough in scope to meet the indenture requirements. Typical instruments that can be listed are U.S. Treasury securities, government agency securities, certificates of deposit and banker's acceptances issued by major credit-sound banks, commercial paper, and other corporate obligations rated in one of the top two rating categories by Moody's or Standard & Poor's. If others involved in the borrowing process disagree with this list they should make it known so that the list can be negotiated to one that is acceptable to all parties. However, the health care financial manager, after researching the appropriate investments to be included, should initiate a list of acceptable investments and not wait until the indenture is essentially complete before submitting it to the underwriter.

Another area of concern, with respect to the process of investing bond proceeds, is the specific approach of actually implementing these investments within the approved list of instruments included in the indentutre. In considering the question of investing the proceeds from a bond issue pending their final disbursement, it is important to recognize the arbitrage provisions of the tax code. Briefly stated, these provisions will not allow the borrowing institution to benefit from any profit received on the investment of funds from a bond issue. Specifically, if the interest earned on the funds from a bond issue exceeds the cost of the interest on the money borrowed by the bond issue, that excess must be returned to the federal government. The intent of the provisions is to discourage entities from borrowing at a low interest cost through the sale of municipal bonds and investing the proceeds at a higher return, if the primary goal is to capture a profit from the privilege of being able to use municipal bonds as a borrowing vehicle.*

Most municipal bond issues are subject to the arbitrage provisions of the tax code. It is obvious that a health care institution will not benefit from any interest earned that is in excess of interest cost unless interest rates fall sharply during the five-year period during which the yield is averaged.* This situation certainly will not provide an incentive to earn maximum interest on the proceeds of the bond issue until such time as the funds are finally disbursed. Therefore, it is important that under no circumstances should aggressive investment techniques be used or higher risks taken simply to earn additional interest income. It takes a substantial amount of additional interest income to equal principal lost through unwise investment of bond proceeds.

These limitations on earned interest are referred to as "permitted yield." Although they provide no incentive to earn yield in excess of interest cost, there are other situations that must be considered. The institution may find itself in a low-interest rate environment and need to be a competitive investor simply to earn the level of return to equal the cost of money borrowed. In this situation it is extremely important that investment yields be taken seriously to minimize the interest cost incurred on municipal bond borrowing.*

Whatever interest conditions prevail at the time the municipal bond issue is brought to market, it is important to be a prudent and efficient investor. There are many alternatives available for the investment of proceeds from the bond issue. In examining these alternatives, the financial manager should be aware of the institution's needs, not only with respect to arbitrage provisions, but also as to internal management capabilities, proper compliance with indenture investment limitations, and sound overall financial practices.

INVESTMENT OF BOND PROCEEDS

The health care institution must examine the responsibility involved in investing proceeds raised from a bond issue pending the distribution of the proceeds for their final use, for example, a construction project or other capital improvement. The complexity of this responsibility has created an investment situation that demands constant and specialized management. Consequently, the selection of an efficient vehicle to accomplish this task creatively is a critical decision.

Investment Alternatives

The health care institution has several choices relating to the investment of its bond proceeds and the management of the investment. They include

- staff management of the investment
- investment package offered by a securities dealer
- guaranteed investment contract with an insurance company
- investment management by bond issue trustee
- fixed-income investment adviser

Staff Management

Investment management of the proceeds from the bond issue may be adequately handled by the financial personnel of the health care institution if the staff has the necessary skills, experience, and resources. The following checklist will assist the institution in assessing its staff and resources.

- Does the staff have experience with fixed-income securities? Have any staff members personally managed a fixed-income securities portfolio?
- Does the institution subscribe to credit rating/review services (i.e., Moody's, Standard & Poor's, or the Keefe BankWatch)?
- Does the institution have access to current financial news dedicated to the fixed-income securities markets?
- Does the institution have a software system that can analyze the best relative values as to yield relationships among instruments and maturity dates and that can validate prices and yields on transactions?
- Does the staff have the time to develop investment skills, perform research, and execute an investment program?

There is normally a broad list of investments that are legal under the bond indenture. Choices must be made among the best possible opportunities for investing the funds. Staff personnel must have sufficient knowledge, skill, and time to perform these duties. Any deficiences must be addressed *prior* to undertaking the investment responsibility.

Investment Package

Allowing a securities dealer to ''sell'' the health care institution a complete package of investments is also referred to as a ''lock-up'' program. In this investment approach, an estimate of the required amounts and due dates for future payments on a construction program are covered by investments made in instruments to mature on each of the respective dates. There are both positive and negative aspects of the investment package. There are basically four positive points:

1. It is convenient because the securities dealer can select investments from the approved list in the indenture and match maturities and amounts to coincide with estimated future disbursement payments.
2. It does not entail the cost of an investment manager; the dealer's profit on the transactions is the only compensation involved.
3. It requires little supervision if the capital funding schedule is close to the original plan.
4. An active investment approach to achieve a higher yield is unnecessary if the earned interest rate is close to the borrowing cost. (A higher yield results in violation of the arbitrage provision of the tax code.)

There are five negative points to consider in a packaged investment:

1. The securities dealer profits from the investments it sells, even though it may be ethical and meet the institution's requirements. The dealer may have a profit incentive to sell certain investments. Also there is a shift of responsibility from the institution to the dealer, but the institution is accountable if a problem develops, and it should be confident of the dealer's skill. (See the investment advisers/dealers checklist in the next section of this chapter.)
2. The "lock-up" approach does not provide for continuing management, and the institution will not know if the credit quality of an investment deteriorates. This may result in violation of indenture requirements or place funds at risk if a default occurs. (This point does not apply if only U.S. Treasury securities are purchased.)
3. The amounts locked up to estimated dates of construction may not be adequate, because these schedules often vary. Problems occur when funds are needed in excess of the forecasted amounts, and an investment cannot be sold to raise funds or when the pay-out schedule is delayed and funds mature before they are needed.
4. A speculative bet on interest rates results when all the funds are invested at one time to cover forecasted needs. The institution essentially is gambling that interest rates will not go up in the future. In a low interest rate environment this may result in yields well below "permitted yield" allowed by tax law.
5. Instruments in these programs may be illiquid, of questionable credit quality, or sold at yields that are unattractive compared with those of other instruments.

Guaranteed Investment Contract

Investing the bond proceeds in a guaranteed investment contract (GIC) to meet disbursement schedules should be carefully considered by a health care institution.

Its good and bad points are similar to investment packages ("lock-up" programs). The GIC is essentially a guarantee from an insurance company that the principal and a stipulated interest rate of return will be paid at some particular point in the future. There are variations on different types of GICs. Some allow early withdrawal of principal, perhaps with a substantial penalty. Others may have a floating rate or include options for extending the maturity date with certain yield guarantees. In addition to the positive and negative points listed under investment packages, special considerations include the following:

- Most insurance companies are rated by A.M. Best, an old and well-known institution for rating the credit quality of these companies. Other firms, such as Standard & Poor's, also provide credit ratings on *some* insurance company obligations. Recent concerns with GICs involve criticism of A.M. Best and other rating agencies for the quality of their GIC credit ratings and large numbers of low-credit-quality junk bonds purchased by many insurance companies in order to generate high yields to cover the rates being paid on GICs.
- GICs are virtually illiquid. Although some can be purchased with provisions for early redemption, this normally results in a severe interest penalty. (This penalty usually does not apply to negotiable fixed-income securities that can be sold prior to maturity for reinvestment or disbursement cash needs.)
- GICs are another case where the institution is making a bet that interest rates will not go up. If they do, opportunity cost can be substantial.

These investment contracts should be viewed from the standpoints of liquidity, credit quality, and suitability to the investor's needs. GICs should be looked upon as only one of several investments to be considered.

Investment Management by Bond Issue Trustee

Under law, the health care institution as the bond issuer must retain a trustee, usually a bank, to act as a fiduciary. The trustee has the responsibility of protecting the interest of the bondholders. This usually includes overseeing the disbursement of funds for the intended use of the bond issue, holding the assets that were created by the bond issue including any uninvested funds, and confirming that instruments purchased with bond proceeds meet indenture requirements. It should not be assumed that investment service is automatically provided because a fee is paid to the trustee for its trustee (fiduciary) and administrative responsibilities. This is usually not the case. If the institution wants the trustee to provide investment management services, it should use the checklist of criteria to select an investment adviser in the next section. It is also important not to confuse the placement of bond proceeds into a trust department money market fund with investment management.

Fixed-Income Investment Adviser

Retaining the services of a fixed-income investment adviser, who is performing properly, offers the institution six positive points:

1. An adviser purchases legally approved investments over a period of time and schedules the investments so they are available for timely distribution to cover payments for construction schedules or other needs.
2. The adviser monitors the trustee's activities with respect to proper accounting of interest income received and segregation of investment proceeds to the various funds (e.g., capitalized interest and reserve fund).
3. Problem prevention is one the adviser's duties, especially when trustees are not timely in their review and reporting responsibilities. Trustees are liable in the event of a problem occurring from an oversight in their responsibilities, but problem prevention is a more prudent approach than later corrective action or litigation.
4. An adviser is expected to select liquid or marketable instruments that will provide funds for unforeseen situations.
5. The adviser makes investments over a period of time, avoiding a "bet" situation on interest rate forecasts.
6. Competitive yields are obtained by the adviser and instruments purchased from several different dealers.

Two negative points are associated with retaining an investment adviser:

1. This type of service entails costs. A typical fee may be up to 1/2 percent of the managed assets or $5,000 per million dollars annually. The institution must determine the "cost-to-benefit" factors in retaining an investment adviser. These factors are discussed before and after this section.
2. Care in selecting an investment adviser is critical, because the institution delegates all decision authority concerning investment of bond proceeds to the adviser. The risk this delegation entails must be seriously considered.

Note of Caution. Many bond counsel are now requesting that any profits, commission, markups, or fees earned by individuals or firms who invest bond proceeds be fully disclosed. The basis for this request concerns the huge profits earned by some investors who are aware of the arbitrage limitations, and the possibility that these profits *may* be unethical.* For example, if an investment adviser or dealer knows a hospital may earn only 7 1/2 percent on the bond issue proceeds, it could purchase a four-year instrument that yields 9-1/8 percent, and mark up its price $55,000 per $1 million face value to reduce its yield to 7-1/2 percent. As a result of this practice, large amounts of money are going into the pockets of the investment adviser or dealer. Some bond counsel view these excessive profits of interest above the arbitrage limits as simply "given away" by the bond issuer.

INVESTMENT ADVISER/DEALER CRITERIA CHECKLIST

It is absolutely vital that the health care institution use a prudent approach in selecting an investment dealer for a "lock-up" program or a management adviser to handle bond proceeds. It should use a "due diligence" analysis to investigate the individual or firm before selection is made. Also, it is wise to document the selection process to show why and how the decision is made. The appropriate time to make the selection is well before the bond proceeds are available for investment. Throughout the investment process, the adviser or dealer should be monitored to assure delivery of promised services.

The following checklist may assist the institution in the selection of an investment dealer or adviser. (*Indicates questions to ask of an investment dealer).

- Are the adviser's fees the only compensation received, or does the adviser receive compensation or services from securities dealers, traders, or salespeople where transactions are executed? (This type of compensation is referred to as "soft dollar payments" as opposed to disclosed flat fee payments which are called "hard dollar payments.")
- Does the adviser initiate questions and invite the institution's comments regarding its viewpoints about investment programs and policy objectives?
- Has the adviser contributed to the body of investment knowledge in any specialty area through research, published articles, educational programs, and investment leadership?
- *Is the adviser or dealer well-qualified in the area of fixed-income securities management? This point is important and should be *verified* by asking the following three questions:
  1. Does the adviser or dealer have any of the following specialized fixed-income-securities information/analysis computer systems:
     - Telerate
     - Reuters
     - Bond Buyer/Munifacts
     - Bloomberg

2. Does the adviser or dealer use any of the following credit review services?
   - Standard & Poor's
   - Moody's Investors Service
   - Keefe BankWatch
   - McCarthy, Crisanti, & Maffei
   - Duff & Phelps
   - Others
3. Does the adviser have software systems specifically tailored to fixed-income securities management that include proper formula evaluation of prices and yield? The specific names of the systems should be verified to ascertain whether they are simply a subsystem of an equity management program.

- *Will the adviser freely provide the institution with written and verbal recommendations from past and present clients?
- Is it easy to communicate with the adviser?
- Does the adviser manage other clients with similar goals in a similar industry holding similar investments?
- Is the investment adviser registered with the United States Securities and Exchange Commission under the Investment Advisors Act of 1940 and also registered as an investment adviser in the state of domicile?
- *Has the adviser or dealer ever been censured for misconduct by the United States Securities and Exchange Commission or any other regulatory body?
- *Has the adviser or dealer ever been involved in any litigation with clients or employees?
- How frequently do key personnel in the adviser's firm turn over? Is there a consistent professional staff to service clients? Has turnover of personnel resulted in inconsistent management of client portfolios?
- What is the experience background of key investment personnel in the adviser's firm?
- What type of clauses may be in the contract between the institution and the adviser to permit quick and easy termination of the adviser's services by either party?
- Does the adviser clearly state how fees are computed?
- Does the adviser clearly state what additional costs may be involved beyond basic fees?
- What type of written reports will the adviser provide, how often, and are they flexible and accurate?
- Can reports be obtained on an ad hoc or special-need basis?

- Does the adviser stress only past investment performance rather than the quality of the firm?
- How long has the firm been in business?
- What is the growth rate of the firm in relation to assets under management?

SUMMARY

Only the health care finance professional can properly assess the institution's needs. The information and checklists in this chapter are intended as guides to assist the institution in assessing the subject of bond proceeds investment. A review of the institution's unique situation and an analysis of possible solutions are required before it can comfortably and *safely* select a course of action.

Index